upscale

About the author

James Silver's career as a journalist began at the BBC, where he was a producer, reporter and documentary-maker at BBC Radio 4 and 5 Live. He went on to write over 400 feature articles and interviews – mostly covering media, technology and politics – for, among others, the *Guardian*, *WIRED* magazine, the *Observer*, *Total Politics*, the *Independent*, the *Evening Standard* and BBC News Online. *Upscale* is his first book.

About Tech Nation

Tech Nation empowers ambitious tech entrepreneurs to scale faster through growth programmes, digital entrepreneurship skills, a visa scheme for exceptional talent, networks and connections, and by championing the UK's digital sector through data, stories and media campaigns.

Founded in 2011 (originally as Tech City), Tech Nation's programmes cater for businesses at all stages of company growth, from initial idea and early stages (The Digital Business Academy, Founders' Network and Rising Stars), right through to the mid and late stages (Upscale and Future Fifty). It also recently launched its first sector-specific programme, covering FinTech, while Cyber, Deep Tech and Blockchain will be launching shortly.

www.technation.io
Twitter @TechNation

upscale

**What it takes to scale a startup.
By the people who've done it.**

JAMES SILVER

**TECH
NATION**

First published in 2018 by Tech Nation

ISBN 978-1-911195-86-3

Also available as an ebook
ISBN 978-1-911195-87-0

And as limited edition in hardback
ISBN 978-1-911195-88-7

Typeset by seagulls.net
Cover design by Mark Ecob
Printed and bound in Great Britain by Clays Ltd, Elcograf S.p.A

Acknowledgements

Tech Nation would like to thank everyone who made Upscale the programme possible and a success, and all those who spared the time to be interviewed for this book.

Scale Coaches
Adam Hale; Alex Depledge; Alex Gayer; Amir Kfir; Andrew Crump; Andrew Graham; Anthony Fletcher; Asi Sharabi; Benjamin Grol; Brad Feld; Brent Hoberman; Bryan Tookey; Cian Weeresinghe; Claire Martin; Dan Hynes; Daniel Campion; Dave Shappell; David Norris; Devin Hunt; Divinia Knowles; Doug Monro; George Berkowski; George Bettany; Greg Marsh; Ian Meyers; Ian Sutherland; James Bilefield; James Routledge; Jerry Collona; Jessica Butcher; Jonathon Southam; Julien Callede; Luke Lang; Malcolm Locke; Matt Buckland; Meri Williams; Niklas Zennstrom; Patrick Campbell; Placid Jover; Romain Bertrand; Sarah Wood; Shane Corstorphine; Sian Keane; Simon Wright; Sophie Miller; Steven Dunne; Steven Rose; Thor Mitchell; Toby Moore; Tracy Doree; Verne Harnish; Will McInnes

Advisors
Andy Young; Davor Hebel; Dominic Jacquesson; Eileen Burbidge; Jamie Coleman; Jon Bradford; Katy Turner; Nic Brisbourne; Reshma Sohoni; Russell Buckley; Simon Calver; Saul Klein; Sitar Teli; Suranga Chandratillake; Tak Lo; Wendy Tan White

Tech Nation
Ashley Hough; Barbara Peric; Becky Smith; Ben Wackett; Caroline Rae; Davina Yanful; EJ Quinn; Gerard Grech; Jos Smart; MB Christie; Orla Browne; Parveen Dhanda; Reiz Evans; Ryan Proctor; Sinead Daly; Tia Mcphee; Ugne Sapezinskaite; Vicki Shiel; Will Dolby; Zheela Qaiser

CONTENTS

INTRODUCTION **Gerard Grech**, CEO Tech Nation.　　　　1

Part One: People

CHAPTER 1: 'Why hiring slow and firing fast is one of the　8
hardest things founders have to do.' **Greg Marsh**, co-founder
and former CEO of onefinestay, on hiring and firing.

CHAPTER 2: 'There is no such thing as a perfect culture　16
– that's known as a cult.' **Neil Rimer**, co-founder of Index
Ventures, alongside key figures from some of the leading
VC firm's portfolio companies, on scaling values and
making culture count.

CHAPTER 3: 'The age of one brain holding all a company's　23
knowledge is over.' Unruly co-founder **Sarah Wood** on the
changing role of leadership (and her company's scaling
challenges).

CHAPTER 4: Total Football, 'crossing the Rubicon' and why　37
startups need a talent brand. **Saul Klein**, founding partner at
LocalGlobe VC, on scaling your team.

CHAPTER 5: 'Skilled coders don't necessarily make the best　47
managers.' **Toby Moore**, co-founder and former CTO at
Space Ape Games, and now venture partner at Entrepreneur
First, on scaling your startup's tech team.

CHAPTER 6: 'Managing your own psychology is the number-　54
one challenge founders face.' **Asi Sharabi**, co-founder and
CEO of Wonderbly (formerly Lost My Name), on founder
psychology.

CHAPTER 7: Riding the rollercoaster. Sanctus founder 62
James Routledge on spotting the warning signs of poor
mental health – and what founders should do about it.

CHAPTER 8: 'Build a talent pipeline', 'Offer employee 73
equity' and 'Beware title inflation'. Index Ventures'
Director of Talent **Dominic Jacquesson** has 19 tips on how
to scale talent.

CHAPTER 9: 'Founders can sometimes be a massively 88
limiting factor in a company's growth.' Entrepreneur-turned-
Balderton Capital partner **Suranga Chandratillake** on why
some founders need to face the music and fire themselves.

Part Two: Company

CHAPTER 10: 'I meet too many entrepreneurs who spend 98
a lot of time jumping on planes, trying to be the hero.'
Anthony Fletcher, CEO of Graze, on what he's learned
from scaling to the US.

CHAPTER 11: 'Send out a fire starter' (but 'open an 110
international office as late as you possibly can').
Shane Corstorphine, Skyscanner's VP of Growth, on
overseas expansion.

CHAPTER 12: The 17 things every scale-up founder should 121
know about boards. BGF Ventures partner, former LOVEFiLM
and Mothercare CEO, and ex-chair of Chemist Direct and
Moo.com **Simon Calver** on boards.

CHAPTER 13: 'Create a sense of scarcity' and 'Don't be too 133
nice'. lastminute.com and Founders Factory co-founder
Brent Hoberman's 11 rules on how startups should go
about partnering with – and selling to – corporates.

CHAPTER 14: 'Brand is critical from day one.' 140
Reshma Sohoni, founding partner at Seedcamp, on
scaling brand.

CHAPTER 15: 'Understand your North Star metric.' 149
Atomico partner and Head of Growth, **Benjamin Grol**, on
scaling growth.

CHAPTER 16: 'Keep your powder dry for big 160
announcements' and 'Don't blog unless you've got
something to say'. Burlington founder and former Director of
Communications at Index Ventures, **Nadia Kelly**, on
scaling comms and coping with crises.

CHAPTER 17: 'Customer care calls would come through 173
to my personal mobile in the early years.' **David Buttress**,
co-founder and ex-CEO of Just Eat, on bootstrapping and
scaling operations.

CHAPTER 18: 'Pay your technical debt continuously' and 185
'Start with *why*'. **Carlos Gonzalez-Cadenas**, Chief Product
and Technology Officer at GoCardless, has these 11 rules
for scaling product.

CHAPTER 19: 'Don't sell umbrellas to camels.' Partnerize 195
CEO **Malcolm Cowley** on scaling an enterprise startup and
why 'B2B companies are judged on revenues early'.

CHAPTER 20: Sheffield Steel. **Aldo Monteforte**, CEO and 206
co-founder of The Floow, on design choices, compensation
and attracting talent outside a major hub.

CHAPTER 21: 'Five years ago we were talking to people 215
who had never heard of machine learning.' **Martina King**,
CEO of Featurespace, on pivoting a business and making
the most of her company's Cambridge roots.

Part Three: Finance & Funding

CHAPTER 22: 'Shareholders are looking for reassurance 226
from the CFO, who must be "the voice of reason" in the
business.' **Alex Gayer**, ex-CFO at SwiftKey and CFO at
Receipt Bank, on scaling finance.

CHAPTER 23: 'Negotiation isn't about bluster and bluffing.' 236
Cherry Freeman, co-founder of LoveCrafts, on how to raise
venture money, when to fight your corner – and what to look
for in investors.

CHAPTER 24: 'Be upfront about past mistakes' and 'Why 252
every signal matters at meetings'. **Megumi Ikeda**, GM and
MD at Hearst Ventures Europe, gives 12 tips on navigating
due diligence with investors.

CHAPTER 25: 'Companies born in up-cycles often don't 260
develop resilience.' **Entrepreneur-turned-investor, BGF advisor
and co-founder of Moonfruit, Wendy Tan White**, on scaling
strategy and growing a business at a time of adversity.

CHAPTER 26: 'The average person doesn't get married 274
after two or three dates; the same goes for finding the right
investor.' **Balderton Capital partner Suranga Chandratillake**
on the pathway to Series B.

INTRODUCTION

by **Gerard Grech**, Chief Executive, Tech Nation

It was 2014 and the Tech Nation (then Tech City UK) team was at Web Summit (a leading technology conference, then held in Dublin), when we first began to notice a glaring gap in the market: a specialist programme for fast growth UK technology startups exclusively focused on scaling.

The early stages of company-building were already well covered by startup accelerator programmes in the UK, while our own Future Fifty was blazing a trail for later-stage companies. But no one was yet serving those founders who were circling that make-or-break moment in the startup journey: the transition from a tight-knit group of multi-tasking entrepreneurs and early hires with a 'Vision', to dozens if not hundreds of team-members, often in multiple offices around the world.

We had recently gone through a similar growth spurt ourselves, as Tech City evolved to become Tech Nation, almost doubling the numbers of employees every year. Having experienced our geographic focus, ambition, budget and staffing levels scale up dramatically, I'd had a taste of the professional and personal adversity that tech entrepreneurs can face during that intense period.

As soon as that red 'scale' button is hit, founders are assailed with challenges from all angles. From ramping up their infrastructure and processes so that they're able to hire at least a person-a-week to building a product or service that works across multiple markets and languages, to fretting about company culture and values which can easily get watered down or even lost as a startup goes into hyper-growth mode, scaling a business can be a white-knuckle ride. Additionally, it's a period where a startup founder is handling decisions and setbacks almost daily. Credible guidance and advice become critical to building the resilience to stay the course.

As the UK's leading network for technology entrepreneurs, we knew we were well positioned to provide this missing piece of the puzzle in startup support. And so, after a period of incubation, Upscale was born.

From its inception, we wanted Upscale to be a market-led programme, driven and shaped by the precise needs of entrepreneurs in the throes of scaling. While many issues which arise are generic - and thus easier to prepare for - others will be unique to founder x, building company y, in sector z at a given moment in time. That meant putting these (mostly) first time-founders in front of people who'd been through the pain and the turmoil, the hard days and sleepless nights, as well as the immeasurable rewards of successfully scaling a business in the face of ferocious competition. So we assembled an ever-evolving team of mentors and coaches who could advise the companies we handpicked to join the programme and respond to the questions they had in real time, across every aspect of company growth.

These individuals were founders and investors who had recently built – or backed – UK companies, in many cases worth hundreds of millions of dollars. Not only did they have the experience and credibility to encourage the next generation of entrepreneurs; they could also talk plainly about the real-world mistakes they had made along the way. The very opposite of an academic programme delving into historic case studies, this would be a living-and-breathing education, running right alongside the inevitable turbulence of scaling a business.

What we went on to create with Upscale was a forum in which entrepreneurs could speak freely about the adversity they faced, secure in the knowledge that none of the proprietary details they shared would leave the room. Crucially, Upscale also became a place where entrepreneurs could use their own experience to advise each other. That network of peers, many of whom went on to form WhatsApp groups and close friendships, has proven an invaluable resource for entrepreneurs across the UK.

After 18 months of Upscale, the conversation turned towards how best we could capture the many valuable insights from the heavy-hitters running the coaching sessions. We were acutely aware that the number of startups invited onto Upscale each year would, by necessity, always be just a tiny fraction of the new digital companies out there. Yet it is a core mission of Tech Nation to help as many new companies as possible. That led us to the idea of having an Upscale 'writer-in-residence' attend the sessions and turn the results into a book.

Work on this book began at the start of Upscale 2017, and one thing quickly became apparent. The presence of writer James Silver at the programme's sessions had an impact on the participants' ability to talk openly; understandably it made them more guarded about sharing sensitive company information. Tackling subjects such as getting rid of a disastrous executive hire *(Greg Marsh in Chapter 1)*, or holding board members to account *(Simon Calver in Chapter 12)*, or the serious emotional toll on your personal life that being an entrepreneur involves *(Asi Sharabi in Chapter 6)* – all of these sparked conversations that not everyone wanted to be in the public domain.

So James opted for a different approach. He would attend as many of the sessions as possible to witness the immediacy of the experience, without inhibiting the honesty and conversational flow. But while that would form the backdrop to the book – and infuse his writing – the material for the chapters themselves would primarily be derived from one-to-one interviews conducted with Upscale's coaches at a later date.

From the outset, we wanted this book to be the antidote to the typical business tone, which is often far removed from the down-in-the-weeds reality of scaling a startup. James received free rein to go wherever his conversations took him, without predetermined angles, even if sometimes interviewees seemed to offer contradictory advice. He would, wherever possible, ask the coaches and mentors to discuss their own experiences - good, bad and terrible - with each interview/chapter highlighting a particular aspect of scaling. Pretty soon, the list of interviewees grew beyond the Upscale programme and even the wider Tech Nation family.

If the goal of this book is to capture the insights and experiences of some of Britain's best-known technology entrepreneurs and investors, there is another underlying aim too. Namely, for the role models featured in these pages to inspire the next wave of founders—those who are currently tinkering with a prototype or a business plan—to get out there and start building the company of their dreams. We have over 15K people in training via Tech Nation's Digital Business Academy, which provides over 60 courses for anyone who wants to start and/or grow a digital business.

There has never been a better moment to create a technology company in the UK, and the evidence shows that today's startups aren't just being successfully launched, but also increasingly scaled in a whole range of locations across the nation. Just look at Skyscanner in Edinburgh *(Shane Corstorphine in Chapter 11)*, The Floow in Sheffield *(Aldo Monteforte in Chapter 20)*, Partnerize *(formerly Performance Horizon)* in Newcastle *(Malcolm Cowley in Chapter 19)* or Featurespace in Cambridge *(Martina King in Chapter 21)*. That's a major change, emblematic of how startups are now a valid career choice for young people across these islands, no matter where they are based.

Crucially this generates momentum. The more companies founded and scaled in cities and towns across the UK, the more 'tech stars' will emerge, many of them with the angel investor capital to plough back into their home cities and into new entrepreneurs eager to follow in their footsteps.

This isn't hype. The digital tech sector is growing an astonishing 2.6 times faster than the rest of the UK economy. In 2017 it was worth nearly £184bn to the UK economy (up from £170bn in 2016) *(Source: Tech Nation, 2018)*. And since 2014, London has moved up to third place in the global startup rankings *(Source: Startup Genome, 2017)*.

I would personally like to thank all our scale coaches, past and present, for enabling the Upscale programme to become what it is today, as well as the entire Tech Nation team. Through our programmes and groundbreaking insights and reports, Tech Nation has so far had the privilege of working closely with over 350 UK companies who have collectively raised more than $7bn over the last five years.

Tech is set to be a major and vital source of Britain's post-Brexit prosperity in the decades to come, with startups and scale-ups providing the jet fuel for jobs and growth. The days of having to go to the Valley to stand a chance of success are over; the vision of being able to grow a world-class digital business in the UK is now a reality.

Scale-up nation is here to stay.

London, October 2018

part one
PEOPLE

CHAPTER 1

'Why hiring slow and firing fast is one of the hardest things founders have to do.'

Greg Marsh, co-founder and former CEO
of onefinestay, on hiring and firing.

The hardest decision CEOs have to make is who to keep and when to fire, says Greg Marsh, co-founder of high-end hospitality firm onefinestay, which was sold to AccorHotels for a widely reported £117m (€148m) in April 2016. Speaking to a roomful of entrepreneurs as part of Tech Nation's Upscale programme at the Goldsmiths' Centre in Clerkenwell, London, he went on to cite Andy Grove, the late, legendary Intel CEO, to bolster his case.

'Grove famously said that about a third of the people he hires are great: they transform the function they're in charge of, they inspire brilliant people and make his business fundamentally better,' summarised Marsh. 'Another third are OK. They don't really do much harm, or much good. And about a third are a disaster, and if he didn't get rid of them quickly, they'd permanently damage his business. And that was Grove's batting average having had a lot of practice and experience.'

Marsh then challenged the group: 'If any of you think your batting average is better than that, you're probably wrong and self-deluded. Hiring executives is incredibly hard; getting it right, *really* right, more than about a third of the time is just luck. It's a second-order skill, and professional CEOs get a bit better at it gradually, until they get about as good, if they're honest with themselves, as Andy Grove.'

At that point, one of the founders present asked about the best way to cope with a promising employee who was unrealistic about their abilities and how quickly they should be able to rise up through the ranks.

Marsh's wry smile was one of recognition. 'The only way to retain really good people is to promote them just a tiny bit faster than you feel comfortable with,' he replied. 'And you can, by the way, develop people at an astonishing rate if they're really good and really engaged...

'But when people are possessed, shall we way, of an irrational faith in their own abilities and skills, you've got a challenge. I think really good people aren't, by the way. The really good ones are pretty dispassionate about what they're good and bad at.

'Interviewing and hiring is a great example. It's a bit like driving. Most people think they're good at it. They're not. Most people are shockingly bad drivers – and interviewers. And they have no idea how bad they are.

'And getting back to your question, you need to have a very honest conversation with that person and say: "I don't want to bring someone external in via a recruiter, I want you to succeed at this – because if you succeed you solve all my problems. It sends the right signals to the rest of the company: I know you and trust you. I know what you're bad at and what you're great at.

'"But I need somebody to achieve the following three things, and I need them to be achieved by this time – and I don't know if you can get there fast enough. So if you can, and I will help you by the way, then the role is yours. But if you can't, then you need to accept that you're not ready for that role."'

'And if they don't scale?' persisted the questioner.

'Then you involve them a bit in the recruitment and selection of the person they report to, and unfortunately – here's the punchline – in almost all cases, they will then choose to leave.'

Pit-of-the-stomach feeling

A few weeks later, in a follow-up interview, Marsh reflects on his choice of words on the hardest decision facing CEOs. 'Perhaps a better way for me to have put it would have been that the most difficult thing for a founder to do quickly or early is to fire fast,' he says. 'It's really easy to say "Hire slow, fire fast", but it's incredibly difficult to do that in practice. Fire too quickly and you risk looking capricious to your other senior execs, your board and others.

'That natural tendency for an entrepreneur, who's in sales mode, to sell the heck out of any potential hire, means that having pumped that individual's stock within the company (whether that's among executives, the broader company, the board community or, God forbid, the public community), if three months later you're beginning to have that pit-of-the-stomach feeling that perhaps you've made a terrible mistake here, admitting that publicly is going to be embarrassing and often very hard,' he says.

'It'll also often have fallout, not only because you've got to replace the person, but you've probably also got to assume their responsibilities while you're replacing them, which makes for a pretty miserable life in the interregnum.'

There are all sorts of good reasons why firing someone is always difficult, not least because it's psychologically difficult to tell people they're failing at something even if you can argue, over the medium term, that you're doing them a favour, continues Marsh.

'Compounding that, though, is that in order to know whether an executive is unlikely to be effective in that role, you're likely to have to give them quite a lot of time to set their stall out and to build the function or turn it around,' he explains. 'And that period is time when, at the very least, the company is not making progress in that strategic capability area – and potentially worse.

'So you've got to give an executive time, but it's time the company can barely afford and you can't reach over their shoulder and micromanage them during that period or you're invalidating your own natural experiment as to their competence. So it's a very tough one,' he says. 'You have to give space to that executive, be incredibly clear about what you're expecting, allow them to make their own mistakes, but put enough pressure on them by setting the expectation of how quickly you expect them to be able to deliver what you need of them.'

In this regard, he continues, the UK is at a natural disadvantage to the US, due to the length of notice periods required for senior executives in established companies.

'It's one of the reasons why executive recruitment is so hard in UK startups. By contrast, in the US, it's typically one- or two-week notice periods for senior executives, and the result is a much more liquid and dynamic senior executive labour market. And in turn, that allows you to get people in and out much more rapidly if they don't work.

'In the UK, often, you go through a recruitment cycle, it takes you three months, you finally find your prince or princess, you bring them in and that person then has three months – or God forbid six months – of notice [to serve] with their existing employer, by which time you're just desperate for anyone with a pulse.

'They join, you've got to give them three, maybe six months to prove what they can't do, by which time when you're finally in a position to make an informed decision, you may now have been without a competent leader in that function for more than a year. That's an awfully long time in a fast-growing company.'

Like the majority of current or former CEOs, Marsh has acute, first-hand experience of the damage failing to pull the trigger quickly on a bad hire can do to an organisation. Describing it as 'a common experience', he estimates that perhaps as many as half the senior executives he hired at onefinestay didn't quite work out for one reason or another. 'And in several of those cases, I left it much too long,' he recalls.

Like a bad relationship

'You often know in your heart when [you should part company with someone]: it's when you don't want to spend one-on-one time with them, when it's no longer exciting to hear them talking about their business, when there's a lack of clarity, a fuzziness about what's really going on, what they're really doing, why things aren't happening. When three, four or five months in, you still aren't seeing output. When people who work closely with them don't tell you how great they are, but dodge your gaze when you ask how it's working out with "Jane Smith"…

'Those are all the signs. It's always easier day by day to ignore the signs than deal with them. But that's like dragging out a bad relationship rather than sitting down and having The Conversation. We're always psychologically averse to having those difficult conversations, but we always feel better once we've had them,' he counsels.

So what are Marsh's tips on mitigating risk over hiring, and thus avoiding such situations arising in the first place?

He advises three key steps for screening candidates thoroughly.

First, he suggests entrepreneurs be upfront and realistic about how bad they almost certainly are at interviewing. 'If you accept, as a premise, that the world's best interviewer is probably only going to get it right about half the time, call that x, then… let's say the probability of failure in any given interview is '$1-x$', how do you reduce the total systemic probability of failure of a process? You raise '$(1-x)$' to the power of n, where n is the number of people taking a view.

'So what does that mean [in practice]? It means don't rely on your own intuitive judgement alone; *also* rely on it, but empower people you trust, who have context, to participate in an interview process. So if there are two founders, each of you separately meet the person and everyone is licensed to veto. If you have a board member whom you trust, then empower him/her to interview, genuinely license them with the power of veto, in fact encourage them to veto if they have any suspicion or anxiety about the recruitment decision, no matter how good the person seems on paper. Now you've raised $(1-x)$ to the power of 3, so if x is 0.5, you are now down to only one in eight in likelihood of hiring a dud.'

Marsh's second step is to test the candidate's true motivation. 'How did we do that at onefinestay? After a few iterations we developed a practice of having quite detailed working sessions with [prospective] senior executive hires. It's very demanding to ask a senior executive to take a few days out of their presumably – if they're any good – busy schedule to prepare notes and thoughts on a presentation in advance of your meeting with them, but it quickly weeds out people who interview well but actually don't think well.

'The attendant risk is that you end up unfairly privileging or favouring people who can present a PowerPoint slide deck really effectively. Ex-consultants tend to be very good at this, but it doesn't necessarily mean they're effective executives of course.'

Reference the heck out of them

Once a candidate has gone through the working session, where they've been challenged to see how they think on their feet, then step three is to, as Marsh terms it, 'reference the heck out of them'. That encompasses both formal referencing through a headhunter, but also informal referencing through back channels, he says.

'Talk to people who are willing to be candid. Don't rely on a printed reference. Don't do referencing only in a confirmatory spirit either; don't soft-peddle what you hear. [Referees] tend to understate a candidate's weaknesses, because very few like to be honest about weaknesses. So every time you hear something that smells like a potential issue, dig and dig and dig. Do it tactfully. And once you hear it in one reference call, take it to your other reference calls too.'

Part of the point to referencing, stresses Marsh, is to try to be better at managing the candidate if and when they join. 'So if after doing three, four or five reference calls a pattern emerges, and that pattern gives you real cause for concern – such as a sales person who isn't good at meeting targets or a marketing person who isn't thoughtful or insightful about customers, or a technologist who isn't that good at technology – then stop and really rethink your decision.'

He's also at pains to emphasise that referencing is no mere formality, and as such it should never be delegated by a founder. 'You should always do your own referencing,' he says. 'You learn far, far more from listening to the pause in someone's answers than anything else.'

Always have a question designed to test for hesitation, he says. 'One of the ones I like is this:

> Q: *On a scale of one to 10 how would you rate Jane Smith*
> *as a marketing professional versus all the other marketing*
> *professionals you've seen or worked with?*
> Pause.
> A: *7.*
> Q: *Interesting. Why? What would it take for her to be a 10,*
> *or why isn't she a 10?*

'And now you're asking the important question,' says Marsh. 'The other one I always asked in reference calls is this:

> Q: *Have you ever had suspicion about the person's character,*
> *ethics or integrity?*

'If there's even a moment's hesitation in the answer to that question, then pass on the candidate no matter how good they look on paper, because you'll live to regret hiring them,' he says, before anticipating my next question. 'And yes, I've been there and done it.'

∨

Inspired by a trip to Pisa in 2009, **Greg Marsh** left leading venture capital firm Index Ventures to start onefinestay, a pioneering luxury hospitality business. Having scaled to a team of over 700, the company was acquired by AccorHotels in 2016. In 2017, Greg was elected to the International Board of Amnesty International. He also sits on the boards of APCOA, Europe's largest car park operator, and a pioneering organic baby food business, Pumpkin. Greg was a co-author of the 2017 Taylor review of modern working practices, commissioned by the British prime minister.

CHAPTER 2

'There is no such thing as a perfect culture – that's known as a cult.'

Neil Rimer, co-founder of Index Ventures, alongside key figures from some of the leading VC firm's portfolio companies, on scaling values and making culture count.

From hammock-strewn breakout areas to free snacks and yoga classes, the perks of tech company culture have become the stuff of industry cliché, ubiquitous in offices from the Bay Area to Barcelona. However, the underlying qualities that mix together to help a company develop a distinctive – and, crucially, durable – culture are far harder to pin down, as is the way founders successfully cleave to those values, as their company grows from perhaps a handful of people in a co-working space to many hundreds scattered around the world.

Few people have a better grasp on all of the above than Didier Elzinga, CEO and co-founder of Culture Amp, which is building a pioneering survey and analytics platform for people and company culture. At the time of writing, the company has surveyed 1.8m employees at 1,400 organisations. 'What we've seen over the years is that the companies that do it best think about culture very much like they do about brand,' he says.

'I like to say if brand is the promise to a customer, then culture is how you deliver on that promise. The companies that have done it well are those that have sat down and intentionally described the experience they want their people to have, and then measure it to see what's *actually happening*.

'It's not just a case of them saying "Here are our values, and here's what we want to be", it's also asking – as the leaders in an organisation – how, for example, management works in your company,' Elzinga continues.

'What should your people expect from their manager? Are they coached or driven? Or when somebody joins the company how should they feel on day one? How should they feel at the end of their first week? Or at the end of their first month? And it's not letting that be something that just happens by chance, but something that's intentionally driven.'

Elzinga describes this approach as 'culture by design', arguing that engaged employees are likely to be more productive, creative and innovative. They are also more likely to have an 'emotional commitment to the organisation and its goals', he adds.

'One of the ways I think about engagement is through the "five o'clock test". The phone rings and somebody's about to walk out of the office – do they answer the call or not? If they care about the company, they will; if they don't care about the company, they won't. That's up to you, as a company, to create a place where people care, so that it's not just about their commitment when they are clocked in, but do you have all that they can bring to your organisation?'

To reinforce the point, he quotes from film-maker Brad Bird, director of *The Incredibles*, among other classics. 'Brad Bird said that if you have low morale as a company, for every dollar you spend you get about 25c of value. If you have high morale, for every dollar you spend you get about $3 of value. That's why companies should pay more attention to morale. I love that, because it just captures the whole idea so powerfully: if you have engaged people, the money you put into your company will go so much further.'

But what makes people engaged in the first place? And how to define company culture, beyond the slogans and taglines that some businesses like to hide behind?

For Index Ventures co-founder and partner Neil Rimer, when it works well, culture isn't something that people in an organisation have to think about; rather, it's a collection of values which kick in instinctively as situations and moments of decision-making arise.

'In great companies, whether it's two people or 200, you find complete consistency and coherence in what two different people will tell you about a company, about a specific challenge or opportunity that it's facing.

'And that's not because they spend every day rehearsing that answer,' he says, 'it's because the company's leadership has been able to distil that into a set of values and principles that they've shared with everybody in the company and that those people have embraced.'

Rimer goes on to explain that it was its uniquely creative culture-by-design that drew the Index team to the Helsinki-based mobile gaming company Supercell – makers of Hay Day, Clash of Clans, Boom Beach and Clash Royale – in which the firm invested in 2013.

'With Supercell, it was all about culture. What makes that company so special was the culture that it created that allowed it to attract and motivate super-creative people, and enable them to come up with an unprecedented number of top-five games.

'But the reason we invested in that company wasn't because of the games they had on the market, it was because of the culture that had led to the creation of those games, and the fact that they had started from first principles in thinking about the culture they wanted to have. Their organisational design came to define Supercell, because of the way it would have small teams, called "cells", which would be able to come up with their own games and take them quite far.

'That was unique versus a typical studio culture, where you have big studios working on lots of different things, with teams in lots of different places (because you needed to chase talent and talent wasn't all in one place). They took a completely different approach and said if you want to work for Supercell, you have to come to Helsinki.'

How important does Rimer think it is for companies to write down such core values and, in effect, codify their culture, particularly as they start to grow?

'The most important thing is they think about it and they're aware of it and they do this deliberately and explicitly, and don't assume that it will just happen because they're working on something interesting or vital,' he replies. 'Culture's something that requires somebody's real attention. Not just to encapsulate it, but also to nurture it and promote it. If the culture is being challenged or stymied by changes in the business or to the team, something needs to be done about that.

'There are companies where – and at Index, we don't really gravitate to those companies – they don't really pay any attention to this kind of thing. They are fewer and further between now, because I think people have understood how important this is.

'But it's not the kind of thing you can just slap on like a tagline or a logo. Or go get somebody to do it for you.

'This has to come from the guts of the company and often the leadership. And whether they write it down or not is less important. In the early days, if there are three people saying it out loud, that's just as good. But as the company scales, clearly it will have to be codified and shared in written or other forms for it to survive,' he says.

One leading company that 'codified' the core values which underpin its mission, as it scaled, is Funding Circle, the world's leading platform for small-business lending.

'They are: "Think Smart", "Make it Happen", "Be Open", "Stand Together" and "Live the Adventure",' says co-founder Andrew Mullinger, rattling them off. 'When you start out, it's basically the behaviours and how the founders and the original employees treat each other which define the culture. But when you get to some scale, you need at least an articulation of what the values of the company are.'

However, continues Mullinger, values and slogans are all well and good, but as a company you don't really know how robust your culture is until you hit rough terrain and what you stand for is put to the test.

'Often a successful culture for a business will be one that's supportive, and where you all play for the greater good and there's an element of selflessness about it all. That sort of culture is strong enough to deal with people who are performing poorly.' But if there are flaws and negative traits, they will rise to the surface at moments of crisis, he explains.

'If you have a business where people are secretive, or you have a very aggressive sales culture, or your company's very hierarchical, or whatever it is, the danger is it can work for a short time, but as soon as problems happen and difficult times come, that same hierarchical culture, for example, leads to bad communication and office politics. And when that happens, everything can quickly start to fall apart.'

While it's relatively easy to define company culture when you're a startup – after all, there are just a few of you, united by a vision and embarking on a shared journey – it becomes exponentially harder as a company grows, as well as even more integral to your success. 'It's not just the expression, it's the DNA that encodes the expression of the values,' says Rimer.

'And it only works if it's self-perpetuating. Probably one of the greatest leverage points of a culture is that it influences – and confirms – hiring decisions. Those hiring decisions will favour people who fit the culture, and also embrace it and propagate it in the people they work with and the hires that they make.'

So how does a culture become self-perpetuating, and how do you retain the same sense of purpose and identity, when you require an aircraft hangar for your end-of-year party, and 'all hands' meetings require dial-ins from offices around the world?

One Index-backed company which knows all about such growing pains is Etsy, the marketplace where millions of people around the world connect, both online and offline, to make, sell and buy unique goods. It has 721 staff members (at the time of writing), in offices stretching from its headquarters in DUMBO, Brooklyn, to Dublin, London, Paris and Berlin.

Nicole Vanderbilt, Etsy's London-based VP of International, says there are two factors which have helped the company maintain its culture as it has scaled.

'Even at the earliest stages of a company's development, the most important thing in establishing a strong culture is the leadership team constantly demonstrating those values through their own behaviours.

'I firmly believe that nothing replaces that. No amount of posters on the wall or policies can replace that.'

For Vanderbilt, this manifested itself most clearly during her pregnancy. 'At the time, I was reporting to Chad [Dickerson], our then CEO, and many times during that period he gave me examples of where he and others in the company were supporting parents in everything that they needed to be both effective workers and parents. He told me a story about our old CTO [Chief Technology Officer] bringing his young daughter to a meeting because he had a childcare crisis. He made it clear that he felt that was a totally reasonable thing to do.

'He also demonstrated this himself as a parent, when he missed one of our team meetings because he went to volunteer at his child's school one morning. It's seeing your values and culture in action in the behaviours of your leaders that matters.

'I've worked at companies where people and policies say that. But when it comes down to it, you've never seen your boss leave to go to his or her child's recital, or, worse, you've seen other people cringe or look down on someone who does do that. Seeing those [positive] behaviours demonstrated so clearly by the Etsy leadership team really reinforces our culture in a way that no handbook alone would ever be able to.'

Vanderbilt's second point stresses the importance of continuing to protect the company's values as it expands. 'Things that you've taken for granted as implicit, you need to make more explicit and spell out,' she says. 'One example at Etsy is that we have a fairly standard interview evaluation form to fill out for new hires. This form used to include a question about their "Etsyness" (which was kind of code for alignment with our culture). In the early days, it was a bit more obvious what we meant by that, and everyone was fairly aligned. But as we grew, it started to wonder. Did this mean that they know how to knit? Or that they like to code? Or that they're vegetarians? In absence of clarity, each person started to assign their own, and often slightly different, attributes to it.

'One of the things the HR team has done recently has been to take a step back and say, "OK, let's put some more definition around this. Let's give people more of a guide, and some tools and questions that they can use to help us get better answers and better data." It's a great example of where something that feels informal, obvious and implicit early on benefits from being more codified and explicit as you grow.'

While maintaining a strong and authentic culture is essential for all great companies, striving for ideological perfection is rather less so. As a company grows, cultural purity becomes harder to pull off, which is no bad thing, says Funding Circle's Mullinger. 'It's a lot easier when you are sub-100 or 150 people [to be pure]. Once you get bigger and bigger, the nature of it is that there will always be a slight level of hypocrisy around what you stand for as a company, because life unfortunately is like that – messy.

'But the good people that you have will understand that that's the nature of growing a large business, and as long as they see you are getting eight out of ten things right, then usually they are very pleased.'

For his part, Culture Amp's Elzinga agrees. 'You're never going to get it perfect, particularly in large companies,' he says. 'As we like to say, there is no such thing as a perfect culture – that's known as a cult.'

∨

Neil Rimer co-founded Index Ventures in 1996. Previously he spent four years with Montgomery Securities in San Francisco before joining Index Securities in 1990. He has invested in market-defining companies from across the spectrum including Betfair (LSE: BET), Funding Circle, the Climate Corporation (MON), Deliveroo, Last.fm (CBS), Moo.com and Supercell. He has served on the board of UC Sampdoria, and currently serves on the board of Human Rights Watch.

CHAPTER 3

'The age of one brain holding all a company's knowledge is over.'

Unruly co-founder **Sarah Wood** on the changing role of leadership (and her own company's scaling challenges).

In her 2017 book *Stepping Up: How to accelerate your leadership potential*, Sarah Wood, co-founder and chair of the celebrated advertising tech company Unruly, argues that in today's more fluid, tech-powered world, everyone has leadership potential – it's just that the notion of what it means to be a leader needs to be reset. 'Leadership isn't about leading a team, necessarily, there are different types of leader and different types of leadership,' she says.

'There's thought leadership, market leadership, as well as managing and leading people. In *Stepping Up* [which was written with Niamh O'Keeffe], I hope I was making it very clear that not only do we all have the potential to be a leader, but actually lots of us are already leaders, we just might not be leaders in the business context. We may be planning trips for our friends, or running a book club, or coaching our daughter's football team, or we're caring for elderly parents, managing their hospital appointments. These are all ways that we lead in our everyday lives. They're just not the way that leadership is traditionally conceived.'

Yet surely the 'traditional' definition of leadership is one that still holds true for most people, I point out. Aren't we very clear that by the 'leader' of a startup, we mean the CEO – the man or woman who calls the shots and with whom the buck ultimately comes to a juddering halt?

'Depends which business you're working in,' Wood responds. 'I'm sure you can find plenty of businesses with a lone wolf leader sat at the top hogging the steering wheel. That's just not the kind of business – or business culture – I wanted to create at Unruly. And it's not the kind of business that necessarily flourishes in a digital age where business is ever more complicated and you need shared knowledge and collaborative decision-making.

'You can't just have one brain holding all knowledge in their head and claiming to know where everybody is going anymore. You need lots of empowered employees at various points of the business who can function as the linchpins, the change-makers, the facilitators and the trainers – and without all those people you'll struggle to build a successful business where the most talented people want to work.'

She proceeds to namecheck an Unruly colleague, Hilary Goldsmith. 'Hilary's a phenomenon. She came to us as an intern about eight years ago, and moved her way up to Senior Vice President of our Global Ad Operations team. During a panel discussion on leadership recently held at News UK [part of News Corporation, which acquired Unruly in 2015 for £114m], Hilary said: "You hear about these leaders who are on the deck of the ship, steering the wheel, but I just think that's an old-fashioned idea of leadership. My idea of leadership is everybody is pulling together and you're probably not even going to be able to see the leader, because they'll be down at the bottom of the ship shovelling coal."

'I really liked that metaphor. If you want to lead today, then be the leader who's powering the ship and enabling everyone else to do their jobs, because we are in such a complex moment of time, businesses need to absorb and factor in expertise and perspectives from right across and up and down the company.'

Yet very different ideas of what it takes to be a leader – how he or she should act – persist, whether it's the ship's captain barking orders, or project managers on shows like *The Apprentice* yelling at each other.

'That's business for dinosaurs,' quips Wood.

Maybe so. But figures like Lord (Alan) Sugar, Rupert Murdoch, even former WPP boss Sir Martin Sorrell are seen as heavyweights because they are men who lead in an old-school way, loudly and volubly from the front. Does Wood think that particular breed of leader is on the way out?

Turns out I'm making Wood's point for her. 'We certainly need a broader range of role models – Carolyn McCall, Alison Brittain, Harriet Green, Karren Brady – these are some of the UK business leaders I most admire. Sir Martin very generously contributed his ideas to *Stepping Up*, and I find he's a very empowering leader, the face and [formerly] the driving force of one of the UK's most successful businesses.

'Rupert is highly entrepreneurial and enabling, very encouraging, and News UK, led by Rebekah Brooks, is extremely meritocratic and that is why, when you look across the various businesses in the group, you see so many brilliant women and you see people from all different kinds of backgrounds.

'Your school tie doesn't matter at News Corp, and I think that's one of the things I most respect about the business. It's not just about gender, either. It's about economic background, it's about race, it's about sexuality. People today just want to be in a businesses where they can be themselves, because if you're going to do your best work, you have to be able to bring [your genuine self] to work. That's absolutely key.

'So, yes, we are seeing a new type of leader. And one of the reasons we're seeing a new type of leader is because the emerging workforce is demanding a new type of leadership. And this is a good thing. The millennial workforce is much more motivated by purpose, much more motivated by working somewhere where diversity and inclusion are valued, and they also want to be somewhere where they get continuous feedback, where they are invested in and are given the opportunity to progress in their careers.'

Fluid structure

'And you can understand why they want all these things. So many of them have seen the housing ladder pulled up beyond their reach, they're saddled with massive debts from university, they've got more job insecurity than any other generation – and with the pervasiveness of social media creating an audience and an echo chamber for judgements and generalisations, they are also the most judged generation in history.

'So it's not at all unreasonable for younger employees to ask for continuous feedback, to seek clarity on where they might be going, to expect investment in their professional development. To be working for a company that has purpose. So, yes, I would argue that to some extent the changing needs and desires of the workforce are helping to shape a shift in the types of leaders that we have.

'Whether we're talking about Westminster or [Harvey] Weinstein, the Presidents Club or [some] Oxfam aid workers, we have a crisis in leadership and it's a moral crisis as much as anything. Old models of leadership just don't work: you can't exert your power in that way anymore and expect people to simply do as they're told. They simply will not accept that behaviour from their leaders and that's a change for the good.'

That's not the only factor having an impact on leadership however, Wood notes. She also points to the rapid and constant technological upheaval in most industries as having 'the biggest impact on the shift in must-have leadership attributes'.

She says, 'The biggest changes are being brought about by wave after wave of digital disruption. Because technologies are changing so quickly, you can no longer have one person who sees themselves as the steward of a business or the gatekeeper for new ideas. Businesses need to be agile and responsive, and this creates the need for a much more fluid structure and a more open idea of leadership, where everybody is expected to be innovating, to be leaning into what's next, and shaping the future so that fresh ideas can be surfaced in the business and then acted upon quickly.'

In that context, every business leader needs to view themselves as an entrepreneur, she says. 'If they don't see themselves in that way in 2017, they're unlikely to be here in 2027. It's the new intelligence – it's entrepreneurial intelligence. We're familiar with IQ, and with EQ, but we're just beginning to recognise the importance of entrepreneurial intelligence, of digital intelligence and of inclusion intelligence, which is super-important if you want to realise the potential of the whole workforce.'

Extreme communications

When it comes to her own experience of scaling Unruly, Wood says the most acute growing pains – particularly around Series A stage – included the three Cs: communication/clarity, culture and consistency (especially of product).

'Communication became more challenging as we grew because we were no longer sitting around the same bank of desks, but we were sitting around four banks and then we were sitting across two offices, three offices, four offices… There's no simple way to solve that, other than extreme communications: making sure that the communications are two-way dialogues and not just one-way broadcasts, and having regular contact – whether that's through hangouts, stand-ups, or weekly one-to-ones with managers.

'We're a global business, and each functional team, including our exec team, meets over Google Hangout or on the phone every day just to catch each other up. Then we'll have weekly bulletins and monthly "show and tells" so everyone around the business has the chance to see what's new. We also have quarterly town halls, where everyone can ask questions and we can be transparent about strategic goals, financial performance and employee engagement, which we measure using the Net Promoter Score (NPS), giving us a regular pulse on how people are feeling about working within the business.

'Then, every 18 months, we have our all-hands UnrulyFest, where everyone comes together in London for training, for celebrations, to meet each other in person and to make sure we're spending time together building relationships. As a leader, instilling clarity becomes more important than ever before when you're in the scale-up phase, because it's very easy for people to know that you want to grow, but they might have very different ideas about how to achieve the growth, which can lead to lots of people pulling passionately – but pointlessly – in different directions.

'That's why it's so important to have the vision, the mission, and the values for the long haul; to have clarity around strategic priorities for the next 12 months, quarterly objectives, fortnightly sprints, weekly objectives for the team and daily to-do lists, with stand-ups so you are publicly accountable on a daily basis.'

While she acknowledges that this represents 'a lot of communications overhead', Wood insists it's worth the price because it enables a startup to prioritise the correct work-streams and makes people much less likely to roar off at 100mph in the wrong direction. 'It's also much more rewarding to be in the sort of environment where people take the time to explain why,' she says.

'If you don't know *why* you are doing something and you don't know *why* it contributes to the team goals and the company goals, then it's probably not a good idea to start doing the task until you do understand the context and why it's important. Because there's never a shortage of things to do in a startup.'

'I don't ever want to fetishise culture'

The second scaling challenge the company faced was culture. 'I don't ever want to fetishise culture,' she says, 'because there's too much fetishizing of culture as though it's something that is sacrosanct, that comes from the founders and needs to be conserved at all costs. I just don't buy that. Having run a company for 12 years, I see that culture evolves. And that's appropriate; a culture should progress and evolve with the business.

Wood recalls writing Unruly's maternity policy when she was 30 weeks pregnant. 'And it was a shitty maternity policy because I was a busy entrepreneur who didn't have time to do a proper policy and wanted to get back to work quickly because I had a lot of video campaigns that I wanted to smash out of the park. It was only as we grew to be bigger that we brought in a chief people officer, who explained that, er, this [policy] wouldn't be appropriate for everybody else and we could do better.

'So we became much more aware of how having a hard-driving startup culture excludes a lot of people from the business. It excludes people with families, it excludes people who might have other interests outside the startup. Again I think there are some myths around working in a startup or being a founder, and really all these myths do is perpetuate homogeneous forms of leadership and keep out people who have valuable expertise, and a lot to give, but don't necessarily conform to the stereotype of working 24/7 and just keeping at it until the job is done. You can do that for a short time, and maybe in the very early days it's helpful to have that approach, but it's not sustainable. That's not a long-term sustainable business that is going to ride the waves of many industry changes.'

Practical measures like offering more flexibility and more agile working practices will help encourage a more diverse workforce, and see more women in particular drawn to work in startups, she says. 'But more than that, we need to be crafting and telling different stories about our industry. The future, the digital economy, will largely depend on the stories we tell ourselves right now.

'If we want to shape a future that is more diverse, that doesn't just have *Blade Runner*-style male heroes, then we need to start telling stories that include different types of heroes, and that's absolutely fundamental to seeing a meaningful shift. Today's stereotypes are holding us back from making progress – too often, our expectations and aspirations are set by the advertising we watch, and by the media we consume, and until we change those stories it's going to be very hard to change perceptions about women in tech/business/ leadership positions.'

Emerging workplace

Wood goes on to argue that excluding people with young families or outside passions is actually harmful to a business. It's missing a trick, she says. 'Some of our best team-players and our most effective members of staff are new mums. They come back after they've had baby number one, then again after they've had baby number two, and they know the business inside and out, they are very organised, super-grounded and very loyal – and loyalty counts for a lot in an industry where there is a war for talent.

'So I think it's about turning some things that have traditionally been seen as disadvantages into strengths. People often look at our senior leadership team and say: "Wow, that's unusually female for a tech company!" That's because we're happy for people to take time off to take their kids in in the morning, to pick their kids up in the afternoon. Then eventually what happens is it's not just the mums that do that, it's the dads that do that as well. It then stops being a "mum's issue" or a "woman's issue" and it just becomes about having a more flexible, family-friendly workplace. That's another big shift we're seeing in the emerging workplace.'

At the time of writing, Unruly had recently launched an initiative called 'Uncovering flexibility', to formalise processes which had hitherto been more informal and ad hoc. 'What we found was that flexibility was causing some resentment because, for example, not everyone realised they could have a sabbatical after five years of service, or that they could flex their holiday allowance, or leave the office early to go to a concert they'd been desperate to go to. So it was a case of putting those things into a policy to ensure consistency across different teams and regions.'

Similarly, the initiative explained that Unruly team members can take up to a month travelling, and do their work in any of the company's various offices around the world, so long as they pay for their own travel and accommodation expenses. 'This is a win-win: a win for the individuals who get the opportunity to work across the business in different markets, and a win for the company because we get to share and disseminate culture and expertise, but without having to spend a huge amount on relocating people.'

Mission versus boomerang

The final scaling challenge Wood cites was one of finding consistency, particularly when it comes to product. 'If your startup is operating in multiple markets, then you will know only too well that markets [evolve] at different speeds and therefore product requirements vary wildly,' she says. 'With Unruly, we found that some markets moved to programmatic advertising much faster than others, some are more interested in the creative features of our [Unruly] Player than the rest, while others prioritise the quality of the media environment.'

In a fast-moving digital landscape, advertisers ultimately need to reach audiences wherever they are, on whatever medium or platform they are using, she continues: 'One of the reasons brands work with us is because we have scale. What that means is we need to be making long-term bets on where the technology is moving. Also, at the same time, as a startup and scale-up we needed to make sure we were here to survive in the long term, and we could only do that by making sure we won deals on a day-to-day basis.'

To ensure consistency, as well as survival, the company's leadership team introduced a development methodology – called

XP, otherwise known as 'extreme programming' – that has proven incredibly successful as Unruly scaled, particularly in responding to changing market requirements.

'Essentially, it's an extreme flavour of agile software development where everyone codes in pairs – no exceptions – and there are daily stand-ups, fortnightly sprints, continuous delivery, rigorous pre-testing, all practised scrupulously,' she explains. 'So where I say there are "no exceptions", there would never be a coder coding alone on the platform, they always work in pairs, which means we have very robust technology and an inbuilt mechanism for sharing knowledge of the code base.'

It also means the company is geared up to respond rapidly to what its clients want in market, which can bring its own distinct challenges. 'One client may need a product feature to go live next week, while another needs a different feature to go live a couple of weeks later, and it can then be difficult to balance those short-term customer needs against a sustainable long-term growth strategy,' says Wood.

'It took us years to get this right. I don't know that any company ever gets it perfectly right, there's always a bit of a pendulum where you're swinging from one side to the other.'

A solution employed at Unruly was to split the company's development capabilities. 'We have a team that's set up for longer-term strategic builds. We call that the "Mission Team", and they're focused on projects that may not bring in revenue this quarter or even next quarter, but we know we need to do that work to make sure we're future-proofed and staying ahead of the game. The other team is our "Boomerang Team", which – as the name suggests – can turn around requests and get them out into market very rapidly.'

XP has become a critical part of the company's DNA, she says, which helps embed consistency, particularly around product. 'It's a connective cultural tissue because it ensures that the development team and the commercial team are aligned. Every two weeks they come and sit together in a room, and discuss what the most important stories [pieces of code] are.

'Each story has a commercial sponsor who argues for it, and explains what the value is, over the next quarter, the next year and so on, and what the opportunity cost is of not doing the story. And they can fight for that story to be at the top of the prioritisation queue. That way we ensure rigorous debate about which product features get built.'

So what are the missteps that Wood most often sees Series A and post-Series A founders make? 'One area is specifically communication with investors. People often underestimate how much you have to communicate with your new investors, as well as your board, following a Series A.

'As you scale, your stakeholder group grows exponentially, including your staff, customers, board members, investors, suppliers – and with the board, in particular, if you don't invest the time giving them the information that they need, preparing it well in advance, making sure they are consulted on the agenda for each of the board meetings, then you can be storing up real trouble.'

Hiring sprees

The second thing to watch out for is retaining focus, she says. 'When you've had a Series A and you've just raised a lot of money, it's very easy to go on a hiring spree and lose sight of the most important roles and also of the behavioural traits that make your employees successful. One of the mistakes we made after our Series A was precisely this; we were so excited to fill the roles that we just started hiring people because they had experience – they were brought in as the "voices of experience". But we stopped doing that very quickly.'

Asked why, Wood replies that once they'd raised their Series A, Unruly began attracting a different type of person. 'We started attracting people who wanted to work in a cool office for a trendy VC-backed company. What we really wanted, though, were people who were passionate about advertising, who loved video and who wanted to come in and roll up their sleeves and do the impossible every day.

'The other thing that happened was, we started hiring middle managers. We were always being told that the people who were right at the early stage of the company wouldn't necessarily be right [when you start to scale]. But my advice is: give them a chance to succeed.

'Before you decide that you need someone with five years' experience from a large corporate or tech platform, give your home-grown talent a chance to succeed, because the grass is always greener. When you look at candidates from other bigger companies and you think: "Wouldn't it be wonderful to hire someone from Google or Facebook?" the answer to that is: "Maybe." Or maybe you're just hiring someone who's used to being a cog in a wheel and those people may struggle to have an impact and they may also struggle to integrate within a startup culture where you've got young, passionate, go-getting employees who are actually really keen to step up and be given that opportunity to lead.

'Sure, there's going to be an ability gap, a skills gap, but I will always say that in our experience it's been worth investing in our home-grown talent. That's why we have Hilary on our exec now. It's why we have Cat Jones, who also came to us as an intern; she's now our brilliant SVP for Data. Our best hires have been our interns who have risen through the company really fast – just give them the opportunity and clear their path and give them the coaching and the training and the opportunities to lead they need, and they will rise to the challenge.

'When you watch people like that rise up, it gives everybody confidence across the whole company, because you know you're in a company that rewards hard work and that is a meritocracy. And it isn't a company that is going to bring in outside talent just for the sake of it because they like the fact that someone has worked at a big-name corporate before.'

Office design

When it comes to devolving leadership to international offices – Unruly now has over 300 people across 20 offices globally – Wood says one key to success is charismatic local leaders, who can lead a team and convey all the excitement and enthusiasm to be found in a company's headquarters that often gets lost in translation by the time it reaches local markets. But, she adds, once you have these local general managers or country managers in place, they must be empowered.

'There's always a tension about how you achieve that – I don't think there's a perfect way, because if you give too much autonomy to [the local office] then you can end up with inconsistency: inconsistency of product, inconsistency of service, inconsistency of culture and staff experience. So there's always a balance to be had there, but that's where the constant two-way communication comes into its own.'

One element that has helped Unruly unify its culture across its hubs has been office design. 'We have our brilliant SVP Global Creative Dan Bernardo, who has been with us for eight years, and as we've opened up new offices, he's 'Unrulyified' each of the spaces, and far more cheaply than any local contractor.'

Unrulyified?

Wood smiles. 'I guess we have a shared understanding of what it means to be Unruly in terms of a workspace. There's going to be a gaming console, there are going to be lots of games and space to play, comfortable spaces to talk and work quietly, there's going to be a kitchen table, places where you can be informal, be yourself, discuss ideas, have difficult conversations and do that in a setting which is conducive to honesty rather than sitting across desks. Once the spaces feel unified, you've got a really good basis for building a unified culture,' she says.

Similarly, a quarterly 'Oneruly day' helps crystallise vision across the entire business. 'This is a brilliant 24-hour hack across the whole company, where we all focus our efforts on achieving a single global goal.' (On the day when this interview took place, Unruly was holding a company-wide 'Mexican wave' for sourcing developer talent.) 'We're on a big global recruitment drive at the moment, as News has given us additional investment for further programmatic development,' she explains. 'They're really excited about what we are doing, investing in our platform and bringing safety at scale to global advertisers, so how do we get all of our offices around the world excited about it too? And how do we make sure they're referring the best candidates?

'The answer is you throw a party, and you do that in each office. So each team has an hour within a day, where they have nachos, Mexican hats and a soundtrack, and they all sit together with laptops to scour our LinkedIn contacts, film the team doing a Mexican wave and then pass it on to the next team. The winning team is the one that logs the most relevant referrals in an hour. It's a simple way of turning a chore into a team sport and making sure that everyone round the business is clear about our number-one priority.'

Crucially, says Wood, leaders across the business must join in and support these sorts of initiatives. 'I'll make sure that I'm there this afternoon, sharing my contacts, sharing the role, joining the Mexican wave – the magic happens because everybody is participating. Creating a participative culture is one of the keys to success in any company, but it does need time and investment. As much time and investment, in many ways, as the product itself.'

∨

Sarah Wood is the co-founder and chair of Unruly, one of the world's most innovative advertising technology companies. Alongside co-founders Scott Button and Matt Cooke, she successfully developed the company, opening 20 offices and working with 90% of Ad Age 100 brands before selling to News Corporation in 2015 for £114m. Unruly now employs over 300 people globally. Sarah was awarded City AM Entrepreneur of the Year in 2015, and CEO of the Year at TechCrunch's Europas Awards in 2016. She was also named Veuve Clicquot Business Woman of the Year in 2016.

CHAPTER 4

Total Football, 'crossing the Rubicon' and why startups need a talent brand.

Saul Klein, founding partner at LocalGlobe VC, on scaling your team.

'Break points.'

Companies, says serial entrepreneur and investor Saul Klein, have naturally occurring 'break points' on their scaling journeys. The first 10 people is one such moment. The next comes as the company scales from 10 to a team of 50. There's another at around 200 people. A fourth at 1,000. And so on.

'In each of those phases, the scaling challenges are very different,' he says. 'Post-Series A companies, for example, are evolving from a group of people who do a little bit of everything and have degrees of specialisation, to increased levels of specialisation and management.

'Then when you get full specialisation, plus management, plus senior management, plus international, you have another level of complexity.

'It's a truism but, as you scale, the organisation and the people within it, how they're organised, the business design, and not just the product design, become increasingly important.'

'There are five key things in any business…'

… that a founder is keeping in mind at any one time, no matter the stage, Klein continues. He lists them as:

- Product
- Team
- Growth
- Underlying unit economics
- Capital and cash flow.

'As a leader, as a founder, certainly as a CEO, you're permanently juggling all five of those things,' he says. 'But as you scale, you need to start to build around yourself a team that can take functional and operational control of those areas, so that you're gradually putting yourself in a position where someone else increasingly has full ownership of them – and over [every other aspect of the business, including] product, hiring, operations, revenue and cash flow.

'That means trusting them to have oversight and provide support and direction for the teams in those areas, because without that you'll end up being too down-in-the-weeds, which can take your eye off the ball and stop you seeing the bigger picture.'

It can also make you too interventionist as a manager or a leader, adds Klein, one of the UK's highest-profile tech investors.

'Delegation is key.'

'This is really all about building a team around yourself increasingly of people whom you feel can deal with each particular area of your business on a day-to-day basis better than you could yourself,' he says.

'Your job then becomes balancing those five key areas and making sure that everything is pointing in the right direction, knowing that at any one time at least one or two of those things are going to be out of balance or problematic.

'If you don't have good people taking control of those areas, who are able to step up and be accountable for key issues like hiring, product and growth, then you won't really know where to turn as a founder.'

'Communication and ongoing dialogue are critical.'

As a founder, you need to make sure that your teams – right down to specialists, if you're a software company, such as your back-end and front-end developers, data scientists and DevOps person – are talking to one another, and that people are pointed in the same direction. Obviously the more people you have in the organisation, the more challenging that becomes to manage and orchestrate.

'That's where things like strategy, culture, goals and objectives become really important because the larger, the more complex the organisation becomes, the more you need things that really bind people together.'

'Total Football.'

Klein argues that one of the ways of achieving that all-important bond is through the concept of 'Total Football', which is defined by the Cambridge English Dictionary as 'an attacking style of playing football in which all the players in a team except the goalkeeper can change positions during the game'.

Says Klein: 'The key idea there is that every single member of the team, other than the goalkeeper, theoretically should be able to play in every other position. Now obviously a software developer is not necessarily going to write great marketing copy, and a sales person is unlikely to be able to write Python. But the real principle that applies to teams is that it's very hard to get the most out of people unless they understand and respect each other's roles.'

It's common, he says, to see divisiveness in organisations between engineering and marketing or sales and marketing or finance and product – particularly in scaling companies.

'While it's unlikely that people will be able to swap in and out of these very different roles – Total Football-style – at the best types of organisations, certainly people in leadership roles understand and respect the roles that other people are playing and also understand that "while I'm not going to understand your piece of the business as well as I understand my own, the better I understand your piece of the business the better I'll be able to work with you and the more successful my piece of the business will be".'

'You can't retrofit organisational DNA.'

The teams Klein currently works with at LocalGlobe are still typically sub-20 people. But he and the other partners prioritise helping the founders in their portfolio get the DNA and culture right as early as possible, 'because it's very hard to retrofit a culture and a set of organisational values and behaviours', he explains.

'The more you grow, the more institutionalised your values and your behaviour and your culture become. It's very hard to turn the clock back and say: "Time out! We want to do things this way now."

'We try as much as we can, at this very early stage, to help founders and CEOs think about how to build teams in the right way.'

'As a scaling VC firm, we really try to deliver on the notion of Total Football too.'

To emphasise the point, Klein says that LocalGlobe portfolio companies are not just working with a single investor, they're working with the entire investment team, and indeed with the operations team too.

'The operations team at LocalGlobe is very involved with supporting the founders and the teams after we've made the investment. Our view is that without them being part of the initial investment process and understanding why it is we were attracted to investing in this company in the first place, without them being in the investment presentation and then the investment committee decision, it's very hard then to say: "Here's a company, now go work with these people!"

'But if they'd seen the institutional evolution of: "This is why this company's interesting; these are the things we think are exciting; here are the challenges that they have." If they'd met that team and they'd seen them present, then their ability to do their job as an operations team – i.e. to support these people – is greatly increased and enhanced.'

Similarly, at follow-up meetings, milestone meetings and board meetings LocalGlobe has a minimum of three in attendance – two from the investment team and one from the operations team – meaning that no single person within the organisation owns the relationship with that founder and/or CEO – something scaling startups can learn from, Klein says.

'The companies we back genuinely have a relationship with us as a team, as a group. So hopefully that means they get better support, but it also means that internally you're building redundancy into your organisation, so theoretically anyone on our eight-person team [at the time of writing] should be able to step in and help any of our startups at any time.

'Translating this to the way an organisation works means you have to know enough about what is going on so that you can step in and help out if an opportunity presents itself, or if a problem arises. Unless you have this value system where there is an acknowledgement that everyone in this organisation plays an important role regardless of their department or where they are in the hierarchy, it's very hard to really get the most out of people.'

'For this kind of culture to thrive, you need systems and work flows that optimise for information transparency and collaboration.'

Klein points out that there are lots of great tools allowing companies to do that today, but ultimately it's a set of systems and values that optimise for it.

He concedes that not all companies follow this model, and some very successful companies, Apple included, operate through information silos and probably believe that you can give people too much information and that too much information can be distracting. But such an approach is probably more applicable to large later-stage organisations, he says.

'The kind of people you want in your first 50, 100, 200 people, by and large, will not only be really knowledgeable, but born into the mission.'

'You also want them to be agile and flexible. It's very hard to recruit and retain those kinds of people unless you're giving them a lot of access, a lot of information and a lot of autonomy.'

'Crossing the Rubicon.'

Klein refers to another key aspect of successfully scaling a team as 'Crossing the Rubicon', in a reference to Julius Caesar's decision to cross the Rubicon river in 49 BC, a strategic move that he knew would be viewed as an act of war by the Senate in Rome.

'The real point of the analogy about crossing the Rubicon is to say that when you are confronted with a tough decision – where there is not necessarily a single answer or where there are very good reasons why you could stay on your side of the river – and you make your choice, having discussed it at length, you cannot then disown it.

'So this is about team coherence and cohesiveness, because you make tough calls as a team, you have the debate, you may be right, you may be wrong, but this is the decision you've made. And once it's made, you all own it as a team.'

'There are at least five to ten decisions a day, big and small alike, being made inside an organisation.'

That's why it always comes back to creating a culture based around teamwork, he says.

'So the point about crossing the Rubicon is, thrash it out, have the discussions, have the debates, but don't paralyse yourself because there is (often) no right answer. When you do make a decision, make it proactively; one of the rules about crossing the Rubicon is that you don't look back and you don't turn around to your colleagues, when you cross the river, and say "I told you this wasn't going to work" or even "I told you this *was* going to work and now I'm going to take credit for it".

'It's really about making sure that when decisions get made, people move forward. They don't look back.

'Again, it's not about a decision being right or wrong – and this ties in very closely to the culture of Total Football – it's where you recognise and acknowledge other people's views and perspectives.

'Really effective teams become highly skilled at arguing, debating and discussing tough issues – and when they move forward, they move forward together.'

'The point of having a weekly management or partner meeting, or quarterly off-sites, or whatever it is, is the rhythm you establish is actually a forum where people can have these "Crossing the Rubicon" discussions.'

'You can put stuff on the table, you can honestly discuss and debate issues, but you then move on as a team,' Klein says. 'And if you can't, you stay on your side of the river.'

Far better to have these hard conversations and decide either to go on together or not than to have someone or part of a team dragged along because they weren't really happy with the decision in the first place, says Klein. 'That's the atmosphere and environment that exists in 70% of companies, or more.

'And that is the kind of thing that kill companies.'

'If you're having difficulty as founders in attracting the right talent to be able to achieve all of the above, then you need to focus on building a talent brand.'

Companies spend time on their corporate and product branding, but the best ones spend an enormous amount of time and energy on their talent brand, Klein says. They ask an all-important question…

'What makes us the most interesting place to work at?'

'It obviously depends a little bit on what you're doing, but by and large, to me, this is not necessarily about benefits or environment.

'Often what people are looking for, particularly in that first 20–50 people in an expanding company, is:

- What is the challenge that you guys are going after?
- What makes what you are doing difficult, yet important?
- Who are all the other smart people that I'm going to be working with?

'Often companies have [interesting answers to these questions], they just don't always take the time either to articulate them or expose them, because they don't think that recruiting is a place where they have to be building their brand.

'They're wrong.'

'Everyone wants to hire the best people – but the best people have a lot of options.'

Particularly as a young startup with only Series A funding and few-to-zero customers, you are essentially selling people a dream, says Klein.

'You're often asking them to forgo the safety and security of alternative career routes. And sometimes you're asking people to not start their own thing but to join your thing instead.

'So I think really understanding how you articulate your unique talent proposition to that calibre of person is really challenging – and really important.

'Many of the best companies do that brilliantly,' he says. 'People want to go work at those places not just because they pay x amount or they have free food or whatever.

'It's because they're doing something that people will think: "Wow! If I can help solve this problem" – and it could be a technical problem, it could be a social problem, it could be an economic problem, whatever it is – "then I'll get a lot of personal gratification."'

'By and large all of the research, as well as one's own experience and common sense, suggests that the type of people who are attracted to startups are attracted by mission and challenges...'

'Quite frankly that's happening even more now in larger companies too, but it's certainly true in smaller companies.'

∨

Saul Klein is co-founder and partner of London seed-stage VC LocalGlobe. Previously he was at Index Ventures, which he joined in 2007 and where he was a partner until May 2015. A serial entrepreneur with two decades of experience building and exiting companies in the US, Israel and Europe, Saul has a passion for working with seed- and early-stage businesses. Most recently he co-founded Kano and Seedcamp. He co-founded and was CEO of LOVEFiLM International (acquired by Amazon) and was also part of the original executive team at Skype (acquired by eBay).

CHAPTER 5

'Skilled coders don't necessarily make the best managers.'

Toby Moore, co-founder and former CTO at
Space Ape Games, and now venture partner at
Entrepreneur First, on scaling your startup's tech team.

When Toby Moore first moved to London as a Java developer over a decade ago, he assumed he was going to go into banking, 'because that's what Java developers did in those days'. A chance conversation with a recruiter, however, led to an interview – and ultimately a job – at Mind Candy, which was then a startup 'operating out of a small shed in Battersea', having only recently closed its Series A.

Moore would go on to stay at the startup, which became one of the poster children of the UK's tech scene, for more than six years, taking over the tech and product teams after the company pivoted from Perplex City to Moshi Monsters. 'I was just a senior engineer at that point, and didn't really have any of the skills required [to be a CTO],' he said, addressing a roomful of Upscale tech leads.

But that certainly didn't hold him back. Fast-forward to mid-2012, and in the wake of raising its Series B round, the entertainment company had scaled explosively to about 250 people, clocking up hundreds of millions of dollars in sales and 90m users. Moore's tech team, meanwhile, had grown to 80 people.

During the early days of his stint as Mind Candy's CTO, he made what he now considers to be a classic new manager's error. Of the first few people he promoted to management roles, all of them were 'great programmers' – the pick of the bunch. But when, despite being well compensated, one by one they began to consider leaving the company, he asked himself what he'd done wrong.

It soon dawned on him that the belief that the best individual contributors were those most suited to management was inherently flawed. 'People start off as individual contributors and naturally the best of them get recognised for their contribution. But [the bosses] think they should move up the management structure, where it becomes less and less about their contribution and more about managing other individuals,' Moore argues.

'There's an assumption that to get further in your career, to be paid more and have more respect, then you have to move up into management; but that is a very hard transition to make. Not for everyone, maybe, but for most people, it's a pretty hard thing to go from a skilled worker to a skilled manager – they are very different sorts of skills, almost polar opposites in a way. And the assumption is that is that it's easy and natural, when it absolutely is not. I think that's probably the number-one problem among scaling tech teams that I see time and again. It causes a lot of struggle.'

Pure engineering

'In my experience, the best individual contributors didn't really want a management job in the first place,' he says revealingly. 'They just wanted more money and the ability to make more impact.'

At Mind Candy, Moore resolved this by deciding to build a parallel engineering stream, alongside that of management, where the most outstanding talent would have the potential to rise through the ranks to the most senior position of Principal Engineer.

'[That role] was paid about the same if not more than the management role, but it didn't come with any management [duties],' says Moore, who – since leaving his CTO (and co-founder) role at Space Ape Games – has joined company builder Entrepreneur First as Venture Partner, while also coaching a wide variety of founders and CTOs. 'It just recognises excellent work at a pure engineering level.'

That twin-track approach to promotion made a huge difference, he says. 'The conversation with a senior engineer changed from being "Do you want to be a manager?" to "You're at a point now where you can decide whether you want to be a manager or carry on down the technical track – and they come with a similar amount of compensation and the ability to make an impact, just in different ways".

'That's a much better conversation to have and it's something that's stayed with me since making that mistake in the early days,' he adds.

Very different skills

What makes the transition from individual contributor to manager even trickier to negotiate is that many coders have little desire to hang up their keyboards and shelve their primary passion for the sake of career growth. 'The likelihood is that the reason they're coding is that they found, from an early age, that they love doing it, were naturally good at it and put a lot of time and effort into it,' Moore continues.

'It's like telling a talented footballer that they can't play football anymore. So it becomes a question of "Should I give up doing what I really love for a reward that I think I want, but probably won't get much satisfaction from at the end of the day?"'

Although he concedes that opinions differ, Moore is 'strongly' of the belief that to be an effective CTO or tech team manager, you can no longer spend your days coding.

'There aren't enough hours in the day to do that and be a good leader and a good peer to the rest of the management team. I do think engineers want to work with someone who can talk at their level when they want to express issues that they've got, in terms of their code, and they want to work with someone who is [capable] of very good technical work.

'But personally, I believe that to be a very effective leader you can't also be doing the work, because what tends to happen in that situation is that you keep the best coding work for yourself and end up taking the bulk of the recognition for it. And if you're doing that, it's really unfair on the team and really demoralising.'

If talented coders are going to make the transition to CTO and manager, says Moore, it has to be 'a very conscious decision' by the individuals concerned.

'If the differences in the roles are really explained, and it's understood that it's a horizontal move rather than a vertical one, where you actually have to go back to basics and learn a lot of new skills from the beginning, [as well as] give up the coding, then they can make really fantastic CTOs. But it's about bringing some consciousness to the decision to make that change, rather than organically letting it happen and finding yourself in the wrong position.'

So who should CTOs be promoting instead?

'It's the standard leadership and management behaviours that apply,' he replies. 'What makes a good leader or manager in general is probably the question to ask.'

Culture gap

Another issue CTOs in fast-scaling startups often have to adapt to is gelling with the rest of the company's leadership team – particularly around communication. When you're sitting around the top table with other executives in various C-level functions, they all talk in the same vernacular – the jargon-loaded language of business, Moore explains.

'The top executives, HR, finance, and marketing, they all talk in the same way, whereas if you've been doing technical leadership for a long time, the language you use is very different. [Yet] you're kind of expected to have a certain level of business and management understanding, which you often don't have.'

To bridge this culture gap, he urges tech team managers to get up to speed on the principles of business. 'You need to know what P&L is, what a balance sheet is, what's "above the line" and "below the line", what investors are looking for and strategy versus tactics. All these [terms] are commonplace for people in normal business roles, but you don't really talk too much about them when you're in a technical role.'

On the flipside, senior tech folk need to dispense with their 'in-house' tech terminology and acronyms, as well as their distinctive strain of cynicism. 'Quite often tech people appear to be very cynical, but don't really mean it underneath. But if you turn up to a board meeting being very cynical, you're not going to do yourself any favours, because most management teams are very optimistic and cynicism isn't the behaviour expected from someone at the top table.'

Indeed, Moore's own boardroom debut is something of a cautionary tale (although in his case, it was a matter of content rather than tone). 'I was running both product and tech at Mind Candy, and I went into the board meeting thinking that those two areas were about 98% of what was important in the company,' he recalls. 'So I had the expectation that I was going to talk a lot and most of the board meeting would be about what I was doing.

'It didn't take very long for me to realise that I was wrong. Obviously product and tech are very important things in a tech company, but the intricacies of it aren't what the board discussion is about – it's about the company and the strategy, and whether the business as its own entity is healthy. [As a tech lead] you think you're at the centre of the world until you realise that you're not. And then you have to adjust accordingly.'

Coding as art

One further issue which Moore identifies as potentially fraught is what he terms 'the push and pull between coding as an artistic or scientific endeavour and wanting to be excellent at it, and the reality of the constant business demands that mean you have to compromise to meet deadlines or various business goals'.

That conflict happens a lot, he says. 'And unless the company has an extremely strong purpose and mission that people, including the tech team, can get behind, what tends to happen is that the purpose and mission of technical people is to do good technical work that they're proud of – it's like the sort of work an artist would produce if left to their own devices.

'Trying to convert the company's purpose into a technical purpose that is stronger than doing good work for the sake of doing good work is really key [to solving this]. But a lot of people struggle with that,' he adds.

With the road ahead all but certain to turn bumpy for most tech leads and CTOs of fast-scaling startups for any number of reasons, Moore urges first-timers in those roles not to be wary of sourcing advice and support along the way.

'As a coach, this is obviously self-serving, but I really believe getting a mentor or a coach or an advisor, someone who's done it before, to guide you through it, who will work with you in a professional capacity, and not just meet for a beer once a year, but actually spend time with you – ideally compensated – will make a big difference to the individual and the business. I had that at Mind Candy with someone that the board gave me and it was fantastic and transformational.

'I didn't really know coaching existed until then, and when the board recommended it I was worried that they thought I wasn't good enough to do my job, and then I realised that, no, they're just trying to help,' he says.

So how should founders go about tracking down a coach?

'There are networks in London, executive coaching practices, and boards – especially VCs – tend to have people who manage services for their portfolios, so they have an internal database of these kinds of people. But they're not going to offer them to you; you'd have to ask them, normally.'

You are only one or two degrees of connection away from people who can make a significant difference and really help, he says. 'But there's a big difference between meeting someone for a coffee and someone actually engaging with you and being part of your success within that role. It did make a big difference to me, and I've seen it make a big difference for others too.

'The nice thing is that we're now approaching the second or third generation of tech startups in London. I've been there for 12 years now and we've had the Skypes and Last.fms, the Moo.coms and Mind Candys and we've got the third generation coming through now. A lot of people from the second generation are now doing what I'm doing, which is taking a bit of a break before starting another company, and spending it with startups to help them grow.'

∨

Toby Moore has been a technical leader since the early 2000s in a variety of early-stage and scale-up roles, most notably as co-founder and CTO at Space Ape Games, an award-winning mobile gaming studio based in London, and as Mind Candy's CTO for six years, where he helped build and scale the Moshi Monsters entertainment juggernaut. Now a venture partner at Entrepreneur First, Moore is deeply passionate about coaching and helping founders grow themselves and their businesses – he's supported the technology ecosystem as an angel investor, advisor and through mentoring programmes for many years.

CHAPTER 6

'Managing your own psychology is probably the number-one challenge founders face.'

Asi Sharabi, co-founder and CEO of Wonderbly (formerly Lost My Name), on founder psychology.

As an eleventh-hour substitute for 2017's first Upscale mentoring session, Asi Sharabi, co-founder of Wonderbly (previously known as Lost My Name), explored a topic rarely discussed – at least frankly and in public – by the tech community: the daunting personal and psychological challenges faced by founders when launching and growing their startup.

'Beyond the strategic and operational challenges of founders and CEOs, what I personally find the biggest challenge on a day-to-day basis is what I call managing your own psychology: managing the pressure, the anxiety and all the faces you have to put on in internal and external meetings,' he said. 'I realised there are a lot of balancing acts to being a founder, especially when we decided to play the venture-backed game.'

Sharabi – whose startup is a full-stack publisher of personalised books for kids – described the main balancing act as 'Killing it versus shitting it'.

The startup world is awash with testosterone and bravado, and everyone's expected to 'kill it' all the time, he said. 'There is this sense of the founder and CEO as some kind of superhuman. Very rarely do you read about how flawed founders can be – just like any other human being.

'As a first-time founder, I feel like I woke up one morning to find I have a board, investors and 80 people to manage – and I don't have a f***ing clue how to do it,' he joked.

At that point, founders are forced to put on an act at meetings or simply just to get through the day, he said. 'Sometimes you are very synced with that act and you feel very confident – and other times you don't. And this isn't just in a pitching situation, it's standing in front of your own company, or doing a management meeting with your execs. On so many occasions and in so many contexts, you either need [to pretend] to be someone you are not, or you have to hack your way through it when you're not ready.

'Whereas the expectation is that you're supposed to be killing it all the time, the reality is most of the time you're shitting it, because you know you're winging it. You're doing it for the first time and you're hoping for the best. Managing your own psychology at those times is probably the number-one challenge founders face.'

A testosterone-led industry

A week later, at Wonderbly's Hackney warehouse base, Sharabi, who is almost too tall and gangly for the cramped meeting room we're in, says there's something about startups, and VC-backed companies in particular, that places intense pressure on a founder.

'When there's investment involved and you're making some big promises, there's a lot more at stake. [Running and scaling a startup] becomes such a completely all-encompassing experience that you can't afford not to be "all in"; and in many cases of winning, it's 150% or even 200% in. In fact, I can't even imagine someone who managed to found and scale a startup to a desirable outcome, whether in three or ten years, without being 200% all in.'

The result, he says, is that 'it's absolutely impossible' to switch off mentally. '[Your startup] never leaves your head – there's not a single waking hour when this thing is not part of your being.'

But isn't that the case for millions of busy professionals with demanding jobs?

Sharabi demurs. 'This goes way beyond busy. You can optimise for busy. You can clear time for busy. You can be more productive and efficient to work around busy. I'm talking about that added level of mental commitment where it's absolutely impossible to park it mentally.

'Yes, you can say I'm taking a week off to go to Vietnam, that's doable, but the ability to switch off when you get there is a luxury you just don't have. You can optimise the conditions for switching off if you have a very supportive co-founder, that you absolutely trust, but that really isn't what happens in practice.

'Generally speaking, when you're scaling fast, and when things are going in the right direction for a significant amount of time, the company and the commitment grow at the same time – and, [contrary to what you may expect], it doesn't get easier in any shape or form.

'You may convince yourself that you're getting used to it all, you can still get better at managing your time and become more efficient, but that's all tactical stuff. It's such an all-encompassing, all-consuming experience…' He trails off. 'I've been in various roles, in various situations, and nothing compares with how all-consuming [founding a scaling startup] is.'

He goes on to cite the example of a recent family holiday, where his psychological absence sorely tested his family's patience.

'Some weeks ago, I was with my wife's extended family for an annual gathering in the Alps. I was there physically, but not mentally.

'It doesn't matter how much you try, you can't just put on a face and pretend that you're fully engaged when you're not. I was working all the time, but when you're working, at least the others know what you're doing. It's in those couple of hours at least where you're supposedly not working, that you're spending with your family, that they notice you're not really present.

'It's a similar thing with weekends, where you kind of can't wait for the weekend, because who doesn't? But at the same time the weekend can be such a drag. It's almost as if you get to Saturday morning and you're 150mph one minute and hitting the wall the next. And there's no one you can talk to about it.'

Asked whether he thinks many founders are almost complicit in not discussing this aspect of entrepreneurship, for fear of perhaps appearing 'weak', Sharabi is unequivocal. 'I have no doubt. Anecdotally, occasionally, someone will voice something different, but at the end of the day you're living in a testosterone-led industry where it's all about "the gospel of growth". And, mostly, you only hear the good stories.

'If you live in this world and you see the success stories, you develop this notion of the "Superman/Wonderwoman" founder who went through everything, the ups and downs, but came out winning. The expectation from a leader in any context – political, commercial – is to appear strong, optimistic, hopeful, resourceful and to know pretty much everything, at any given time.

'In this regard it's not necessarily only a startup thing, but in the startup world in particular, that's what's expected of you, and especially in this context, where things can change so fast, and in many cases you almost accidently got to this point – if it's going well, and things are scaling,' he says.

'And if you're a first-time founder, then you wake up one morning and there are 80–100 people in the business, and you don't know how to manage them because no one taught you and they weren't there a year ago, when [the startup] was just an idea with a bit of traction.'

That sort of stress is 'definitely not something founders will talk about in a meet-up', says Sharabi, partly because of a reluctance to puncture the mythology of the Superman founder who defies the odds.

'One of the most incredible entrepreneurs and VCs in the world, Ben Horowitz, wrote a great book called *The Hard Thing About Hard Things*, in which he describes in detail the sleepless nights and anxiety attacks [which many founders endure]. But while the book makes you feel like there are a lot of people like you on this crazy emotional rollercoaster, at the same time it does a lot to perpetuate that Superman myth because you see that "Wow this guy went through all of that shit when things were on the absolute cliff edge, but still he survived."

'[Horowitz] talked to many people trying to figure out the core trait that successful entrepreneurs need, and he came to the conclusion that it was the people that didn't quit.

'So it's endurance, stamina, optimism and probably conviction in your own vision and purpose – a mixture of them all – but the common denominator was "I didn't quit". Again, that, to a degree, adds to the myth of the person who goes through walls and just keeps going until he figures it out.'

No simple solutions

Yet if founders are expecting simple solutions to managing their stresses and strains, Sharabi argues that they don't exist. 'The reason why I've started to think about balancing acts and the idea of managing your own psychology is there is no right and wrong way [of going about it]. You can apply one thing that makes a lot of sense in a particular context, but not in others.

'Sometimes, putting on this Superman mask and going for "the kill" is exactly the right thing to do, because it comes more naturally to you. But at other times it doesn't, and it's almost as if you don't have the luxury to say: "Today I don't feel like Superman."'

Despite this, Sharabi is also at pains to stress that founding and running a startup is the best job he's ever had. 'The thrill of the journey, the satisfaction of figuring out how to make it work, the small and big wins – it's still absolutely worth it,' he insists.

Back at the Upscale mentoring session for entrepreneurs, Sharabi drew the session to a close by asking how many founders present had a partner and/or kids. A smattering of hands slowly went up.

As a father of three daughters, he knows only too well how preserving a personal life while scaling a startup entails yet another balancing act – one he terms 'giving it everything versus remembering your wife and kids'.

He told those present: 'I can find myself at home over the whole weekend, but I'm not there. The voices of my kids are just somewhere around me because I'm so completely preoccupied with my meeting on Friday or the one coming on Monday. And it can be incredibly difficult to pull yourself back to the present and be there with your partner and kids. Sometimes you can do it, other times you can't.

'A very supportive partner like my wife is always a great thing to have, but be aware of that. Be aware that the startup is not the only thing that matters and there are others who need some of your attention too. So giving your startup absolutely everything you can, while at the same time not forgetting the other people who want you and need you, is a struggle – and it's a balancing act that I've yet to personally master.' Then he added: 'But I'm doing better than I was six or seven months ago.'

Two more of Asi Sarabi's 'balancing acts' for founders are:

Focus versus opportunism

'This is more of a juggling act. I can't think of a single board meeting I've been to where the board didn't emphasise focus, as in: "You guys need to focus more – and you'll be fine." What they mean by that is that if you spread yourself too thin, you'll end up not achieving anything. If there is an opportunity for 2x growth here and 2x growth there, you cannot juggle the two, you have to decide which one you're going after and apply yourself 100% to that.

'While that makes a lot of sense, it's also very [theoretical]. In many cases, you need to find the right balance, because forcing yourself to focus is a good discipline in itself, but there is also something inherently positive in the mild ADHD [Attention Deficit Hyperactivity Disorder] that good founders have, where they're thinking "What's next?" all the time.

'You can really screw yourself over by not being focused and by spreading yourself so thin that you end up achieving nothing, but at the same time you can focus so hard that you miss some big things – and see your competition come in and pass you by as a result.'

Stepping up versus track record

'This one is a little more practical than psychological: promoting talent internally versus hiring a heavyweight outsider with a proven track record. As a founder, you'll hear successful entrepreneurs and VCs say: "Look, your job is to manage your risks, and hiring [external] senior execs who have been there, done that is one way to de-risk. And because your job is inherently about taking risks, then if there's any way to de-risk, you should take the opportunity [to do so]."

'But at the same time you're saying to yourself, if – in my own case – there was an opening for a CEO role at a tech-led publishing company in London, I probably wouldn't get approached, [despite the fact that] I'm doing this role right now, and doing it relatively OK. Besides, I have lots of examples of Venture-backed companies who, as soon as they raised Series A, hired two or three senior execs, and the business couldn't absorb them. And in those cases, it was a failure because that person was wrong for the business, or they might have performed in one context but couldn't replicate it another. So, as a founder, you have to balance these competing [outlooks].'

∨

Following a short-lived academic career (LSE, Social Psychology) in which he tried to get Israeli and Palestinian children to hate each other a bit less, **Asi Sharabi** moved on to build a career in everything digital. He started Wonderbly (formerly Lost My Name) as a DIY project with some friends. Pretty soon the project changed from being a labour of love to a funded tech and storytelling startup with the ambition of making millions of kids around the world more curious, clever and kind. In three years, Wonderbly has sold over 2.7m copies of its books worldwide.

CHAPTER 7

Riding the rollercoaster.

Sanctus founder **James Routledge** on spotting
the warning signs of poor mental health –
and what founders should do about it.

James Routledge's mental health startup Sanctus was five years
in the making and forged from personal experience. In 2012, he
dropped out of the University of Sheffield, where he'd been studying
History and Politics, to found a social platform for sports fans called
Matchchat. He characterises his three years as founder and CEO at
the Newcastle-based startup – and at a second startup called Now
Native – as a heart-pounding and exhilarating roller-coaster ride.
'I just found myself taking the red pill and disappearing down the
rabbit hole of the tech startup world,' he says.

'We jumped straight onto the accelerator/VC bandwagon and
raised about a million dollars in three years. But I was never really
working on anything that I was truly passionate about. It was just:
"Can we make an app? Can we raise some money? Can we raise even
more money? Can we sell it and be happy and just try to recreate this
startup dream that everyone seems to be chasing? Can we find that
pot of gold at the end of the rainbow?"'

During that period, he says that while he wasn't actively ignoring
his mental health, it was something that he was barely aware of. There
was no history of depression or mental health issues in his family, so
the telltale signs of things starting to fray at the edges simply weren't
discernable. 'Obviously we're not taught about mental health at
school. Then, I suppose, in the world of startups and as a founder, I

just kind of got primed to never really admit that anything was ever going wrong. I got very good at presenting this facade.'

'It can feel a bit like you're on *X Factor*'

'I was raising money, so I was constantly pitching and presenting. Everything was a show and again, in the accelerator world [Matchchat was on the Ignite accelerator programme], it can feel a bit like you are on *X Factor* at times. It's all about pleasing investors and raising money, and for many people that seems to be the goal in itself.

'I got very good at suppressing any negative emotion, whether that was a feeling of isolation or of imposter syndrome, or anxiety around our financial position or where the business was, and I just suppressed all of that. I just never showed any vulnerability at all really. I was very much caught up in the world of "We're smashing it! We're killing it! We're growing really fast!" – and needless to say the business stuttered to a halt and we ended up shutting it down.'

It was after that disappointment that long-suppressed emotions bubbled to the surface, all but engulfing Routledge. 'When the front of "I'm a founder and I'm doing great!" was gone, suddenly there was a gaping hole in my life,' he explains.

Another job followed, this time working for an angel investor, where Routledge helped run the firm's AngelList syndicate. But the role simply offered him another mask to hide behind – a mask which slipped on all too easily. 'I was almost pretending to be a VC at this point,' he recalls, with more than a hint of embarrassment.

But the emotional toll was beginning to weigh heavily. He felt a creeping sense of anxiety which gnawed away at his life. 'For the six to nine months of being in this job, and post-shutting down my business, I just felt constantly anxious, with sweaty palms. My heart was constantly dancing or fluttering. I wasn't really sleeping very well, and I was drinking a lot at the weekends. I was just feeling very off. Underconfident too. My self-esteem was pretty low.'

Like many young, active British blokes, Routledge says he has a Type A personality. Used to concealing uncertainty behind swagger and bluster, he chose neither to confide in anyone nor to see a doctor to discuss his symptoms. 'The reason for that, when I really reflect on it, is that I didn't want to admit [my mental health issues] to myself if I'm honest. People talk about the stigma and the lack of access to mental support, but you know what? [That support] is out there if you're willing to admit that you need it – and I wasn't. I hid it all away, and the only place I did talk about it was in a journal.'

Panic attacks

Throughout that period of his life, Routledge kept a journal in which he would try to describe how he was feeling – his way of making sense of it all. Meanwhile, his symptoms took a turn for the worse. 'They started manifesting in panic attacks. I was having regular episodes of anxiety attacks, or panic attacks, on the Tube. Then I had one in a meeting, and at that point I knew, no matter how stubborn or ignorant I was, I couldn't ignore [the situation] much longer.'

He checks himself, back-pedalling slightly. 'I'm not saying I was at a critical point. There were no suicidal thoughts or anything like that. I just knew that something wasn't quite right. That's when I first started to look into what was happening to me; to try to find out more about it and understand it better.' So he did what almost everyone does today, when faced with medical or mental health issues: he googled his symptoms. 'But everything out there just served to make me feel worse. It was all about anxiety, depression, suicide, generalised anxiety disorder, bipolar. It was charity websites or clunky NHS websites.'

He continues: 'It was Reddit forums, where people were clearly in distress, and I suppose that was when I noticed that everything around mental health that was out there was very disempowering. It made me feel broken, like I needed fixing, or it made me feel like I was ill and I had serious mental health issues [to confront].

'Deep down, I knew that I didn't. I knew that I wasn't right, but actually I was OK and was just going through a bit of a rough patch. I knew that it wouldn't last forever. I had this inner – whatever you want to call it – strength or voice, that knew that I wasn't "broken" or "weak", but seemingly all the conversations out there were telling me that I was.'

That was when his journal led him to writing a blog post entitled 'Mental health in startups'.

'And that was me coming out,' he says.

Raw and honest.

'I'd been presenting this image and this facade of entrepreneur-turned-investor for a long time, which wasn't very authentic. Then I wrote this one post that was just me opening up. It was raw, it was honest. There's not an element of bullshit or blag in there, it's just completely honest. I wouldn't say it was painful to write, but it was difficult to click "Publish" on. And that post did really, really well. Not that that was why I wrote it. I just wrote it because I thought I had to. It got 10,000 views in a couple of days. There were hundreds of messages off the back of it too. As soon as I hit "Publish", things just kind of changed forever for me.'

The key change for Routledge was a reappraisal of his personal attitude to mental health – he began to learn that openness about feelings and being honest about himself could start to ease the burden he'd been carrying in secret.

'That post also kick-started a load of conversations with friends, family and people around me, and even people I'd never met before. I was just really connecting with them and being really honest and having these meaningful chats. I was pretty much training this muscle of authenticity. What I mean by that is it's harder to be yourself than it is to conform, and I'd spent a long time trying to conform and trying to be someone that I thought I should be.

Being open and allowing myself to have these conversations with people felt great.'

It also sparked in him a growing interest in mental health. 'I got really excited. Whilst I'd seen all this narrative around mental health online that had been very dark and depressing, what I was experiencing was quite the opposite. I was experiencing real uplifts. I was experiencing real connection with myself, with others. I was starting to become more emphatic to people around me.

'I was becoming much more self-aware of what works for me and what doesn't, and more compassionate. I was starting to make choices that were good for me, and I put that down to treating my mental health in the same way that I would my physical health. I started to invest in it. I started playing around with meditation, mindfulness, coaching, all these different things.'

That turnaround was also the moment Routledge began thinking about Sanctus. 'What I realised was the reason I didn't open up sooner about how I was feeling was because the perception of mental health was so bad. The perception of mental health was that it was something shameful to talk about, that you were weak if you felt you were having mental health issues, when what I was experiencing was just the opposite.'

The mission that began to take shape gradually in Routledge's mind was about changing the perception of mental health. 'Why don't we create a brand which redefines what mental health means and really focuses on the positive, uplifting and almost aspirational side of mental health? If you can do that, you can inspire people to invest in their mental health proactively, so they treat it like going to the gym and staying fit. Not only will we then prevent these burnouts and people suffering in silence, until the point where they can't cope, we will also raise the bar of where people are at currently, and hopefully help them to become happier and more fulfilled.'

The fallacy of uniqueness

What does Routledge think it is about the startup world – and being a founder in particular – which often leaves entrepreneurs close to the edge and struggling with their mental well-being?

'A good phrase which I came across recently in a book called *10% Happier* [by Dan Harris] is "the fallacy of uniqueness". Startup founders and people who work in the startup world think they are special. They actually also seem to get into this thing of thinking: "We've all got mental health problems because we're all so special and unique and creative and entrepreneurial." If I'm honest, that's bollocks.'

Every profession comes with its stresses, strains and anxieties, he continues. 'It doesn't matter whether you're an entrepreneur, an investor, the office manager at a startup, an engineer, a journalist, lawyer or banker, the environment we put ourselves in is going to have a certain impact on our mental health.

'The way that we've been bought up, our uniqueness and all of our little idiosyncrasies are going to manifest too, and surface in our working environment. Now startups, yes, they have a particular working environment. There are long hours, there's financial pressure, there are all sorts of different things, including open-plan offices, that don't actually serve to make people feel great.

'There are investors putting pressure on founders and founding teams, there's all this kind of stuff, but we shouldn't fall into this trap of thinking that people who work in startups are special because we're not.'

In fact, argues Routledge, the very idea of tech entrepreneurship being on-trend and 'extremely cool', largely derived from the perceived glamour of Silicon Valley's most successful companies and headline-grabbing billion-dollar exits, has the dangerous effect of attracting ego-driven founders to try their hand at the startup game and found companies for 'the wrong reasons'.

'I believe successfully scaling a startup [from those precarious early days] into a profitable business has to be a vocation. It has to be something you were quite possibly born to do. If not, you're not going to have that passion or determination and you risk ending up burnt out. There are a lot of people that are in it for the wrong reasons and they'll get found out eventually.'

Similarly, he decries the tendency among some in the tech startup world to see being a founder as a path that's inherently superior to opting for the well-trodden traditional corporate route. 'The person who works at PwC, for example, is probably also working 18 hours a day and their partner's just left them or whatever it is. The pressures around being a startup founder are not unique. Yes, there are certain cultural challenges in the startup world which can have a particular impact on mental health and they need to be discussed, but this isn't just about tech. There needs to be much more openness about mental health [generally and how mental health issues can affect everyone, whatever your line of work].'

Does he not acknowledge, however, that a somewhat macho culture has now become pervasive in tech, where founders are fearful of looking 'weak' or ineffective in front of each other and, more pertinently, their investors?

Routledge demurs. 'It's your choice, as an individual, whether you conform to that or not. I'm quite opinionated on this, because [no one's forcing you] to put on a front to say you're always smashing it to your investors. You can tell your investors honestly how it's going. That is possible as one human to another; there's nobody stopping you doing that.

'Culturally, yes, that's what the industry is condoning, but as an individual you can make a decision on how open you want to be. So yes, there's a stigma, there's a cultural thing in startups which is "We're all smashing it, we're all killing it!" because that's the nature of the industry. The nature of the industry is this blurred line between perception and reality: you're trying to create something new and you're trying to sell a vision and a dream that doesn't exist yet, so yes, the lines are very blurred. But it's down to you as an individual, as a founder, to decide how open and authentic you want to be. So I don't buy into the fact that you have to act in a certain way.'

He does concede, however, that a founder who comes clean about struggling with mental health issues to VCs who have invested large sums into their startup is taking a big risk. Any investor will prioritise safeguarding their money – and that of their Limited Partners (LPs) – over an entrepreneur enduring a torrid personal time.

'I'm not saying [being open and honest] is easy to do by the way. I'm just saying it can be done. Yes, of course, VCs investing exorbitant sums of money, large multimillion-dollar sums, into a business – or even individual [investors] doing that – massively turns up the pressure dial. And what many startups perhaps don't see is that those individuals are under even more pressure from their LPs. Those investors will be under a huge amount of pressure from the pension funds or the institutional investors or the family offices or the fund of funds which have given them $100m, $500m or even a billion dollars. That pressure just kind of trickles down, and it does make honesty exceptionally hard.

'But you, as a founder, have chosen that route – and that narrative is quite clear now. In a fairly well-developed startup eco-system, people know that if you're going to go down that VC path, it's going to be really hard work. People know the risks, they know the terms, they know what it's going to be like and they've chosen to do it despite all that. So, yes, there's insane pressure when you raise multimillion-pound sums from VCs, but it comes with the territory and it doesn't mean you can't be open and honest with yourself and your investors along the way.'

A mental health gym on the high street

The big vision for Routledge, in co-founding Sanctus, is to step-by-step build a Nike-like brand which inspires people to look after their mental fitness in the same way as their physical fitness.

'We're an aspirational brand which we hope people will want to be tied to, to show they are the kind of person that invests in their mental health. The sort of symbolic mission for that is to one day put a "mental health gym" on the high street. We believe that the day that someone goes into a mental health gym to go and speak to their coach or to go to a group workshop or to go and meditate for 30 minutes is the day that negative perception around mental health really has shifted.'

Currently, Sanctus offers a service to businesses that begins with a company-wide introductory workshop, where the founding team share their story and get the business's leaders to effectively tell their employees that it's OK for them to be open about mental health issues in the workplace.

'They tell them it's OK to talk about what's really going on. Then the ongoing solution we provide is to put a Sanctus coach into that business for a day, two days or four days a month, and open up that space for people to have a one-on-one conversation with a coach. So that's a bit like putting a personal trainer into a business for people to go and have 45-minute sessions with. It's completely impartial, it's completely confidential, it doesn't have to be work-related, it's not performance coaching, it's just for people to sit there and unwind and talk about themselves really.

'There's a lot of space at work to talk about how your career's going or how you're doing in your role, but we try to create a space that's very inclusive; it could be that you talk about a particular challenge, or you talk about the fact you're stressed and you're anxious, or you talk about how you're in a good place and you want to work out how to stay there. How you improve your self-confidence. All sorts of things, really; anything across the whole spectrum of mental health.'

So what does Routledge suggest that founders, in particular, do if and when they struggle to cope with the inevitable turbulence and dark nights of the soul that hit all scaling startups sooner or later?

'It's extremely important when you're in that position to create space in your life that's just purely for yourself and that has nothing to do with your business. For different people, it'll be different solutions. That space could be going to see a coach or therapist, and you sit down with them once a month and you talk about what's going on with you. It could be that you meditate for 10 minutes every single day and you spend that time just checking in with yourself, where your head is at, where your body is at. Or it could be that you go to the gym for an hour every day and you just solely focus on the day ahead.

'It's very important to have these pockets of time throughout your working week where you take time just for you. It resets, it grounds you, it balances you.

'Obviously I wouldn't have started Sanctus if I didn't think coaching was massively valuable – having another person who is truly impartial that you can open up to, that you can be vulnerable with, that you can share the ups and downs with… That doesn't have to be a coach that you pay, it could be your partner or a friend, or an advisor or your co-founder – but it's having that space where you can truly be yourself. Whether you do that by sitting with your eyes closed listening to [meditation app] Headspace or whether you do that by sharing with someone else, it's getting to the point now where it's vital, and I think in the next five to ten years there won't be a founder who doesn't have that in their life in some way.'

Routledge's confidence that attitudes are slowly changing in the tech startup scene is such that he envisages a ripple effect that will increasingly create a marketplace for mental health products and services. 'Mental health has long been treated as a charity case, but that's changing and there's going to be hundreds of businesses like Sanctus. There are going to be thousands of coaches and thousands of meditation practitioners and it's going to diversify and commoditise just like the physical health and fitness markets.'

Over the next decade, he says, people will talk less in terms of 'mental illness' and 'mental health issues', and will refer to 'mental fitness' and 'mental strength' instead. 'People will be talking about how they tap into their inner world and find out who they really are. These phrases and this language that we've long associated with hippies and the spiritual will become pretty normal. And people will be talking about their own inner journey as much as they talk today about their fitness regime.'

∨

James Routledge started his first business at university aged 20, raising $1m in investment and growing his team and product to relative scale. In the process of building his company and subsequently dealing with its failure, he suffered burnout, experiencing anxiety and panic attacks. He set up Sanctus to create the brand that he wishes had existed for him and for millions of others: a brand that aims to redefine mental health. The Sanctus team do this through coaching, community events and working with businesses to create an environment for people to talk openly about mental health.

CHAPTER 8

'Build a talent pipeline', 'Offer employee equity' and 'Beware title inflation'.

Index Ventures' Director of Talent
Dominic Jacquesson has 19 tips
on how to scale talent.

One of the most difficult adjustments founders face, particularly in the immediate aftermath of raising their Series A round, is the change of mindset from 'lean startup' mode to one where they're suddenly required to go hell for leather on growth, argues Index Ventures' Director of Talent, Dominic Jacquesson. And this attitudinal shift is felt particularly keenly in recruitment. 'They have to go from being super-tight and efficient on hiring, and really holding back by doing everything as far as possible themselves, to suddenly having several million in the bank and being told [by investors] to ramp up recruitment to enable them to scale successfully,' he says.

'That shift of gear is tough to do in reality – but I'm always amazed at how much founders are up for the challenge.'

The reason it's such a tall order, says Jacquesson – who has worked with celebrated Index portfolio companies such as Deliveroo, Funding Circle and Secret Escapes – is that they have to think deeply and differently about organisational design; they have to be clear about what their hiring plan is going to be, and what will work best for their particular company. 'To some extent it's: "What have other people done?" But then you have to make it right for your business model, your go-to-market strategy, your culture, your own skills as a founder or as a founding team.

'Obviously there's always going to be some iteration – you have to be agile on organisational design just as you are on everything else in a startup – but you do need to have a solid plan of action that you can continually tweak and modify.'

Here are Jacquesson's 19 tips for founders on how to scale talent:

1.
Hire a head of talent

Suddenly you've got an aggressive hiring plan, and you're ready to fire the starting gun, but you probably haven't developed the recruiting muscles necessary to execute, because up until then you'll have almost certainly hired people in your immediate network, whether it's people you've worked with before or people who've been recommended by your early hires. But that's a very different process to saying, 'Right, over the next six months we have to hire these 40 people.'

That's very daunting. So building that recruiting capacity is a critical area. It involves several things. I always push, in our post-Series A companies, for them to hire a Head of Talent.

If you're an Upscale-stage company or a startup that's been backed by Index or one of our peers, I'd say do this as soon as possible. The average scaling Series A-stage, venture-backed company will expect to hire 30–40 people over the six to nine months post-investment, and that's not going to happen magically by itself. Even if you do somehow manage to do it without a Head of Talent, you're likely to have to hire another 30–40 people in the six months that follow, as you continue to scale, and will you have managed to put in place the necessary checks and balances on quality without one?

So you need to get ahead of the game if you're going to achieve that level and volume of hiring whilst building capacity to do even more hiring beyond that – all while running the business day-to-day. It may take you a few months to find the ideal person, so I'd suggest getting on the case as soon as possible in starting to identify possible candidates.

2.
Think early about employer brand

One thing a smart Head of Talent will push for, besides role-by role hiring, is to focus hard and focus early on defining and promoting your employer/talent brand. That starts to tie in as well with how you think about company culture and values. Why would people want to join your startup as opposed to A N Other, or going to work for one of the big tech companies? How are you going to convince them that this is the place they should be?

You've got to communicate what's distinct about your company, your mission and your culture. To some extent it's selling your vision, as you do to VCs and customers, but it's also tweaking that from the point of view of a potential candidate or employee.

3.
Introduce interview training

Another process I'd encourage founders to implement early on would be interview training. Usually as a founder you're going to be, at this stage, interviewing everybody who comes through the door yourself. But you want to broaden the net and make sure other individuals in the team – who are interviewing people probably at an earlier stage than you are and filtering people out – know how to interview people, particularly for culture-fit. And again this ties in with your employer brand.

You – as the CEO or founder – might have an intuitive sense of whether someone is just going to gel with what you are looking for. But as you grow, those individuals will need to have been pre-filtered by other people in the company, so you have to extend that cultural radar to others in the team.

It goes without saying that you do that when you're hiring for technical competence and experience and whatever else, but particularly around culture, the more you can make that explicit, and figure out how you're going to assess people for it, the better.

4.
Develop you own version of the 'Netflix culture deck'

Netflix have developed a culture slide-deck which has entered into startup legend (google it). So much so that a lot of entrepreneurs know about it and refer to it now. It's brilliant, has obviously taken years to develop and absolutely nails the company's values, which are a key component of what's enabled it to scale into the juggernaut it is today.

So developing your own version of the Netflix culture deck early on is a great idea – and I know a few founders who've done that. It makes your values explicit, and actually you can share it with candidates, perhaps on your website, rather than just saying: 'These are the roles we are hiring for.'

Even if you don't have a full careers page, you can have something upfront describing the sort of people you're looking for. That way, at least some potential applicants will feel they may not be a good fit for your company and won't apply, so it acts as a simple filter. But this is as much about drumming your values in internally, so they become intuitive and second nature to everybody in the organisation – and those involved in hiring in particular.

5.
Build a payment grid

Another thing I advise companies to do early on – or to think about early and get something basic in place – is how they approach compensation and employee equity. Employee stock options is a topic I've recently written a book about, which is downloadable on the Index Ventures website.

The tendency otherwise is to be very ad hoc and to pay individuals what you think you need to land them. Soon, offers to potential hires start to become a fuzzy mess of inconsistencies. And that can become dangerous and create tensions within the team. So, early on, develop a grid of what you intend to pay people.

I'm not suggesting being completely transparent about who earns what, but a grid that says 'for these differences in experience level and in these different functions, this is the range that we pay people' can really help. It makes it much clearer when you can say to candidates: 'For this role, this is the offer we're making, and that's fair because that's what people in the team are making."

It makes it much harder to get pushback. If you don't have something like that to work from as a starting point, then it becomes much more to do with how aggressive candidates are at negotiating.

When you need to sign your 'star striker', then you recognise that that person is coming in at a different level, with a different grade of experience – and their salary offer reflects that section of the grid.

6.
Everyone should have some skin in the game

From an Upscale company's point of view, we are in the fortunate position in the UK to have the Enterprise Management Incentive (EMI) scheme; options here are pretty much the best in the world, and we should leverage them and take advantage of that fact as much as possible.

In my opinion, every staffer in the company, from the receptionist to the leadership team, should be offered employee stock options, so there's alignment and consistency at the company. At the same time, I don't advocate going nuts; it doesn't have to be vast amounts, but everybody should get something and have some skin in the game. Work it out according to functions; generally speaking, execs and engineers would tend to get the most options.

One of the things I advocate in the Index book is, outside of execs and engineers, holding back by not offering significant equity when you hire people, and telling them they'll be eligible for more options once they've been with you for six or twelve months instead. By then you'll have a sense of what value they're adding to the company. Tell them that you're more interested in using the equity to retain people and motivate them than to hire them in the first place.

Outside of those execs and engineering hires, most people in Europe are still not joining startups for the equity. So you can afford to hold off at first, but then when you've got people who are proven high performers, you can really lock them in and keep them highly motivated with generous awards.

7.
When making senior hires, avoid creating layers of management

Post-Series A you are going to be thinking about senior hires, because up to that point all you've probably been doing is hiring mainly experienced software engineers, maybe a designer, someone in product, marketing or community and so on. You're now going to be hiring for a broader range of roles, but also more people who are going to be managing teams.

Whether you need to appoint execs rather than simply senior hires is moot, and depends on the skill set in your founding team – and particularly on the technical skills you have (or don't have). If you've got a co-founding CTO, it reduces the immediate need to hire others. You don't want to create layers of management for the sake of it. Sometimes the issue is there's this sort of cookie-cutter mentality, where founders think: 'We've got to get a Chief Financial Officer (CFO), a Chief Marketing Officer (CMO), a VP Product and so on.' But those can be the wrong hires at that stage. As part of your 'organisational design' thinking, you should think carefully about what senior roles you most urgently need – and focus on them.

8.
Beware of job-title inflation

There are certain howlers I see that make me wince, such as a company with 30 people with a CMO. I wince because that individual is not going to be what I consider a 'true' CMO. It's incredibly unlikely that a Series A-stage founder will have landed someone with the breadth of experience to have developed that left brain/right brain combination that a CMO needs. You're simply not going to be at a stage yet where you can land that sort of heavy-hitter. So giving somebody a CMO title when they're not actually ready for it just means you're going to have to effectively demote them later on.

The general model of titling at post-Series A stage is a layer of individual contributors, then 'Head of X' would be above that, followed by a director level above that, a VP level and C-suite on top. That's the most common way of doing it. So, often at this stage, you are hiring more 'Head of' and director-level people. An exec title is a VP or a C-level person. You might be hiring a couple of those, but it depends what your business model is and the skill set in your founding team.

9.
Avoid bringing in a big-hitting VP Product really early

Another error I see is startups bringing in a big-hitting VP Product really early. That can often backfire, because the founders are neither ready nor willing to let go of that much of the product roadmap so soon – and nor should they be. In fact, it's critical in an early-stage business that the founders are highly involved in product definition and driving product/market fit. What you actually need at Series A stage is more somebody who can execute day-to-day on liaising with engineers, making sure from a project management view that you're delivering and that you're being realistic about how fast you can roll out and ship features. But the really strategic thinking and prioritisation on what your product roadmap looks like should almost always still be done by the founders at that stage.

So if you bring in a heavy-hitter VP Product, they are likely to be frustrated that they're not being given the responsibility and autonomy to do what they need to do. And that leads to clashes and often to a parting of ways, not because there was anything wrong with the individual you hired, but because they weren't the right person in the right role at the right time.

One caveat: depending on your founding team, it can be very effective to bring in a COO [Chief Operating Officer]-style person instead, especially if you are a solo founder or you're a pair of founders, one commercial and one very technical.

10.
Build a bespoke on-boarding process for your startup

As you expand post-Series A, by the time you get to 40–50 people and you're in the thick of talent-acquisition pressure, you'll start to feel the pain points or tensions from the point of view of people operations or HR.

Some of those follow on directly from hiring. The most common ones, where founders often feel they need to become more effective and competent, are around on-boarding. By that I mean those initial few months after somebody has joined, when you're getting them up to speed, making sure that they feel they know what's going on and that there's a team alignment there – and that you're not creating these silos of different groups where people aren't interacting.

There are also the practicalities of on-boarding, where you ensure people have a laptop and somewhere to sit and it can be as basic as that. Part of the whole on-boarding trick is creating the right environment for people and making sure they're set up for success – so devote time to designing an on-boarding process for your company. It'll pay dividends in terms of integrating new arrivals more quickly and effectively.

(A note on workplace: I'm an advocate of staying lean by subletting or working in a co-working space until you are 20 people. But you'll need to assume that you'll be out within six months or less, so be clear in your mind about where you want to be next; sudden, last-minute moves can be highly disruptive.)

11.
Think about the diversity of your team early on

You have to think about diversity as soon as possible – and post-Series A at the latest – because your company's DNA is created in those very early days. Your company is your people, and by the time you are 50–100 people strong, if you are 90%+ white males, with a few women and the occasional person from a BAME background, then any female or minority-background candidate is going to walk into your office space and probably feel that it's not a place they will want to work.

And it's almost impossible to fix it at that point, because it becomes self-perpetuating.

The lack of diversity in your early team, for instance, limits your company's referral network, because at this early stage somewhere between a third and a half of the employees that you hire are likely to come from referrals from your existing employees. This is a good thing and you'll want to encourage it, but you need to ensure that the referral network you're depending on is as diverse as possible, because then you will naturally bake in diversity from the start.

You have to make a real effort at this, because diversity doesn't happen by accident. Yes, it is difficult when you are desperate to ramp up your team, but it's absolutely crucial if you want a genuine selection of candidates.

12.
Ask new hires for the names of the 10 best people they've worked with

Leveraging your referral network is very important. As part of on-boarding, in the first week of someone joining your team you should ask them for the names of the 10 people they've worked with that they really rate, whether they're looking for a job at that moment or not.

Don't be shy about doing it. Your attitude should be: 'We want to build this amazing company, and we've chosen you because we think you're terrific, so we want to know the people you think we should be working with so we can stay in touch with them.' It might be that they don't join for six months or a year, or never do, but it's always worth staying close to and tracking them, because it's all about building a pipeline of talent.

13.
Hire by thirds

You want to have a mix of talent sources and it will vary by role, because when you start to hire for roles that are new to the company your referral network and employer brand are less likely to help you. You're going to get fewer people thinking: 'I should check out this company for this sort of role.'

If you've been hiring engineers principally, which you probably have until that point, you might find it easier to build your talent brand for engineers, but when you want to start hiring salespeople it's a new thing.

I really like the idea that's gained traction in the Valley of 'hiring by thirds', which is the optimal hiring mix that you should aim for as you grow a startup. The idea is, a third of your hires should be from employee referrals, a third of candidates should be sourced, so you're actively going out directly and sourcing them, and a third inbound, who apply – which means your talent brand is building up and you're getting quality inbound candidates.

That's a good mix to aim for. Of course, you're likely to be more reliant on employee referrals and perhaps more on sourcing in the early days as you build up your employer brand, and then over time you should get there. For me, it's a really good principle to have in mind. It also enables you to reach people with skill sets that you don't have in the team or in areas where your referral networks are weak, or when you are trying to look from a diversity perspective as well.

14.
Put some recruiting metrics in place

Another reason for having a Head of Talent is for getting some sort of hiring and recruiting metrics in place. Basic things like where you're sourcing candidates from, how long it's taking you to fill roles, how much time overall in the business is the whole hiring and/or interview process taking, which team members are the most effective interviewers – or whatever you feel is most helpful. Then you can measure and try to optimise around that.

15.
Install an applicant tracking system (ATS) very early

The entire hiring process will be much easier to manage if you've got an ATS in place.

One of the London-based SaaS (software as a service) startups Index backed in 2017, Beamery, has the tagline 'Treat candidates like customers' – and that's exactly the right approach to recruitment. Measure your recruiting process in the same way you measure sales – i.e. building a pipeline to source leads from, how the funnel breaks down, which parts are inefficient, what's your conversion rate, and so on. That's what their software does, particularly in combination with an ATS. So think about the recruiting process overall in that way.

16.
Make sure you have a consistent message across your external employer pages

As part of your employer branding effort, make sure you've tidied up your Glassdoor, GitHub, Stack Overflow and LinkedIn pages. On those four in particular, having an appealing presence and consistent message, perhaps describing your values as a company, is essential. They should absolutely chime with your own site – the reality is you are likely to be using a range of sites for sourcing talent as you scale.

17.
Regular management training sessions can help forestall conflict

The key change, as you make the transition in size, that drives most of the other challenges you face in terms of retaining and developing talent is the fact that you have a management layer in between the founders and all the people in the team. As soon as you have a tier in between it means there is less connectivity and:

i) the founders don't know everything that's going on;
ii) messages can become garbled;
iii) there may be differences in emphasis between the founding team and the managers they appoint.

Some of those managers might have been promoted from within the team and have never managed people before, so they don't have the skills yet. Or maybe you shouldn't have made them people managers or team managers and you have to find other ways of rewarding them.

It's a cliché because it's true, but often your best engineer or salesperson will be the worst manager of those respective teams. (By the way, that's not to discredit those individuals at all, they are brilliant as individuals and they can have a massive and continuing impact on the company, but you have to find a different pathway for them to keep them motivated and retain them without them thinking it's 'up or out'.)

Similarly, appointing external candidates to management roles carries risk too, because they haven't lived and breathed the journey and they are joining in a more senior role than many people who have been there from day one. That creates a lot of potential for tension of the 'That's not how things work here!' variety, which may entail the founders stepping in to resolve it.

Obviously you want those individuals in part because they are bringing in something fresh and new, but it's got to be aligned with the rest of your team and culture. So I'd recommend having some forum or regular training for all of your management team on soft skills – things like performance management, giving feedback and dealing with conflict.

18.
Step up your internal communications game

Again, it's not like in the early days when you just have a daily stand-up and everybody knows pretty much everything that's going on; you're living and breathing everything in the company as individuals. You now actually need to have some way to communicate more broadly.

So you've got your weekly all-hands meeting, but how are you going to get the most out of that? One tried-and-tested way is to have a different team doing a team presentation at each all-hands, focusing on a particular thing they're working on. You want to make sure you're not just recognising the engineering or product people, and that you're hearing from voices from all areas of your business, that need to be heard and that also have critical things to say.

And the complexity multiplies if, for instance, like a lot of UK startups, you've got an engineering team which is off-shored. Probably a quarter to a third of London startups have off-shored engineering from very early on. So effective internal communications is a pretty common issue.

19.
Gradually introduce a performance management system

In the early days of a company's life you need to step towards a performance management system – although you don't want to over-engineer the process too early. For me, the key thing is management training and having discipline around giving prompt, regular and timely feedback. Better that than holding formal appraisals every six months.

Good managers will give positive, useful feedback as a matter of course, and, when they need to, take people aside and say 'I don't think you should have done that' or 'You could have handled that in a different way', or whatever it may be. And they should do that in real time. Again, it's the whole agile approach to scaling that ripples through to how you handle HR or people issues.

But that deftness doesn't come naturally to most people. It's a skill, and it's something to make people aware of so they know what sort of language they should use or how they should do it. Otherwise you get people ducking out of it and it causes problems or tensions in the team later, or leads to some managers being overly tough and shaming or embarrassing people (who will probably then leave).

Those sorts of things have to be focused on super-early because they are what become your culture. Obviously your culture is carried by everybody in the organisation, but those in the management layer are the key transmitters for how you live up to what your culture says you should be. And if your managers aren't living up to those values and behaviours, then you've got a problem.

∨

Dominic Jacquesson works across the global Index portfolio, but particularly with Europe-based founders and senior executives, on talent-related issues including executive searches, international expansion, building in-house talent operations and providing expertise in various HR areas such as compensation and organisational design. Prior to joining Index in 2012, Dominic served twice as a Chief Operating Officer, in New York and London. He has first-hand experience of scaling companies between 1 and 400 people, and the challenges of building executive teams, managing multi-site and international operations, and steering company culture through periods of growth, crisis, M&A and public listings.

CHAPTER 9

'Founders can sometimes be a massively limiting factor in a company's growth.'

Entrepreneur-turned-Balderton Capital partner
Suranga Chandratillake on why some founders
need to face the music and fire themselves.

It may be something of a taboo topic in entrepreneurial circles – but it's a vital, perhaps even make-or-break issue nonetheless: sometimes the person who founded a company and steered it through its bootstrapped early years – through hustling initial funding to co-working spaces to raising seed – is simply not the right person to see it through scale-up to subsequent rounds and quite possibly acquisitions. So argues Balderton Capital partner Suranga Chandratillake, who has been in this very predicament himself.

'The reality is that it's not just that the founder him or herself changes; companies, too, change dramatically as they scale,' he says.

'What that means is that people who are right for a certain phase may not be right for the next phase. It works in both directions – there have been plenty of cases where a startup has brought in a very senior, highly experienced person with a glittering CV, but they've failed to make an impact and they've taken the company backwards because they joined too early.

'But equally, you're going to also have leaders or individuals in an organisation who were brilliant early on, but at some point in time just don't scale with the needs of the company. I don't think that's necessarily a negative, from that person's point of view. It's easy to think that bigger is better, therefore if you can't cope as it gets bigger that means you're not as good. But it just means a different kind of focus.

'There are lots of people who simply can't do what is required in the early days. Similarly, there are people who can't do what is required later on.'

So how does Chandratillake explain this? 'Some of it is to do with talent and ability, some of it is to do with training and experience, and some of it is to do with what you actually enjoy doing,' he replies.

'I do think that founders, along with other people, can sometimes be a massively limiting factor in a company's growth. All the skills and talents, and almost even the kind of approach that made them so successful in the early days, can sometimes start to work against them as the company gets bigger.'

Salt-and-pepper executives

In a blog post entitled 'A Founder's Guide to Replacing Yourself', about why Chandratillake decided to stand aside as CEO of blinkx – the intelligent search engine for video and audio he founded in 2004, which went on to achieve a peak market cap of more than $1bn – he argued that founders have a great deal to worry about, including whether their board will 'someday decide to unceremoniously shove you aside in favour of a more experienced salt-and-pepper executive'.

While he concedes that 'it's a worry some founders have, although not every founder', Chandratillake says that it has driven some very high-profile founders to opt for 'slightly paranoid share structures', which are popular in the US and afford them some protection against being ousted. Since Mark Zuckerberg, among others, insulated himself as Facebook's leader, the two founders of Snap – Evan Spiegel and Bobby Murphy – have done the same thing. 'They have this special class of shares which means they are in control, and if either of them passes away or leaves, the other gets control so they keep it between them,' he says.

'So there's definitely a level of concern amongst founders that they won't be able to have long-term control. There are legal ways of doing it, of course. One easy way is a set share structure like that, but the reality is that these things only really work for as long as the company is successful and profitable enough that it doesn't require any kind of desperate measures.

'You can have all the share structures you want, but if you're running out of cash and you need to raise new money, then the people who can provide that new money can demand that you change any existing share structure if they want to. So I always think people who come up with these elaborate schemes are slightly missing the point, because in the extreme case it's not going to help you anyway.'

Much more important, he says, is to think about how long you – as a founder – really want to run the company for.

'The answer to that can be "for the foreseeable future", and then when you work with investors or decide which investor to go with, look them in the eye and really discuss this issue with them and consider how you think they're going to respond. That's what you are trying to do: you're trying to [assess] the person. The legal barriers can always be worked around if people really want to.

'So if the founder is thinking they only want to be in it for a certain period and then they want to hand over, it's really important to talk about that before you take on an investor. Similarly, if you really want to be in charge for as long as you can see going forward, and you're nervous at all that the investor may not see it in the same way, then you should also be very straightforward about that conversation as well.'

The straw and the camel's back

For Chandratillake himself, the way his job evolved over time from being about new products, closing sales deals and exciting new marketing initiatives to instead becoming primarily about shareholders, legal process, administrative areas like HR, litigation and acquisitions convinced him that being CEO of a large and growing tech company – with more than $100m in annual revenues – wasn't for him.

'I found all of those things interesting at first and really kind of enjoyed the first two or three times I went through each of them, because anything new is always kind of interesting, at least to me. But over time I realised that that was all my job was. It was just that on repeat. And I saw a future where that was all it was ever going to be.

'The straw that broke the camel's back was when I was negotiating a particular acquisition we were doing and I suddenly realised I hadn't left my hotel room for 48 hours and I'd barely had any sleep in that time. Everything I'd done in that period was honestly stuff that I did not enjoy that much.

'Meanwhile my co-founder and CTO was doing exactly the kind of stuff I really enjoyed doing, on the other side of planet. I sort of woke up and thought: "I need to change this, because it is not what I signed up to do."'

'A switch went off in my head'

Chandratillake stresses that there was no immediate hurry as the company was thriving, nor was he collapsing under the weight of his responsibilities as leader. 'But a switch went off in my head and made me realise that this was something I just had to change.

'Then I was able to talk to my board and figure out what actually was in the end quite a lengthy process of transfer, because we had to find the right person and make sure he or she was ready for it before we finally made the change.'

So what are the warning lights founders should look out for that, while they were the ideal candidate to lead their startup through its early challenges, they may not be the right person to do so as it rapidly scales?

Chandratillake has two suggestions. First, that all founders should have trusted people within their organisation whom they can rely on to give them the unvarnished truth on an issue, rather than sugarcoat it because they are the founder or the CEO.

'Sometimes that may be a co-founder; sometimes it's actually someone who's known you for long enough and they're in touch with the pulse of what's going on in the company. They're confident enough in their position and their relationship with you that they don't mind telling you how it is. I think that's really helpful because those people can turn round and say to you, "Look I'm hearing from different people in different groups that you're the barrier, you're the bottleneck, you're the person who's stopping things from happening," or whatever it might be. Having that kind of insight is very useful.

'You need to know who can do that for you, and to really listen to what that person tells you. Not every day; you don't have to be obsessive about this. But if that person starts to get a level of noise that seems compelling and it's coming from multiple places, then you know there might be an issue.

'You can dig into what they're saying and ask yourself: "Are these things that I know I'm purposely blocking because I want to? Or are they [indications] that I've lost sight of the [overall] goal or I'm slowing down and can't actually cope with the rate of progress we're going through?"'

Irrationalist-in-chief

Second, Chandratillake advocates that founders should be self-aware and attuned to their own moods. 'Much more than any kind of rational thing that you can analyse like your performance, your decision-making or how fast the business is growing, what we're all actually very good at – if we listen to ourselves – is where our heart is and where our soul is on things.

'If you find yourself spending a majority of the time being frustrated, annoyed, bored, trying to avoid things you know you have to do, then you know your job has turned into something that is no longer really well-set for your particular interests.

'Obviously every startup job, particularly as a founder, is really hard. You're going to have a chunk of moments [where you feel frustrated], but if you find the balance of the stuff you don't enjoy completely outweighing the bits you do – and it's not just measured by time, it's measured by level of emotion – then perhaps you need to change something, from just altering the way you work to the extreme of replacing yourself entirely.

'We went through months at a time where everything seemed to go badly, but then there was a day where it would all break through and that made it all worthwhile. However, I just realised that I'd lost that point, just grinding endlessly. I think you can be aware of that kind of feeling, which is also a very valuable sign.'

The best founders tend to have 'a bit of a dual personality – that's just the reality of the beast', continues Chandratillake. The reason for this is founding venture-backed technology startups is a completely irrational activity.

'There's absolutely no reason to believe that five or ten people sitting in a garage or a bedroom somewhere can build something that will be worth billions of dollars and take over the world and [in the process] completely mess up existing [companies] that have hundreds if not thousands of people, who are smart and hard-working, working for them.

'It makes no sense whatsoever, it's a completely irrational thing to do. Anyone who thinks it isn't is kidding themselves.

'As CEO you're basically irrationalist-in-chief, because every human being at some point – however irrational they are at times and however OK they are with coping with this irrationality – will have moments when they stare into the abyss and ask themselves: "What the hell am I doing? How am I having the audacity to imagine this could ever work? It's clearly going to go wrong."

'We all go through those moments, and as a CEO your job is to be the cheerleader at those times to stop your team from looking down into that abyss and deciding to quit. That's a really important thing, and the bigger the organisation grows, the more people you have who are likely to look at that irrationality; and [simultaneously] the more constituents you have, whether it's shareholders or customers and so on.

'[Your role as CEO] is to create a reality-distortion field around what you're doing, and somehow give people the belief and hope that it's going to work. That always exists, and you can never escape that part of the job.'

Mind the gap

But then the question becomes: how much time must you devote to this, and what's your personal threshold for the gap between the reality you know to be true and the version of it you're projecting to your employees, customers and investors?

'Every minute, every day that you [tolerate the gap] has an emotional cost, and has a toll – and each of us has a different bank account from which we can pay that deficit. At some point you can just have too much of it – and when that happens, then I think you [can] start to crumble.'

The reality, says Chandratillake, is that some leaders can keep people going indefinitely, but others cannot. That's a really important thing to watch out for, and when things genuinely are going well, it's really important to start to reflect that and replenish your well. 'You have to exploit the good times, to get yourself girded and ready for the bad,' he adds.

The mark of Cain

When asked whether founders should be worried about carrying a stigma or even 'the mark of Cain' as far as future startups or roles at other companies are concerned if they opt to step down, he is unequivocal. 'My experience, honestly and personally, was that it was a fleeting issue.' He quickly corrects himself. 'In fact, it wasn't even a fleeting issue; I don't think I really had any issues at all.'

The reason for that is that 'the people who matter have all been through tough situations and totally get it', he says.

'No founder I've ever talked to didn't understand. Anyone who reads my blog [on why I fired myself] and is a founder nods instinctively. Any great investor – and good investors are people who have been in those seats themselves before – will get it too.

'Sometimes you'll meet a naive investor, who's only ever been a pen-pusher behind an Excel spreadsheet their whole life, who may not get it because it's not an equation they can find in Excel. But to be honest that's not the kind of investor you want anyway.

'The same with chairmen and chairwomen, and even with people in your company. I was really afraid of admitting it to the executive team. I didn't know how they were going to look at it. I didn't know if they were going to feel disappointed or feel I'd let them down.

'In the event, they didn't at all because they'd also all gone through hard journeys, and they'd witnessed my journey – and they knew it was tough on me.'

It's an entirely natural fear to have and difficult to dispel, Chandratillake says. 'But I can say, as one who survived it, it's actually not nearly as bad as you probably think it's going to be.'

∨

Suranga Chandratillake joined Balderton as a general partner in 2014. Previously an entrepreneur and engineer, he founded blinkx, the intelligent search engine for video and audio content, in

Cambridge in 2004. He then led the company for eight years as CEO through its journey of moving to San Francisco, building a profitable business and going public in London, where it achieved a peak market capitalisation in excess of $1bn. Before founding blinkx, Suranga was an early employee at Autonomy Corporation - joining as an engineer in the Cambridge R&D team and ultimately serving as the company's US CTO in San Francisco.

part two

COMPANY

CHAPTER 10

'I meet too many entrepreneurs who spend a lot of time jumping on planes, trying to be the hero.'

Anthony Fletcher, CEO of Graze,
on what he's learned from scaling to the US.

As head of innovation at Innocent drinks, where he was involved in 14 new market launches (some of which were decidedly bumpy rides), Anthony Fletcher makes no bones about the pain high-growth businesses can endure when expanding internationally. He rattles through the issues, scarcely drawing breath.

'It's very hard to know what consumers in other countries want. It's very hard to know who the true competitors are in other countries. It's very hard to understand the structure of the market and how it works. It's also hard to raise your brand awareness and get your product right. All of these things mean that when you move into another country, if you've got any of them wrong, it can compromise your entire business model,' he says.

He isn't finished. 'Furthermore, what many founders find is that as soon as they internationalise their business, especially if they start opening extra offices, the complexity of the business goes up dramatically... This requires a different set of skills to handle different processes: your ability to nurture culture, your ability to communicate your vision, your ability to get them all to communicate and work together even if they're not in the same location.'

So how did his experience at Innocent shape how he approached Graze's expansion to the USA?

Fletcher replies that he believes it is easier to expand overseas as an online business than as one in traditional retail. 'I believe that technology has invented a number of useful mentalities or behaviours which are useful when going international.

'When Graze went overseas it did a Minimum Viable Product [MVP] test in America, which involved two developers going over for eight weeks to make a website to measure over 100 Key Performance Indicators (KPIs) of what was going on in the local market. This meant that when we went to market we could invest a large amount of money because we were more confident it would work, so [we could] go in with a certain aggression, while being very clear on what the issues we had to solve were.'

There were, he says, just two key issues to address in the end, which meant the company had 'real clarity that to conquer America we need to solve these two things, put teams on them and make sure they had the resources to solve them'.

He continues: 'That isn't how a "normal" international launch works. There's lots going on, lots of different information is arriving at different times. You often find that strategically you haven't got it right, and [you have to ask yourself] how you get everyone to work out what the real plan is. How you then reorganise the business, the product, the marketing and the expenditure plan to solve those problems.'

The two blazing headaches Fletcher and his team needed to address were product and logistics. 'For us, the product wasn't right, but it was nearly right. So you had to take our product and tweak cultural allusions, health positioning and taste profile to make it suit the American market. Not hugely difficult if you have a lot of data coming in telling you when you do get it right and wrong – which we did.

'And, second, logistics in America do not function the same way as in the UK.'

Headache #1: Product

Having been involved in multiple offline overseas market pushes (for Innocent), Fletcher already knew that the traditional approach to new market entry – namely, doing painstaking market research and strategising – was far from a guarantee of success.

'It would still probably go wrong,' he says, 'and so lose you huge amounts of time.' By contrast, the American experience with Graze was radically different, involving focusing on generating an MVP and planning the rest of the firm's strategy off the back of it instead.

Continuous streams of data meant that, from an organisational perspective, the entire business knew it had to 'solve' the product – and answer three questions in particular:

1. Do Americans want larger portion sizes?
2. Will Graze products have a price premium?
3. Are they only going to be wanted in America's coastal (i.e. more sophisticated) cities?

There were universal theories on those topics, says Fletcher, but there's no way a startup has the organisational bandwidth to tackle them all competently without mining data and iterating accordingly. 'Ultimately, getting the product right along those three vectors was mainly done because we got 15,000 product ratings per hour back from our Grazers about what they liked and what they didn't like.

'So it was literally like a game: every week we launched three products. We'd see how they performed, remove the three worst, go and get, say, BBQ sauce working, give up on the Indian flavours, because we decided they were never going to work in America, and so on. Over six months you just gradually make things better and better. Of course, the first wins are always the easiest and then it gets a bit harder later on.'

Headache #2: Logistics

Logistics were another matter. Or 'hugely difficult', as Fletcher puts it. 'This was probably the largest risk we took as a business because we started the full launch process, including securing and building fulfilment centres, while we hadn't solved this problem.'

The specific issue his small team had to crack was that the United States Postal Service (USPS) did not have rich data on its own performance. Or, if they had, they couldn't source it. For a producer of healthy snacks, dependent on slick and seamless distribution, this was of course a major problem.

'So we had two possible theories on how to solve it,' he recalls. 'Plan A was we were going to make a bendable Graze box to flow through the USPS's sorting machines. There was even a guy in Indonesia looking at bamboo moulding [for the boxes] for us.'

And Plan B? 'Plan B was somehow we'd just get the existing service to work, using data. It was the Plan B team who came through in the end with: "OK we need a data set, so we'll just generate our own."

'We got so frustrated with not actually understanding where the boxes were going. We were posting them in New Jersey and they were taking 14 days to reach [nearby] Manhattan. It even got to the point where we were considering putting trackers in the boxes, but it was a time of heightened security concerns and we thought radio transmitters were not a good idea.' He smiles.

'Then someone asked: "Can't you just pay to have these things scanned?" It turned out you could, at seven different places. You just chunked up the money and did it once and did a data science piece [based on] posting them on different days, different strategies, and posting them in different places.'

As a UK-headquartered startup on a limited budget exploring logistics across a vast and complex country, the team ultimately took an imaginative, entrepreneurial approach: namely, one that involved cardboard rabbits.

'We posted cardboard bunny rabbits with tracking barcodes on to understand the mail system there and how it worked,' he explains. 'And from there we then came up with an algorithm for how we should use the USPS. There are all sorts of different tactics and strategies and ways of interacting with it. We actually ended up giving our data back to the USPS to help them improve their understanding of their own e-commerce solutions and why they may be not working.'

Fletcher thinks it was 'the clarity of the problem and the excitement' which got the team's entrepreneurial juices flowing. 'Here's a really exciting challenge, and either you're crushed by it as a business or you go: "We're up for this!" And it's either going to be bendable bamboo boxes or cardboard rabbits.'

While he admits it makes for a 'killer story', the underlying lesson for scaling startups is that if you take a small group of talented people and you can give them a really clear task, most of the time they'll figure out a way to overcome almost any obstacle in their path – often with highly creative solutions.

Conversely, he believes that if Graze had launched in America with a full team and then set about solving the same problem in a less fleet-footed way, six months would have flown by and 'a ton of money' would have been blown, along with significant disruption to the core business.

Fast-forward to the tail end of 2017 and Graze's stateside launch has proven successful. 'It's pretty much 50% of our revenues now,' he says. 'But America has challenged us in different ways, and it's still consuming our focus and capital.'

∧

Asked to reflect on the key factors founders should bear in mind when scaling internationally, Fletcher says if they genuinely want to have offices in multiple countries and internationalise their business, rather than simply export or ship products internationally they need to lean into the changes they've got to make within their organisation.

'They've got to ask themselves questions like: What are you going to standardise versus localise? How can you articulate your culture so that if you've got someone hiring in a different country they can seek the right people? How do you embed that culture in the new organisation? How do you systemise processes, so people in that office can understand how the business works and how they get things done in it? There's basically an enormous list of things which you can get away with not doing when you're all in the same building.'

Here, he describes some of them:

1.
Can you get a signal?

When considering whether to scale into new markets with local offices, Fletcher suggests leadership teams search for signals. 'I met one guy once who worked for a B2B business and said he won't open an office in a new country until he has his first contract. He said: "I believe that you can close the first contract without a local office, by flying team members into the new market. Then, when I have that contract, I know there's revenue coming in and I need to service that first customer, so that's when I open the new office." That's always felt like it makes a lot of sense to me.'

Signals come from a wide variety of sources, he says, including early customers, trade shows, MVPs, exporting and search traffic – and often a combination of the above.

2.
Be obsessive about product/market fit

'As I've described, the advantage of technology is that you can iterate your product/market fit,' says Fletcher. 'You get a constant stream of data, some of it almost in real time, when you have a digital product or physical product. Graze has both. Data-led, high-speed, iterative ways of working can help you solve the product/market fit rapidly.'

3.
Be obsessive about your culture

Culture is always critical, Fletcher argues. 'If one bit of the organisation behaves in one way and another one behaves in another way, you're going to have a lot of trouble in getting them to see eye to eye or feel on the same page on things like appetite for risk and all sorts of things.'

4.
Consider carefully where you're going standardise, and what you're going to localise and adapt

As soon as you launch internationally, you need to decide for a whole range of things: do you want to standardise, i.e. impose on a local market and keep your business the same, or do you want to go – 'the local market is different and hence we need to adapt'?

This, Fletcher says, covers almost every strand of the business you can think of, from whether the brand visuals and health claims, for example, should be the same as in your home market to whether you should be targeting the same customer. And so on.

'So the more you adapt, the more you fit the local market. But at the same time, the more you have to reinvent or do additional work and the more debates you have to have on what is the right approach.

'What you tend to find is that your people in the local countries want to adapt heavily. That's because they can see the consumer and they naturally want to change things to suit him or her. Also people in local offices tend to want control. "I'm sitting here, so I'd rather be in control of lots of things" is a natural human tendency.

'Meanwhile the people in-group – i.e. your headquarters – tend to want to try to keep the business as simple as possible. You've normally got to a bigger size by this time. The business has learned some lessons from simplification, and just having really clear processes and not coming up with little fiddly things for different markets [makes life easier].

'So for a whole range of things from processes to people to your brand to your product, you're going to have to ask: "Is there a reason to change it all or should we keep it the same?"

5.
Most people think they need a local office as soon as they decide to launch in a new market – they don't

Do not underestimate – as soon as you open an international office – how much more complex your life is going to be. 'It's back to the "standardisation versus localisation/adaptation" question – do you really need an office or can you hold back for just a little bit?'

When Graze first launched in the US and was carrying out its groundwork, the team used a WeWork office in Manhattan, although it had already leased its own fulfilment centre in New Jersey, says Fletcher.

'It kept coming back to how much complexity do you want? Do you get an office that's this big or this big?' he asks, demonstrating office size much like a fisherman would a prize catch. 'We hadn't quite worked out how big the team was going to be. We were still having strategic debates on questions like "Do we really need these local experts or don't we?" So by holding it back, again you've got more signals from the market, which helps you make those strategy calls.'

Jumping in with both feet from day one is rarely the answer, he adds. 'It's why some companies lose lots of money going international. Often you take these big punts, you hire an office that's too big or you hire a whole team you realise later that you don't need.'

And beyond blowing a large chunk of (usually) investment capital, if such decisions go awry, there invariably follows a painful period of unpicking. 'Emotionally it's quite difficult to disassemble some of these networks,' he says. 'It's not pleasant to remove a whole team, and you feel pretty bad as a CEO that you made the wrong call.'

6.
Double down on data

Data has been the critical underpinning of Graze's international push. Fletcher describes it as 'very group, as in we believe it's a special area and the job of our data team is to produce data which can be democratised through to bits of the organisation'.

If fellow CEOs at a similar scale-up stage are doing their job well, they will be gathering the relevant data and reorganising it so that people in the local markets can have the tools to do their job, he says.

7.
Send out a seasoned, trusted and – crucially – entrepreneurial team member to head up your new international office – and get *them* to do the local hiring

The idea of getting on a plane, finding and hiring a local executive in your new market and then dropping them in an office on their own and expecting them to succeed is an approach Fletcher characterises as 'mind-boggling' in terms of risk. As is simply picking a team member and sending them out into a new market – because their inevitable naivety will likely prove fatal. 'They won't have the faintest idea about how it all works – even in a country like America,' he says.

Instead, he urges founders to send out someone who is firmly established in the group business, who knows how it works, who has more of entrepreneurial 'can do' attitude. 'It's the "I don't care if the lights aren't working it's all good fun" kind of person. Then identify what the skills you need to bring in locally are.'

Ultimately, Fletcher says, founders probably need a senior hire early on, who knows how everything works locally, alongside the seasoned, entrepreneurial team member who's 'excited about making it happen' and knows how to wire the two operations – headquarters and the new office – together.

'That person will also give you a lot of chat on what's really going on in the market. You often trust them, so if they say "We're screwed because X doesn't work" or "They like the product" then you know what you have to do. If you hire locally, then you won't have built up the trust in that employee, meaning it can be difficult to get that kind of clarity.'

8.
That approach to hiring will set the tone and help you scale company culture

It really matters who the first person you send out is, because they know who to hire and those local hires will copy them, argues Fletcher.

'The first four [local] hires will rock up in the office – and hopefully you've hired people who are a good cultural fit – and they'll look at the person you sent out, and say: "Look at this guy, he's can-do, or he wants to have fun, or he's very analytical and he wants to see me present data to back up my decisions."

'And because he was the first one in, they copy him, which means for the next group of people coming in, you've established a norm.'

9.
Build your own marketing tools –
and do it early

In the early days, the Graze team built a series of performance-marketing tools in-house, says Fletcher. They also developed a culture around how to deploy them to very rapidly test different marketing channels and make almost by-the-day decisions on how to scale them with both digital and traditional media.

'We then gave the American team these tools and taught them how to use them in a way that meant they could rapidly penetrate the market,' he says. 'We knew we'd have to be very good at paid marketing to win in that market.

'Our view on performance marketing is that you have to empower the people doing the marketing every day, rather than have a hierarchical structure where decisions [are made over their heads]. You want your marketing team to have the ability to make the right decisions based on data. And that's what most of our tools are there for – basically to make it very easy for them to see whether things are working or not, and whether they're getting ROI [return on investment] or not.'

10.
Too many entrepreneurs spend a
lot of time jumping on planes

When it comes to how 'hands-on' a company's headquarters should be with the running of satellite offices, Fletcher argues it comes back to having a good debate on 'standardisation versus localisation/adaptation', enabling a team to have clarity early on.

'You need to be able to say the team in the local market's job is x, but for them to succeed they need the support of the group [HQ], who need to do y, which may mean delivering a different product, say, or providing data so that the local market team can serve their consumer better or understand the [components of] a perfectly functioning supply chain.

'So it starts with what your strategy is, and of course being aware of the pitfalls, such as how most of the local people want to do more themselves and that the group is more established, but maybe a bit slower, bureaucratic even, in a medium-sized business. The trick as a CEO and a management team then is to make the right decisions, but what I feel is that most of them don't even realise they should be making those decisions in the first place, and they're being very instinctive instead.

'I meet a lot of entrepreneurs who spend a lot of time jumping on planes trying to be the hero, or the entire management team becoming obsessed with a new country launch and almost leaping into the problem rather than trying to build the organisation which can solve the problem.'

For his own part, Fletcher jetted to the US roughly once every few weeks. 'Would it have been a good thing for me to go more often?' he muses. 'Yes. Did I think that succeeding in America was mostly about transforming the entire business? More so the latter than the former.

'[The team] were doing a good job out there. They had a clear remit, they were very talented, and they had the money required to succeed – and what they wanted to feel from us was that the business could support them in what they needed to do.'

∨

Anthony Fletcher is the CEO of Graze, the healthy snack brand which designs, manufactures and sells its snacks both online and offline in the UK and US. He was responsible for taking the business to the US, achieving a $32m run rate in the first year. He led the company's sale to the private equity group Carlyle in 2012 and launched the brand through traditional FMCG channels in the UK and US, becoming the fastest selling healthy snack in retailers such as WHSmith, Sainsbury's and Boots. Previously, Anthony held various roles at Innocent Drinks.

CHAPTER 11

'Send out a fire starter' (but 'open an international office as late as you possibly can').

Shane Corstorphine, Skyscanner's VP
of Growth, on overseas expansion.

From complex logistics to distribution, taxes and licences to shipping, when e-commerce businesses start to open up international offices, they encounter a labyrinth of challenges (see Chapter 10's interview with Graze CEO Anthony Fletcher). No wonder then, says Shane Corstorphine, Skyscanner's Miami-based VP of Growth, that even a titan like Amazon has a physical presence in a relatively small number of countries (about 30). 'You assume Amazon has localised marketplaces across the world, but it absolutely does not. That's because localisation as well as distribution, warehouses and logistics are all incredibly complicated,' he says.

While digital-only businesses like Skyscanner – the leading global travel-search site – get to sidestep logistics and bricks-and-mortar-shaped headaches, they still face significant challenges, largely orientated around talent and localisation.

Skyscanner has three 'growth hubs': Miami, which covers North and Latin America; Edinburgh, which covers EMEA; and Singapore for APAC. They also have dedicated teams in Japan and China. 'The big thing you need in each hub is at least one high-quality university and a range of spoken languages. You want a real melting pot of nationalities, because as a scaling digital business, the last thing you want is to be opening up an office in every single market – in Peru, say, and try to hire Peruvians. It won't work.'

The location of each hub has nothing to do with the physical market Skyscanner wants to be in, explains Corstorphine somewhat bafflingly. 'It's not about the local Singaporean market or Florida. It's about the scale of the Growth, Engineering and Product operation we want to build out in that region. We have Singapore, Edinburgh and Miami because it allows us to cover the bulk of major markets and hire people from those major markets. In Miami, it's still difficult to hire growth-hacking skills. But the universities there are very strong, so you can build your own pipeline of skilled people if you're happy to invest.'

Moreover, Skyscanner does not plan to open any more hubs. 'We can do the globe from our hubs as we've currently got them. Our Russian team has six Russians in it, but they're all based out of Edinburgh. By finding cosmopolitan cities, you can get nationals there who can do the role you need them to do. Our offices are right next door to the University of Edinburgh for that reason. It allows us to get great engineers, growth hackers, and all kinds of talent right out of the university.'

Clearly those locations make sense for Skyscanner's global reach – its products are available in 30 languages and 70 currencies. But for founders of other types of digital business, what are the signals entrepreneurs should be looking for when it comes to deciding where to open their first overseas offices?

'The first thing you're looking for is product/market fit,' replies Corstorphine. 'And I don't believe you need to set up an operation or office on the ground in a market just to see whether you're starting to achieve product/market fit or not. In lean-startup principles you would chuck the product out there, you would push it a little bit, you might spend a little bit of money on advertising just to try to get some traffic to your site. Then you'd test it; product/market fit tends to be measurable primarily in terms of retention, but also activation metrics.

'So if you push it out in a market and you discover that no one is coming back to use it a second time, or that uninstall rates are super high or whatever it might be, you want to fix that stuff before you start investing in a major office. And you can get it to a satisfactory level, if not a really great level, over time. But it takes time to build trust that feeds into retention, brand and relationships, and you don't want to be incurring a lot of costs along the way.

'Initially you need to be able to answer the question: "Is there a cohort of people that are repeatedly coming back to my product?" You can achieve this by putting people on planes to do sales deals, effectively camping over there to see if you can get that traction and retention and those repeat bookings. And you keep iterating your product. But you don't need an office on the ground initially. There's also a high probability of never reaching product/market fit in some markets, so again, it's best to learn that before you open an office.

'When you start to get much better retention and product/market fit signals that you want to amplify, then *that's* the time to invest. That either means building a team that has nationals working on the ground – if you are online-only like we are, then ideally doing that from a hub office – otherwise it may mean a physical office there.'

Open an office as late as you possibly can

It is not just about the cost, but about the noise and distraction too, says Corstorphine.

'For example, I'm flying to Singapore in two weeks' time, and I fly from Miami on a Sunday night and arrive on the Tuesday morning. I have Tuesday and Wednesday there and then Thursday night I fly back here. That's a 24-and-a-half-hour flight, and I probably need to do that four times a year. Your senior team spends a lot of time flying around just taking temperature checks in these offices – that's a lot of time travelling and not necessarily executing.'

Opening an on-the-ground office also poses risks to a company's culture. 'Stopping your culture from going feral in different offices might also be a challenge. Sharing of best practice can be difficult. I have a 6.30am call every Tuesday, Wednesday and Thursday, and because I'm on it I want the UK on it and I need Singapore on it and it's 6.30*pm* for them. But it's very difficult to build trust through video calls without being present and spending time with them, and to be able to identify what they are going through, what their challenges are.'

Understanding the specific local challenges can be a tall order, too, especially in a new market, he says. 'You turn up, you get a hit list of stuff. But is X really an issue or is it just people venting on stuff? Similarly, what challenges am I not finding out because I'm not here long enough?'

The leadership 'distraction' of having multiple offices is also really significant. While some leaders can get excited by the glamorous or ego-driven side of having more offices, the all-important 'maintaining element' is frequently underestimated, says Corstorphine, who now oversees more than 150 people.

Fly out entrepreneurial fire-starter types to run the local market

Fire starters are ideal people to get a new office up and running, but over time a challenge emerges. 'Centrally, you're always evolving,' Corstorphine says. 'As you're scaling up you're going from 80 people to 1,000 people, and the 1,000 people org will be much more sophisticated and professional by definition than the 80 people org was.

'The skill set you need to grow that team from nothing and establishing it is different from the skill set needed to scale that team.

The skill sets need to be evolved to allow the local team to operate with the professionalism required when they are part of a 1,000 people org. In not doing so, there's a danger they end up operating in a different way than the rest of the organisation.'

So what does he suggest, should that scenario arise?

It's about anticipating that that might happen and sending the right people out at the right time, he replies. 'I would suggest an 18-month secondment, which you might extend by a year, where you rotate out the person who was right for the early stage, and replace them with someone for the next phase.'

Furthermore, instead of opening a new office, if you decide to acquire a business locally which has an existing team, there's always work to do when it comes to integrating that team.

'We actually use many qualitative as well as quantitative metrics to assess the success of an integration. For instance, we'll look at their approach to embedding with our culture. We also spend a lot of money on travel to send the [overseas] people back to the UK to go through inductions,' he says.

Every new start at Skyscanner goes to the UK for induction

Skyscanner has a 'super intense' induction programme which flies new hires to the UK to get to know the company culture, and build relationships and bridges between departments.

'Let's say we were hiring a person a day, which we have done for years, we'd start the induction every Monday rather than randomly throughout the week,' he says. 'We also have this vertical startup belief, where at least a week before a person arrives, we'll make sure that laptops are ready, email accounts are set up, business cards and mobile phones – if needed – are approved and signed off, so that when the new start arrives at their desk they feel genuinely wanted.'

And the induction sessions will already be detailed in their calendar. 'We fly in all the new starts for a sprint, which happens every few months, and they'll get to know their starting group – as well as the various presenters from across the company – so they understand who the experts are in key areas. They'll get an idea of the company landscape and a feel for the culture, which they also get in the regional offices (because they'll have sometimes been working in the regional office for two months before the induction starts) and they'll realise it's not that different.

'Yes, it's very expensive – as a company we generally fly people around a lot anyway – but it does ensure we keep a consistency across regions from a cultural point of view.'

What you DO and DON'T localise

Then you get into the nuances associated with a new market, Corstorphine continues, and the issue becomes slightly more challenging. 'It's then a question of what you allow to be localised versus what you don't. What's a core offering versus what's not? What you ideally want is for core features to be put into a configuration service that allows markets to A/B test lots of different localisations without needing engineering support. Where it's configurable at market level you're not having to tie up engineering time to test little bits and pieces, such as testing a particular type of imagery. Imagery for Mexico, for example, is really different from imagery for Colombia – albeit we use the same language on the two sites.

'And then teams are also localising channels such as building local Facebook landing pages as opposed to a global Facebook landing page, so it's localised from a language point of view, and on and on it goes.'

Ask yourself: 'What do I need to win in this market?'

'Building to win at a market level is highly complicated and a lot of people get this wrong because they start centrally and look at what they should be doing in a new region, and only then do they look at what they should be doing at market level.

'Actually, they should flip it the other way round and ask themselves: "What do I need to do to win in this market?" The answer is everything from designers to engineers – and in an ideal world, that's 100+ people to beat the incumbent domestic player – because every market has a really strong domestic player, who gets the benefits of being really well localised but loses out on network effects and the economies of scale of being global.'

Now, you're unlikely to want 100 people for every market, Corstorphine says, so you then need to ask 'What do I need to have that is specific to that market, and then what do I degrade to regional and what can I degrade to central/global?' – and not the other way around.

From a hiring point of view, accept that sometimes the person who got you from 0 to 50 people won't be the one to get you to 500 or 1,000

Despite the demands of scaling, founders should hire slowly and put a robust hiring process in place to ensure consistency, he says, as well as double down on those who can help them make that journey, with leadership coaching.

If a company is doubling in size every year, you've got to double in capability too, as complexities continually ramp up.

'I recommend being upfront with people – and speaking to them as a group, not just one-on-one, and telling them they're doing a great job but they should push themselves to grow and develop as much as they can. The reality is that the complexity of your business is likely compounding daily.'

Shane Corstorphine's playbook for new markets

- First we do a market prioritisation to see which markets have the most potential. The market is handled by a team dedicated to launching and building the foundations of that market.
- Then we do the technical stuff that's free to do and easy. We drive unpaid traffic. So we would create a domain, or a forward-slash 'en' or a forward-slash 'en-gb' or whatever it might be, or we'd create an app for that market, depending on the market needs.
- Then we start building the market foundations: creating a commercial roadmap where we identify what partners we might need to incorporate to have a truly local product, and identifying any specific product needs that are local to the market. Once the market has achieved the minimum product/market fit, we start testing different growth channels from SEO to paid media, affiliation, etc.
- If the traction is looking good and the product/market fit is looking good, we might hire somebody or incorporate that market into an incubation squad that looks at four or five different markets with three or four different people in it.
- From there, each market becomes like a little startup. The team will continue to work on it, start testing more channels – including starting to look at the paid side too – but still predominantly unpaid, SEO-link building, ASO for app, re-engagement strategies, email or whatever it might be, and they'll start to set all this stuff up. They'll look at the product and the funnel analysis – taking a very data-led approach.
- Then, when it's ready, we spin it out of the incubation squad to become a dedicated market with a dedicated squad of maybe three or four people within it. And those are, broadly, the first steps...

An example of that is how lines of communication within a company explode when you keep doubling in size. 'Supporting people through these changes is a major challenge, as is helping people to understand and accept it – to challenge themselves and continually develop and adapt their skill sets. This is probably the most important thing for any scale-up to get right.'

Does that mean that you are inevitably going to lose a lot of key staff when you reach scale-up size – including those you would prefer to keep?

'Not always, but if care isn't taken, this is a risk,' he says, adding that hiring for a fast-scaling company is complex due to the difficulties founders face in attracting the right senior talent for the particular stage of a business, when it's continually evolving.

Finding stage-appropriate senior talent is a serious challenge

'Founders usually haven't really worked with scale-up C-level people. They may well have come out of corporates themselves and seen senior people blocking growth, or emerged from startups where they've worked with startup people. So identifying the correct hires is incredibly hard for someone in that position.'

The perception of a typical corporate is that it has a lack of innovation, a lack of fun, slow decision-making processes (with multiple sign-offs on nearly everything), blue carpets and a lack of autonomy at a lower-down level of the company – but, crucially, corporate companies tend to be professional and scalable, says Corstorphine.

The trick founders have to pull off when scaling is 'avoid becoming corporate – apart from "professional" and "scalable"'.

'When you start putting scalable solutions in place, what happens is a lot your current staff start saying: "We're becoming corporate." When you ask them what they mean, they list similar things to those I've just said. That's why it's really important to use things like staff opinion surveys to track sentiment around questions like "Are we an innovative company?" and "Do you feel we are innovative?" Your ideal place to get to is where you can say: "We're more innovative, more creative and more fun, but we're *now also* professional and scalable." And that's a difficult place to reach.'

Getting that model right is at the heart of everything when you're scaling up

It can be a long and tortuous road, Corstorphine adds, which is why companies need a board and investors who are 'in it for the long run of the scale-up', rather than looking to monetise early. Most of the seed to proof-of-concept stage has been 'First we prove it, now we monetise it' – but when you're scaling up, you're delaying monetisation even further.

'At Skyscanner, whilst growing revenue quickly, we held our EBITDA (earnings before interest, tax, depreciation and amortisation) at around $20m for four years, and over that time we just hired more aggressively and opened new offices. We kept that cushion though, as we knew we needed to deal with rainy days, whilst also scaling aggressively. Then, when you slow that fixed-cost growth as you start to mature, the operational gearing of your cost base – which has mostly been people – should start to kick in and you should get incredibly profitable quite quickly. Understanding that is really important for scale-ups.'

Invest in leadership coaching

'Hiring senior people for scale-up stage companies can be very hard, because often they've come from a large corporate that does things in a certain way – and culturally they're not quite the right fit,' he continues. 'So being able to identify who can make that transition is key, and by investing in them, they will be more likely to succeed.

'We spend a huge amount of money on external leadership coaching. It's a really worthwhile investment for the longer term.'

∨

Shane Corstorphine is VP of Growth and heads up Regional Growth at Skyscanner, overseeing the travel search company's accelerated growth in more than 30 markets globally. Shane joined Skyscanner as CFO in 2012 and has seen the company grow from 140 employees in two offices to a global organisation of 10 offices and over 900 employees. He previously ran his own startup and was also Director of Performance for Barclays Bank.

CHAPTER 12

The 17 things every scale-up founder should know about boards.

BGF Ventures partner, former LOVEFiLM and Mothercare CEO, and ex-chair of Chemist Direct and Moo.com **Simon Calver** on boards.

1.
The board doesn't run your company – you do

It's easy to fall into the trap of thinking that the board are the people who really run the company, but they're not; the CEO and leadership team are. The board are the ones who help ensure that the strategy is on track and moving in the right direction and that the shareholders' rights are protected. They're there to check the company's being well run and to help support and coach the executive team. But it's the latter who actually run the business.

That's a really important lesson for people. When founders are looking to pull together a board to help them, they should think about the sorts of skills and experience they'll need on the journey they're about to embark upon, and how the board can help them on that journey.

At times it might be that a board member gets really heavily involved in a particular issue because that's their area of expertise – and that's a good thing – but you've got to remember that they're then going to step back and become board members and non-exec board members again, while you and your team have to carry on running the business.

That's why it's so vital to get that balance right. One of the early bits of advice I got from [Index Ventures partner] Danny Rimer was: 'Don't come to us asking about strategy. Come to us and present the strategy. And it's our role to challenge it – but ultimately we, as investors, are backing an executive team, and as the CEO, we're backing you, to lead it, to run it and make the decisions.'

Don't be afraid to do that – be positive. Make the right calls and get help, support and nudging in the right direction along the way, rather than go to the board for the answers.

2.
Go to your board and say: 'These are the three or four things I need help with'

Don't just go to a board meeting with your KPIs and how you're tracking against them and say, 'Thanks very much, see you next time.' That's really not the right approach – you should always give people the data, but let them read it in their own time so that when you're together as a board (and that time is precious), you can make the most of it and ensure that you're discussing the issues that are really important for you or that you really need help with and input on. And that help and input can range from support with recruiting to help with strategic direction or securing the next round of funding.

3.
Minimise the size of your board as much as you can

For a post-Series A company, you need to be able to reach out easily to all the different board members and make quick decisions. That's why if you have six, seven or eight board members, that can become more complicated to manage and board meetings require more orchestrating.

But in the end there isn't a one-size-fits-all answer to what the optimal number of board members should be, because if you're operating, for example, in a very complex market, or you have many different routes to market, then those challenges may mean that you need more contacts, more help and wider coverage than you would normally.

So it really is horses for courses, but don't feel you have to put every executive team member on the board, or that you have to have a board that consists of eight or more people.

The key question you need to ask yourself is this: what is the correct balance to enable you to get the right speed of decision-making?

4.
The more investors you have, the more investors will want to get in around the table (especially if they're writing large cheques)

The number of investors on your board depends on the size of the company and the stage you're at. It also depends on how many investors [in your business] you have in the first place. If investors put a significant amount of money into a business, then they'll want a seat at the table to try to understand how their investment is going – and help.

Typically the best thing to do, when it comes to board size and numbers, is to think about each investment round in turn and ask if there's an opportunity to change the board at that time. And have those discussions early with people, rather than leave it until later on in a round, otherwise it can sometimes get a bit fractious.

You have to respect new money coming in, and you also have to let people know that you want to keep a board light and agile. But the common truth is that the more investors you have, the more investors will want to get in around the table, especially if they're writing large cheques. It's therefore all the more important that you pick your investors wisely.

5.

Help your board by not sending them 50-page board packs at the last minute

Some of your board members may sit on as many as eight or nine boards, so try to help them out by not sending out a 50-page slide deck a day or two before the board meeting. It's going to be hard in any scenario – public or private, small or large – for board members to have read that thoroughly and to have thought through the issues.

Founders and CEOs can also help members of their board by trying to focus down on the three or four key issues that they need to consider. Think differently. Maybe start with those issues, rather than do a page turn through the numbers. In fact, you shouldn't be doing a page turn anyway; people should come having read it – and it becomes pretty clear who hasn't read it when you start to ask: 'Are there any Questions about Section 1 Financials? OK, fine, let's move on to Section 2.'

Your board will soon learn to read the papers ahead of the meeting if you start doing that.

6.

Have a board meeting every other month

More sophisticated, more challenging environments may require more frequent board meetings, but personally I'm a fan of having one every other month. It's amazing how quickly monthly board meetings come around. And actually, you can end up not focusing on some of the key issues facing the business when they're too frequent.

If you need to give a board update – in between meetings – there's nothing wrong with doing so on the phone if that's what's needed, just to keep people on track. Or even sending out a metrics or information pack, so people can ask questions if they need to.

I'm not necessarily arguing that 'less is best' when it comes to board meetings, rather that it's more a question of finding the rhythm that works best for you.

7.
Your board should be tracking the same reports that you are

Make sure that the board are looking at the same reports you are using internally. Don't go out and say: 'I've got to create a board pack of different reports, in order to satisfy board requirements.' Instead, you've got to ensure that what people are looking at are the very things that you are using week in, week out, month in and month out in the business.

There are two reasons for this. First, it gives the board a real understanding of the metrics that you prioritise as a company.

Second, it's no extra work. It's just sending the board three or four reports that you use on a weekly basis anyway, to talk about what's going on.

A board meeting isn't a reporting session – clearly, it's an update on how well the business is going, but it's also an opportunity to get input on the strategy, the focus areas, the concerns, and to make sure the business is moving in the right direction.

8.
Get the whole board together socially a couple of times a year

The board is like any other team. You get out of it what you put in, and the more time you can spend together, talking about issues around the table, the better. I don't think that means before every board meeting you need to have a social, but certainly once or twice a year, I'd get the whole board together, have a dinner and talk about some of the issues, and use it as an informal way to talk about the business.

9.
Always keep minutes of every board meeting

The minutes don't need to be four or five pages long, they can be just half a dozen key bullet points of what's been discussed and decided. But part of why keeping minutes is so vital is that you, as a board member, want to ensure that you're understanding the decisions that have been made, that you're tracking against progress, and that you're capturing the discussions and agreements that you have as a board.

The other reason keeping minutes is really important is that at various times as a board member you are legally required to sign off various items, such as disability policy or health and safety policy. You have to have discussed and approved pension requirements as a board as well as your company accounts – and sign them off, as well as minute that you have approved them. These are all important things in the life of the company, from a fiduciary point of view.

10.
The chemistry between the CEO
and the chair is incredibly important

I have heard of situations where CEOs have said: 'I can't discuss that with my chair because there'll be an issue with x and y.' That's missing most of the benefit of having a chair in the first place. You've got to be able to have a completely open relationship talking about the business, and have a 'no surprises' policy from both sides.

If you do that, then I think your chair can really help you with any issues that are going on and give a useful perspective. And also, your chair can meet you between board meetings – they shouldn't just rock up, sit down for a couple of hours and say, 'See you at the next one!' That's not really their role.

A chair is supposed to help support you and potentially even help some of the executive team. They can be an independent point of view and a sounding board when you need one.

It's really hard running a business, getting a startup off the ground, hiring people, making all that work – and the help you can get from people who've been there and done that or who have a slightly different perspective is really important. So at the appropriate time, a chair is a great addition to the boardroom and also can help keep the board running smoothly so that you don't have to spend a third of your time managing the board and you can get on with the most important thing – running your business.

11.
When you're on the hunt for a chair, put the word out with people you know or that you meet at events (or, failing that, use a headhunter)

As a post-Series A startup, you're not looking for a classic FTSE 100-type chair, but simply for someone who'll be a wise counsel, who can help you through some of the bumps on the way that happen as the company scales. You're looking for someone who's going to help align you with the investors, when there are different sets of objectives and when conflicts occur, which do happen from time to time and can't be avoided, given the nature of the work itself.

To find him or her, you should reach out to people you know, or when you meet people at events, always ask them if they know anyone who might be relevant. If you can't find someone doing those things, you can always use a headhunter or recruiter. At LOVEFiLM, a headhunter helped us find Charles Gurassa, who was a really good chair and wise counsel for me, and that relationship was incredibly important in the ongoing success of LOVEFiLM.

In terms of qualities, it's the chemistry and the value-add and the way the chair can help you that are going to be most important. If you have a City grandee, for example, who is completely intimidating and that you're afraid to put on the spot with questions, then I don't think that's really a value-add for any new or first-time founder.

12.
Having an experienced independent chair, who's able to bring that experience to bear in a board meeting, can be invaluable

My advice is always, at an appropriate time – and that differs by company – make sure that you potentially get an independent chair, for two reasons.

The first is to help you manage your investor base, especially if there are more than a few investors around the table. There will inevitably be a time when the goals of the investors are different from that of management. Having an independent chair at this stage is really useful.

Second, they should also be coaches and mentors, and a source of advice for you as a founder, so that you can have somebody around the table whom you can have discussions with, whom you trust and have a relationship with, and who is aligned to doing what's best for the business.

13.
Don't jump into finding someone for the sake of finding someone

If you can't find the right person to be an independent chair, then don't rush into it. There are advisors than can help; some of your angel investors can help you in certain situations, and then over time those people may evolve to take on a more formal role with your company.

For example, I was a mentor to Richard Moross, founder and CEO of Moo.com, for three or four years before I stepped in as chair. So there are other ways to build a relationship with people, and get an understanding of what you think is important and build that chemistry, because when things get tough in a startup and cash gets tight, it's really hard and you need to have trust and openness and the right dialogue to move the business forward quickly.

That's where a good chair or mentor-advisor that you've built a relationship with can really make the difference. It's less about the board meeting in an early-stage business, and more about the advice you can call up.

14.
Never be defensive in a board meeting

It's really hard when you're sitting there as a non-exec or a chairman and you ask a question and the defences go up and you don't get an answer, or it becomes difficult to ask the question. And then what happens is you get a breakdown in the ability to ask open questions and talk freely about how the business is really going.

Everybody around the table, typically, is completely aligned in wanting the business to be a success, and if you approach it from that point of view, where everyone is trying to make it work, then I think that mindset can help in the quality of discussions that you have.

When the founder and/or CEO gets defensive and the barriers go up, then it inhibits the ability to have a really good, open discussion – and that's often when misunderstandings and miscommunications can take place.

15.
Don't be afraid to hold board directors to account

If you have the sort of relationship with the board where you have an open dialogue with people, then you can always ask the questions: 'How do you feel about the board meetings? What's working? What isn't?'

Ask yourself: "Is it time to do a formal review with each director?' (Typically the chair, if you have one, will actually do the review.) But if not, go out there and have discussions with each of the board members individually. Make sure you're meeting board members outside of the board meeting itself – first, to help build a relationship, get that understanding and build that trust. And second, to get a sense of how they're honestly feeling about things.

Often, if you have these sorts of difficult discussions, board members who are not pulling their weight will either change, which is good for the company, or they'll recognise they need to change, which is also good for the company.

But there can't be any harm in having an open discussion and holding directors to account when they're not living up to the expectations of their role as a director of the company. Even investor-directors have a fiduciary responsibility to the company to ensure that it performs as best it can.

16.
Beware of toxic behaviours on boards

A not uncommon example of this is when you've got two or three investors around the table, and sometimes those investors appear more interested in competing against each other than they are in focusing on the company's issues, particularly when it comes to times of exits or big transactions. Sometimes that can prove challenging.

My advice in those cases is again to spend time trying to create an open relationship with and between board members, so people can have really open discussions.

A board is no different from any other team in the organisation: if a founder were to think about the quality of the executive team and the interactions they would want, it would be the ability to have open discussions and the ability to challenge (and for people not to take things personally).

Again, that has to be exactly the same on the board. Taking a bit of time to build those board relationships so that can happen is really important.

17.
For Series A-stage businesses, having too many board sub-committees becomes quite onerous

If you've got a small board, then don't set up sub-committees too soon. Sub-committees really have a role when there are at least eight or nine people on the board and you just can't get everybody together all the time.

My view on sub-committees at this point in a company's life is that if you need to sign off the accounts, then do it in the half an hour before the board meeting, so you're not having separate meetings and trying to arrange them all the time.

If you're having a discussion about budgets, then make sure you have the time to do that in the board meeting. For Series A-stage businesses, having too many subcommittees can become a distraction.

∨

Simon Calver is best known for his seven-year tenure as CEO at LOVEFiLM, one of the early successes of the UK venture industry – leading the eventual exit to Amazon in 2011. He went on to become CEO of Mothercare, kick-starting the turnaround plan and accelerating international expansion in over 30 countries. Before this he worked at multinationals such as Unilever, led PepsiCo in the UK, and was General Manager at Dell. He was previously chairman of Moo.com and Chemist Direct and is currently a founding partner of BGF Ventures, where he is on the boards of various UK technology companies.

CHAPTER 13

'Create a sense of scarcity' and 'Don't be too nice'

lastminute.com and Founders Factory co-founder
Brent Hoberman's 11 rules on how startups should
go about partnering with – and selling to – corporates.

1.
Corporates must feel like they've got nothing to lose from working with you – and, potentially, everything to gain

When I was at lastminute.com, 30% of the business was B2B – and our suppliers were brands like BA, Virgin, Lufthansa, Alitalia and Air France. We made sure they didn't have to change their business processes to work with us – that's why we accepted, for example, faxes (yes, it was that long ago). We did all the heavy lifting we could on our side, rather than on their end – although that changed over time when we became bigger.

The second thing we did was help them recognise that they could learn from us about the innovation that was starting to sweep across our industry.

Third, in the same way that 'nobody ever got fired for working with IBM', we tried to position ourselves in such a way that if they didn't work with us, they would be left out.

And then fourth, lastminute.com was about unsold inventory, so of course there was no downside for corporates in teaming up with us.

2.
Get to the point where the one person who doesn't do a deal with you will get fired

The bosses at some corporates would expect their teams to be innovative. So you need to make their team leaders worry about being left out of the 'innovation press release' (announcing new partnerships, acquisitions and initiatives).

With others, special deals and inducements were required to get them to do more with us – we offered BA and Virgin Atlantic a 'warrant instrument' (entitling them to buy stock at a fixed price) should they drive disproportionate market share through our platform.

But, ultimately, it was all about creating this sense of urgency, that their rivals are on our platform and they couldn't afford not to be.

I wanted to get to the point where, with all the top brands working with us, the one person who didn't do a deal with us would look like a Luddite and get fired.

3.
To get a foot in the door with major brands, first you need to establish a sense of gravitas and credibility

Credibility comes from many things – who's on your board, who your investors are, who your other suppliers are, your employees, the amount of capital you raise, who's on your advisory board – any and all of these are signs of gravitas which can distinguish you from the also-rans.

We went all out to attract heavyweight board members at lastminute.com and MyDeco.com (now MONOQI).

At lastminute.com, when we were just about 10 people, we got Pieter Bouw, the former chairman of [Dutch flag carrier] KLM to be our chairman at the very beginning. We went to a top headhunter early on to find him. So then it was a question of relevance. We were bringing him relevance and understanding of what the next generation of the industry was going to look like. That was, for him, what made it work.

In a similar way, when we got Sir Terence Conran and Philippe Starck to be co-chairs of our design advisory board at MyDeco, we approached them offering the opportunity to be part of a new type of company, where design meets digital, encompassing community, open source design, innovation and 3D.

We said: 'We're going to be trying all of those things, so if you want to be at the cutting edge, then join our journey.'

The thing about having those sorts of names onboard, is that one great name attracts others. A high-profile board member helps you hire a great COO, say.

It also brings you the gravitas and introductions you need to get meetings with corporates.

4.
Always find out who the decision-maker is – there's no point in taking meeting after meeting with people who can't say yes (or no)

Aside from creating that sense of FOMO (fear of missing out), do everything you can to understand the (often quite convoluted) processes at every corporate you approach. Find out who the real decision-makers are, where the sign-off will come from – and try to understand that journey as soon as you can.

Then work out how to get in a room with that individual.

Too many people are just too nice and tread too carefully. Ask up front about a corporate's processes – and if the person you're meeting with isn't the decision-maker, then quickly find out who is.

But also be realistic, and accept that with some of the bigger companies you do need to persevere and it may take you six months.

The only way to progress really is urgency, and to make them feel that there's 'only one slot left'.

In other words, creating a sense of scarcity by saying: 'We only have space for one more partner at these terms, so you don't want to miss the boat.'

5.
Do your research to find the corporates who are geared up to work with startups

Corporates who are set up to work with startups should be on the radar of people like our own Founders Intelligence – Founders Forum's innovation consultancy which helps large brands work with startups.

It's not just a question of targeting the corporate angle; do the reverse look-up too – by looking at case studies of the startups which are already working with corporates, particularly in your industry, and try to learn from their journey.

A good starting point would be to look for the big brands with open innovation programmes for startups, such as Aviva's Digital Garage, the Unilever Foundry, Diageo Technology Ventures and L'Oréal too. Go to LinkedIn and do general internet searches to find the titles of the people at corporates who run these programmes and use them as an entry point.

6.
CEOs should lead the way

CEOs are often great salespeople, and if partnering with or selling to corporates is important enough to them, then these initiatives should really be led by them.

You can, as you get bigger, have the CEO go in with a brilliant biz dev person, of course – and then the biz dev person will take the lead knowing that they have top-level support.

7.
An introduction made on your behalf should feel like a favour on both sides of the equation

Access is everything, so if you can get a warm introduction and/or proper recommendation from someone, then that's obviously the best approach.

Although there are very few tech industry events where you have very high-level access, there are some where you can introduce yourself. Make the most of them.

LinkedIn can also be very powerful for working out those three degrees of separation between you and the person you want to meet, and who in your network can introduce you to them.

But always bear in mind that you do need to have enough credibility to earn that introduction, because – speaking from personal experience – I get some pretty random people asking me to make an introduction for them, and if there's no quality, qualification or gravitas behind the ask, then I'll probably just ignore the request.

A good rule of thumb is that it has to feel like an introduction's a favour on both ends of the equation rather than just on one side.

8.
Be realistic and don't try to monetise your relationship with a corporate too soon

If you're looking to get into the corporate world, make a profit from the deal *and* get them to expend resources to get something live, then I think you really are in a weak position [from a deal-making perspective].

Instead, if you're able to say 'I'm going to build this service for free or at cost, and then we can talk about monetising it' – then you're in a much stronger position.

Ultimately, partnerships [from a startup's perspective] are, initially at least, about building credibility – and we've got one of our companies doing this right now with Aviva, where they're currently getting their prototype adopted. The whole experience has been incredibly powerful for the team.

9.
Tenacity is a vital ingredient, but so is flexibility

Success in life is not about luck, it's about a mix of grit, passion and tenacity. So that's what you want to look for in your team.

But you don't want blind tenacity. It's critical also to have teams who are responsive; who listen and adapt accordingly.

Too many times you see founders veer towards having a monologue, instead of being receptive and able to change according to the needs of the large corporates. That's the DNA you want to bottle up and replicate.

10.
Know when to call it quits

Knowing when to give up is probably the hardest thing— there are quotes from people like Sir Richard Branson that if you just keep going for long enough you'll eventually always succeed.

That's definitely not right, in my experience. You've got to be able to understand when you've run out of rope.

Normally, in the end, the market will tell you that. But you don't want to cling on indefinitely, because once you lose your credibility, you lose your ability to attract and retain great talent. And that's when the game's up.

11.
Early hires are critical – get it wrong and it's the kiss of death

If you're looking to partner with or sell to major brands – as with everything else – early hires are critical.

Get it right with your fourth, fifth and sixth employees and you'll get it in your DNA.

On the flipside, get the DNA of your company wrong early on, and it's often unfixable.

Brent Hoberman is chairman and co-founder of Founders Factory, a corporate-backed incubator/accelerator based in London. He is also the co-founder and board director of made.com, a direct-from-factory consumer crowd-sourced homewares retailer in the UK. He co-founded PROfounders Capital in 2009. In April 1998, Brent co-founded lastminute.com. He was CEO from its inception, and the team took the company to profit and gross bookings of over $2bn. In 2005, lastminute.com was sold to Sabre for $1.1bn. Brent sits on the advisory board for LetterOne Technology (a $16bn investment fund) and the UK government's Digital Advisory Board.

CHAPTER 14

'Brand is critical from day one.'

Reshma Sohoni, founding partner
at Seedcamp, on scaling brand.

As soon as Seedcamp makes a new investment, it invites the startup's founders to an on-boarding week – essentially a crash course in early-stage business fundamentals. Among the very first topics to be covered at these sessions is brand, says Reshma Sohoni, who co-founded the seed fund with Saul Klein in 2007 and is now its managing partner. 'Along with fundraising, which will be so important to them a few months after our round, and some basic finance and networking things, our view is that brand is always critical – and it's critical from day one.

'Brand is the fundamental DNA within an organisation and it impacts on so many things, not least a company's culture and its early adopters, all the way through until it – hopefully – goes mass market.'

As you start to shift through the gears from pre-seed to seed, through Series A, B and beyond, the challenges for your brand evolve, Sohoni goes on to argue. 'So whereas an early adopter has a certain view on your brand, product, service and your story as a brand, all of those things are starting to get challenged in terms of consistency. Is your brand being talked about in the same way? Is it eliciting the same emotional response? Are your customers' expectations the same? Those are the sorts of issues we see with our companies.'

Consistent brand story

'The companies who are successful as they start to scale through to growth stage have been lucky or talented – or both – in terms of always having a consistent brand story.'

Luck, rather like its twin – timing – is one of those hard-to-pin-down factors that can help make or break a company. Yet, as Sohoni points out, the best startups tend to have the talent or instinct to engineer their own luck – particularly when it comes to brand.

TransferWise – the currency transfer service valued at $1bn+, which was Seedcamp's breakout investment – is a case point. Founders Kristo Käärmann and Taavet Hinrikus have a backstory, which is exquisite in its simplicity, that has passed into tech startup folklore. It also has the virtue of being true.

While one founder was continually transferring money from his Estonian bank to his London account, the other – with a mortgage back in Estonia – was doing the reverse. With both hit by sky-high bank transfer fees, the pair realised they could save a truckload of cash by paying each other's expenses instead, thereby cutting out the 'middle-man'.

Consistency is all, says Sohoni. 'The thing about that story is that it hasn't changed – and it is exactly what the currency transfer business is, whether it's someone transferring to another person, or transacting with an institution or a P2P service. So I count that as lucky that they had this story and maybe their talent lay in spotting that it would play a big part in taking them through to where they are now – all the way to millions of users and a billion-plus valuation.'

Authenticity

However, the thing about a brand story, Sohoni continues, is that in order to have staying power it needs to be authentic – it cannot be bolted on retrospectively at the scaling stage.

'Hindsight is great for articulating the points of resonance for a story, but you need an authentic story of an Airbnb type or TransferWise type or indeed a Seedcamp type for it to play through across [the years].'

By the time companies reach their Series A, let alone B, something, she says, 'has gone seriously right'. When you're right at the beginning, part of the reason your startup may not be resonating is that you don't have a story which elicits an emotional connection with your product or service.

'But when you're at Series A or B, you've probably sold a million or so of your product, or you have anywhere upwards of a few hundred thousand users, so I believe by then the problem is one of articulating rather than not having an authentic story in the first place.'

So what does she advise companies without sticky TransferWise-style backstories do to ensure their brand resonates?

'Even if you haven't got a powerful personal story, there's something [persuasive] in solving a problem of some kind – look at Slack or Dropbox – that can be emotional, or "sexy" even. If large numbers of people are starting to use your product or service, they're doing it for compelling reasons, and that should become the heart of your brand.

'When our startups come to us or others and ask, "How do we create a brand out of this or create more of a brand out of this?", we will suggest they tap into the stories of why people are using their product or service.

'Take Thriva, a home blood-testing kit. The team got this incredible note the other day from somebody who had discovered they had thyroid cancer thanks to their test showing there were some inconsistencies in their results, which prompted them to go to the doctor. Through that, there was an early diagnosis, when most cancers of that type are not diagnosed until it's quite late.

'If you don't have that personal "Me and my friend did x and y and so the company was born", then if you can pull out these sorts of success stories – and they could be in the cybersecurity field too, where an app helped solve a hacking scandal, for example – you can use them to champion your brand.'

Irreplaceable

For B2B companies too, startups can build a brand around the expectation that customers have of a product or service. But in such instances, Sohoni argues, it becomes even more about 'ease of use'.

'Are you able to get better employee engagement? What's the service or product of that brand that allows you to get championship of it? It's interesting that Salesforce, for example, isn't a brand people feel emotional about, but there's clearly incredible utility to it. Some of our companies have come to us saying: "If I'm trying to sell this, my customers are requiring me to have these Salesforce integrations."

'So it's become that foundational tool within startups and enterprises. It's so ingrained – and we talk a lot about that because the Holy Grail for brands is: "How do you become irreplaceable? How do you become so widely used across a company, across a set of systems, across entire sectors, that you just can't be replaced?" If you can [pull that off], then that's your brand.'

As a company reaches scale-up stage, growing from its first 10 or so original employees to 100 or more, the founders often face a range of urgent issues surrounding their brand – however compelling the brand was when the startup could utilise its insurgent or underdog status.

'Somewhere on that journey to 100 employees, or whatever it is, everything around your brand breaks,' says Sohoni.

'[Your brand's] colour usage, the typography, the brand story, what your brand and product do and so on – all of those things break at that point. What entrepreneurs fight against especially is you need much more standardisation, and as an entrepreneur who hates routine and instinctively wants to fight against standardisation, unfortunately it becomes so crucial.

'Again, the simpler your storyline is, the easier and less onerous standardisation is as you're growing. That's probably the biggest thing [for scale-ups].'

What's more, your 100th employee needs to be able to tell the brand backstory (or proposition) with as much conviction as your earliest hires, she says. 'If your slogan is "Faster, cheaper, better", then all your employees need to adhere to those core brand promises in everything they do.

'From our standpoint, we recommend that all the elements of your brand – from the website or app's colour scheme to your backstory and your promise to customers – fit together in a single thread that carries right across the brand in a coherent way.

'You want to be able to see that your brand resonates three or five years down the line with your 500th and 1,000th employee being able to tell that same story. That's your ideal path. But if that's not happening, then, as a scaling company, you can find other ways to achieve the same result. As I said earlier, you might look for brand champions – customers whose lives have changed as a result of your product or service, or whose organisation you've transformed.'

Similarly, strong brands tend to go hand in hand with company culture, she says, which is why it's so integral to a startup's success. 'It's a chicken-and-egg situation between brand and culture. If you have the right culture and the DNA in those first two, three, four people – or even that one person – who started the company, they're always also obsessed with brand.

'If you're obsessed with brand, you'll end up having a pretty good culture. Of course, that cuts both ways, depending on what your brand values are. For a hugely successful company like Airbnb, its distinctive and inclusive brand is plain to see in its culture too.'

Scaling companies' brands also face particular growing pains around international expansion. Often when a company is getting pretty dominant or nears critical mass in the UK, they then need to figure out how their brand and marketing strategies will resonate across borders to different markets, says Sohoni.

'That's particularly the case when it's not specifically a cross-border product or service [such as a marketplace or social network]. Another of your biggest challenges as a founder will arise when you need to grow cross-segment. What I mean by that is when you already have 200,000 or half a million users in a specific segment but you need to keep growing, which involves appealing to other [groups and demographics].

'Again, you need your brand to resonate with different audiences, and that doesn't happen by default. Those two areas – international and cross-segment expansion – are probably your two biggest challenges as a scaling startup, alongside how your team grows and retains its culture across different employee locations.'

Iconoclastic

Marketing, too, must always be consistent with your brand, Sohoni says. TransferWise, who've taken a guerrilla-style, stunt-based approach to marketing – with, for example their #Nothing2Hide campaign featuring a group of near-naked people converging on the Bank of England – have always ensured their core messaging of speed, ease of use, low prices and transparency is at the fore.

Despite – presumably – disquiet in their boardroom that the ads were a gamble and would either work brilliantly or fall flat, they were nonetheless painstakingly in keeping with the unicorn's iconoclastic brand positioning, she says.

'Even in their swimming campaign [where the founders emerge from the icy, wintry waters of New York City's Hudson River in their wetsuits], there's just that authenticity – and that's why it works. To me, the whole thing was a bit tongue-in-cheek, because if you're a TransferWise-user you're transferring a fair amount of money, it's not a few quid here and there. So that kind of joke again only resonates with their customers or people who are likely customers.

'It doesn't necessarily resonate with a mass community of people who have to work in different currencies. But that's the brilliance of it – the people who were in on the joke were precisely the people the TransferWise founders wanted as customers – and that's still the case.'

The team tapped into the same subversive strain with another campaign which targeted the banks – who were Enemy No. 1 in some quarters at the time – and their 'hidden' fees in particular. Sohoni reflects that it was something of a soft, and therefore low-risk target, given the animosity towards Big Banks in the wake of the credit crunch.

'So the timing really works there as well. But you'll hear the founders talk a lot about the way they built TransferWise, and continue to build it today, is always to ask themselves: "What's the least we can charge and what are the basics we need to do business, and stay in business, while providing a faster, cheaper, better product and service to our customers?"

'They don't talk about, for instance, the fattest, healthiest profit margins that they can have. It's always: "What is the least we need to do to be an ongoing business so that we can serve our customers in 10 years' time?" [So their brand values] are all about authenticity, coupled with careful timing. And you can't underestimate the power of timing in going against an incumbent sector, like the banking industry, and how it was the perfect moment to be doing that.'

Long-term challenge

Another issue companies face with brand – as scaling speeds up exponentially and upstarts become the incumbents – is retaining an emotional link with users. Sohoni points to Facebook's long-term challenge, in that it started by sparking an emotional reaction from users in the first decade of its life, which has seeped away for a variety of reasons of late.

'Major brands have that over time because it's hard to retain that exact positive emotional feeling for a brand into the second, third or fourth decade of its life. Microsoft, I guess, would be an example of that.

'That would also be TransferWise's challenge, probably not for the next five years, but sometime after their ten-year anniversary – but they'll be well prepared for it, I'm sure.'

It's a challenge which Seedcamp itself – once the European disruptor and answer to Silicon Valley's Y Combinator, but now in its second decade – also faces.

While Sohoni's startup blazed a trail as Europe's first seed-stage startup accelerator, according to the European Accelerator Report there are now at least 113 tech accelerators across Europe – a host of rivals and also-rans against which Seedcamp must continue to stand out. Today, like Y Combinator, it has been repositioned as a seed fund.

'People are invested in our old story because it's emotional and it was well known [in the industry]. There is that embedding in people's consciousness about who we were and, as we evolve, that in itself becomes the challenge.

'Our challenge also is – and I think this happens more with B2B companies than B2C – as you develop features you get known by certain customers. So, for example, people know you as the high-speed transfer service for large files. And those features become your brand.

'It's the same for us. The ways in which we support our companies: those different features become our brand and we're trying not to be defined by them.

'I go back to Airbnb; that same story really works. They're [reportedly] going into the more luxury end of the market, but there's a core bit of that story that is still about finding an experience, whether that's a home or a room or whatever – that resonates from the original story. TransferWise has that too. Few brands really do. Brands like ours have a challenge because our story doesn't necessarily resonate in the same way that it once did, when we're talking about now participating in €1m–€2m rounds. That's not [aimed at] the same entrepreneur that we invested in back in the day.'

Inevitably, as Seedcamp's role and audience have shifted, as it has scaled, the team gets a little frustrated by the way they're still thought of in a particular way, as the plucky upstart, perhaps – a hangover from their earlier market-defining success. 'Why do people still think we're *x* or *y*? Maybe it's the "camp" part of our name?' Sohoni laughs as she ponders.

'Rather than Seedcamp as a campfire of boy and girl scouts – we're trying to think of Seedcamp as base camp of Mount Everest. Everyone wants to reach the summit, so that's an IPO [initial public offering] or M&A [mergers & acquisitions], or whatever it is, but they always want to pass through base camp along the way.

'So that's how we started, saying: "Seedcamp is your base camp." Whether you want it to be a $100m, $1bn or $10bn business, you're still going to go through a base camp to get there – and that's us,' she says, before conceding: 'But trying to get that angle across in our brand is very difficult.'

∨

Reshma Sohoni co-founded Seedcamp in 2007 with a strong belief that European entrepreneurs have the power to compete on a global scale. A decade later, Seedcamp has invested in over 250 companies, including the likes of fintech unicorn TransferWise, Revolut and UiPath. Reshma is passionate about the intersection of business and technology, and has degrees in Engineering and Business from UPenn and M&T as well as an MBA from INSEAD. She describes starting Seedcamp as a 'once-in-a-lifetime opportunity and one that I jumped into with a strong desire to help the European founder realise global success'.

CHAPTER 15

'Understand your North Star metric.'

Atomico partner and Head of Growth, **Benjamin Grol**, on scaling growth.

When he first joined Atomico in 2016, Benjamin Grol told an interviewer that it was his ambition to help bring some of the latest growth learnings from Silicon Valley to Europe. When asked what he meant by that, he begins by pointing out that customer/user acquisition is a continually evolving space. Tactics such as Facebook and Plaxo's 'Invite All' email blast schemes, which were an effective if blunt instrument a decade or so ago, were 'pretty hostile and wouldn't work in 2018', he argues.

Indeed, rather than a one-size-fits-all approach, today the way to acquire users – as well as activate and retain them, and then generate referrals – depends not only on the kind of business you are in, but also the subset within that category. 'Are you a marketplace? Are you a digital or physical marketplace? Are you a fully managed marketplace? Each one has its own best practices, and they are constantly shifting with time,' says Grol, speaking after holding an Upscale session on the topic.

'Email isn't as great for acquiring users as it once was (but can still be very powerful for re-engagement and getting users to the "magic moment" of the product), but now Slack is in a golden age where you can actually, for a certain category of businesses, use Slack and Slackbots very effectively to acquire people.'

The same goes for mobile messaging, he adds. 'I have seen indicators that SMS, WhatsApp, [Facebook] Messenger and Instagram are going to be coming into a golden age for acquiring users as well. So these shifts are continually happening, and as a result you have these relatively narrow category approaches.'

Retention is everything

So what, then, are the 'big picture' aspects and drivers of growth for founders of scaling companies to bear in mind?

Grol – who previously worked in product and growth leadership roles on four billion-user products: Gmail, Google Maps, Facebook and Facebook Messenger – says that for every sector, excluding maybe some sorts of travel businesses ('because they are their own beast'), the number-one thing is user retention. 'Whether it's SaaS businesses, marketplaces, consumer, games, fintech, I would say the main thing for those businesses would probably be keeping a user once you have got them; retention is everything.'

The problem is, while most founders focus hard on acquisition, fewer devote the same energy to retention, he says. '[Typically] they'll think about page views, and clicks on their sign-up button. But I would say that helping people get value out of your product as quickly and as simply as possible is the core strategy for retaining users. In growth parlance, that's called "activation".'

'So registration is if you go to a website you put in your email, set up a password, pick your username – hipsterkebab33 – and you're on the social network or whatever app it is. What are the things that then need to happen on that application to maximise your probability of turning that registered user into a retained one?'

The magic moment

'For example, immediately after registration on Facebook, they get you to connect with your friends. On Messenger, users get 30 messages –

inbound or outbound – to three distinct groups. On Pinterest, you have to select at least five topics or themes. So for each of these apps, there is something that you need to go through to experience what they call "the magic moment" – and at its core, user growth is around optimising, understanding, and as quickly as possible driving users to that magic moment. And then amplifying it.'

Where many people go wrong with the process, continues Grol, is failing to think about activation. 'They don't think enough about "What do users have to do or experience to have the magic (aka 'AH HA!') moment?" A typical tendency I've seen is that people are so deeply into the weeds or the specifics of their business, that to them it's self-evident why the product is great. So they build something, and the underpinnings of it, the way it's built, is sometimes prioritised over the user getting to the value as simply and quickly as possible.'

Instead, a growth specialist may look at, for example, the button to complete a fundamental action and notice that it is small and tucked into the corner of the page. One could argue that if the core action is to get the user to tap that particular button, then it should be presented in an appropriately prominent way (like a popover dialogue). The goal is to get the user to the core value directly and immediately.

'Ask yourself what's the one tagline at the top of the page that'll make it clear why they want to click on the button,' urges Grol. 'So really focus on getting the user excited, reducing friction and walking them through this journey of getting the most value out of the app as quickly as possible.'

That can sometimes be a tweak as simple as changing the name of a button – or removing a particular step and putting it much later in the process, he says. It could even be having a pop-up that clarifies the next step, or refocusing on email capture rather than a full (and often laborious) registration process.

'In some businesses, you can follow up and acquire the user later with email drip campaigns. That is the kind of thinking I just don't see as much of as I would like. I think it will be a secular shift into the future, and a decade from now everybody will think that way; it'll become normal that you do it like that.'

Benchmarks

'Next,' continues Grol, 'I would probably look at benchmarks. What are you building? Is it an e-commerce app? Is it a newsreader app? Is it a game? And then understand in that category what good looks like and then really go for it; build something better than that.

'The best retained "app" of all time is probably Google search. We don't know that for sure, because you can use Google search from many devices: your work computer, your home computer, your phone, and you're oftentimes not logged in while you're on it. But the imperfect data we do see shows very high retention. Which makes sense: it's incredibly useful, very easy to use and cheap.

'WhatsApp is somewhere in the 70–72% long-term retention rate – that's a remarkable, heady number. Facebook is 63%. Messenger is in the 50s, Snapchat is in the 40s, Instagram is in the 50s and LinkedIn is 40% "day 30" retention, and it sticks around there – so these are really kind of the best numbers you can achieve.'

Retention loops

If benchmarks serve as a guide for how an app is performing (or underperforming) against category leaders, boosting retention is all about developing habits and identifying useful triggers so people come back to the product. There are multiple ways of doing this, explains Grol, ranging from emails or push notifications of new updates the user may be interested in, explicitly establishing a habit that the user creates themselves (like setting up a reminder to exercise at 6.30am with the 8fit app) to a coffee shop-style loyalty card that gamifies a habit.

'Uber Eats, for example, is throwing money at the problem and trying to develop a habit with people by building all of these loyalty schemes. This mechanism is known as a retention loop. [As a founder] ask yourself what the mechanism is that will trigger your users to come back repeatedly to your product or service?'

A retention loop that's worked for Grol, as a customer, is one that's deployed by the UK on-demand laundry service Laundrapp. 'Once your laundry is delivered back to you, you get an email saying "Hey Ben, you've unlocked a reward" – and it'll be a discount or some kind of interesting incentive for using them next time. They use a powerful psychological lever called variable rewards. I don't know what the reward's going to be on the third time, and that curiosity, the same curiosity that has me pulling the slot machines in a Monaco casino, has me coming back to try Laundrapp for the third time.

'So there are many of these psychological levers wired into all aspects of growth. A fun one to share with you is related to loyalty cards. It's called "the goal gradient effect" and it's based on a well-known psychological principle: the closer a human is to a goal, the more motivated they are to achieve it.

'For example, two coffee shops, shops A and B, set up a loyalty-card scheme for their customers. Once the customer stamps every icon on the card, they receive a free coffee. Shop A created a card that had 10 empty icons. Shop B created a card with 12 icons with two of them already stamped.

'The customers of coffee shop B completed their cards on average 20% faster than those of card A in an experiment run in 2006. In a world where attention span is stretched thin, and motivation can be marginal for new services, this kind of change could be the difference between activating a customer and losing them.'

'It's fascinating, right? If you're looking at getting started flows in an app, you can consider the first "get started" action as step 1, so the first screen that asks for information about you – like confirming your phone number or asking your name – can show that it is step 2 of 7. Based on the research above, the motivation the user has to complete a process is greater when they are at step 2 of 7 than when they are at step 1 of 7. In various tests I've seen, this generally improves conversion.'

Similarly, user growth of highly 'addictive' games like the enduringly popular Candy Crush Saga (by King Games) is, in part, driven by the sights, sounds and reassuring simplicity of the casino, says Grol.

'What I see when I play Candy Crush is a lot of the elements of a casino. It's very easy; there are not a lot of challenging mechanics. It does become challenging at some level and the mastery of visualising how things will move to get the four-in-a-row blocks is quite a challenge. But you can always get out of it by paying. It's never so hard that you can't pay a little bit and get yourself out of a sticky episode, which are few and far between anyway. So you'll go through 15 easy ones and have one properly hard one.

'So for the people who desire mastery, you have it and it's actually quite rewarding when you finally, after days, complete it. And for the people who just want the easy diversion and are willing to spend 99p to get the power booster to break through, they can do that instead. It's in some ways an absolutely perfect game, which satisfies both the "I want to level up and develop mastery of this medium" and "I just want a diversion, combined with tons of these casino-style variable-rewards play dynamics" urges.'

Acquisition loops

Generally speaking, after your product's retention is roughly where you want it be, it's time to start growing the user base. The rule of thumb is to get great retention first, then acquire users.

Acquisition loops are mechanisms that give your user acquisition efforts a measurable turbo-boost. Let's follow an illustrative example with **fictional** numbers.

For every 1,000 people who sign up to Facebook, 100 of those invite others. On average, they invite 6 people each. And of those 6 invitees, half of them accept the invitation. So, following the maths:

1,000 new users ➜ 100 inviters ➜ 600 invitations ➜ 300 acceptances

Then of those 300 new users from the invites,

300 new users ➜ 30 inviters ➜ 180 invitations ➜ 90 acceptances

Then of those 90 new users from the invites,

90 new users ➜ 9 inviters ➜ 54 invitations ➜ 27 acceptances

Then of those 27 new users from the invites,

27 new users ➜ 3 inviters ➜ 18 invitations ➜ 9 acceptances

Then of those 9 new users from the invites,

9 new users ➜ 1 inviters ➜ 6 invitations ➜ 3 acceptances

Then of those 3 new users from the invites,

3 new users ➜ 0 inviters ➜ 0 invitations ➜ 0 acceptances

Now, you add up all of the accepted invites in this recurrence of invitations and see:

300 + 90 + 27 + 9 + 3 = 429 net new users via invitation.

From a base of 1,000 new users, this leads to a net of 1,429 users for this cohort, or in growth language, a growth multiplier of 1.429.

This is powerful. Since these invitations are effectively 'free', you could say that my effective cost to acquire new customers can be divided by this growth multiplier.

For example, if I paid £500 to acquire those initial 1,000 users, after factoring in all of the invitations, it's no longer a spend of 50p per customer, it's now 50p divided by 1.429, giving me a ~35p cost-per-user to acquire those 1,429 people. A nearly 30% cost reduction per user based on the virality of the product. This kind of shift in customer acquisition cost can be foundational for the success or failure of a business.

High school dropout

Unusually for a VC (although it's not so rare in the entrepreneurial world generally), Benjamin Grol walked out of high school one morning and never went back. 'I just got up one day in a study hall and the teacher said, "What are you doing?" and I said some rough language and just walked out. I was 16, in my sophomore year. I just went home and I played video games for the day; *Super Mario 3*, I believe. It was time to mull over what to do with life, and the minimum-security prison of school didn't feel like the right venue.'

Grol recalls feeling trapped and limited in school, by both its discipline and curriculum. 'I had little interest in reading Jane Austen – it felt really disconnected to anything in the world I was seeing. At the time, I couldn't fix a car, I didn't understand how to do taxes, I didn't know how to fix a toilet, I knew nothing about investing money, I knew nothing about writing effective business emails. Anything that is of use in adult life wasn't covered in school. They were anchored to this curriculum from a 100 years ago and that wasn't going to change any time soon (and arguably still hasn't).'

Instead, Grol – inspired by TV Food Network, which had just started to take off in the US back then (it was 1995) – went to Europe to learn to become a cook. Later, he attended the Culinary Institute of America, where he received a degree in culinary arts. But after a few years as a full-time chef, he hung up his apron on coming to a realisation that it wasn't a fulfilling long-term career (for him); nor did it stretch him intellectually. 'Certain parts of your brain are not exercised [when you're cooking]. It's fun and you can be good at it and there's a craft and you learn new techniques, but there's some analytical problem-solving and a kind of teamwork that's just not part of the day-to-day and I really crave that.'

He rebooted, instead focusing on computer science, earning a BS from Stanford. Today, Grol draws a contrast between what he terms 'the loners' who toil in kitchen and the collaboration which tech engenders. 'In tech, collaboration was much more of a thing. In the kitchen, if one person isn't contributing they are immediately fired. Maybe they get one warning and then somebody else replaces them. It just doesn't work that way in tech. So I feel like that was one huge difference, where you really had to learn to be collaborative, a team player and develop empathy to be really effective and get the most out of the team.

'Tech is like an incredible breakfast buffet at a high-end hotel for the brain. You go in and you're at a company like Google or Facebook, and the things you can do ... there's advertising, there's growth, there's working on engagement, there's AI, there's internal infrastructure to make people deploy their code faster, which is really a challenging thing to do. You can just do almost anything.'

North Star metric

For companies seeking to speed up their drumbeat of growth, Grol offers two key rules.

'For businesses (except maybe some travel businesses), the first rule is to understand your retention. In many cases, when you do that, you might realise there are some places where you're under-serving your user: it might be hard for them to sign up, or the value of your product isn't really made evident. Sometimes it's as simple as sending a follow-up email to them 20 minutes after they sign up that has an animated GIF showing what the product does and why it's useful, and they can "Click here" to learn more. Or a "Click here to chat with somebody if you have questions".

'That doesn't apply to all categories of businesses, but in some when you are charging a $10-a-month fee, it probably is worth it to you, if you consider the cost of having a support agent to help that person. So really understand your retention, is number one.'

The second is understanding your 'North Star metric' as a business. 'I've seen some businesses where they have a lot of data, but how do you [identify the critical data amid the deluge]? They've got a hundred dashboards – the activation rate, the resurrection rate, the conversion of the homepage rate, daily active, monthly active, weekly active users, the number of photos uploaded, the number of comments made, and so on. So what matters?

'For most categories of businesses, there are standard North Star metrics derived from experience. So if you're a SaaS business, for instance, monthly recurring revenue (MRR) is likely to be your North Star metric, and anything you do that sustainably and ethically drives that up is going to be a good thing.

'If you're a communication medium like Facebook or Slack, depending on the nature of the communication, you'll pick either monthly active usage or daily active usage. So, for example, Facebook has monthly active usage as a North Star metric, and has done since at least 2007 – and they obviously want much more than once-a-month usage. But you start with the monthly active usage and then you drive them up from there into a daily active user, into more time spent. There are teams that layer on top of teams, but at its core you want the reach and retention of 2bn monthly active users.'

For Slack, it's daily active usage, Grol says. 'If you're not using Slack each day at the office then there's something wrong with the product and it's not providing value to people. Facebook Messenger chose monthly active usage as their North Star because reach is always a struggle for networks, so they figured the best way to get reach was to get monthly active usage, which I agree with. With [digital] games, I'd say daily active usage.

'With marketplaces, it's usually a liquidity metric. The example I'll give is Airbnb, which is nights booked. So you have a supply side, and you have a demand side. When there's a successful transaction in the form of night units for Airbnb, that's the sign of the marketplace working. So anything you do that's driving up nights booked [or equivalent] is what you want to do for a marketplace.

'For Uber and Lyft, it's rides booked. So they don't say kilometres driven; they could, and then you could incentivise people to do longer rides, but the theory is that ride length is not very elastic, so using these ride-sharing services for more rides is the right reflection of the utility of those apps.'

And while it's not always immediately obvious what a company's North Star metric is, says Grol, without knowing it you are going to have a much more challenging time accelerating the growth of your business.

∨

Benjamin Grol is a partner and the Head of Growth at leading VC firm Atomico, where he focuses on helping portfolio companies grow and evaluating new investment opportunities. Previously, Benjamin worked in product and growth leadership roles on four billion-user products: Gmail, Google Maps, Facebook and Facebook Messenger. Prior to working in technology, Benjamin was a professional chef. He worked in top restaurants across the US, Italy and France refining his craft, but eventually the draw of 'bits over bites' was too much for him to resist.

CHAPTER 16

'Keep your powder dry for big announcements' and 'Don't blog unless you've got something to say'.

Burlington founder and former Director of
Communications at Index Ventures, **Nadia Kelly**,
on scaling comms and coping with crises.

Ubiquity is a terrible communications strategy

There are an unprecedented number of ways to communicate today. But 'owned' media – and by that I mean blogs, Medium, and above all social media outlets such as Twitter and LinkedIn – are the most fraught with danger. Yes, social platforms allow you to speak with immediacy and frankness, in an unfiltered way. For those who are natural-born bloggers or tweeters – or industry media gurus like Saul Klein – they can be a boon. They can help companies differentiate themselves and connect with target audiences in an authentic and timely way. Yet the flipside is that their very availability and ubiquity creates a tendency in some not just to shoot their mouth off, but also to tweet/post *just because they can*.

Let's rewind a bit. As a scaling startup, begin by asking yourself what your comms objective is. Too often I see companies fall into the trap of feeling like 'X is doing it that way and it's working for them, so we should be doing that too'. But every case is different. What works for X may be a terrible idea for Y and Z. If you are a B2B business, for example, or your customers aren't likely to be on social media in droves, then all you are doing by implementing an active social strategy is wasting time, effort and resources, all of which could be better spent elsewhere.

The other risk is that sometimes, if you don't have any significant presence, you're just shouting into a void. For me, few things are worse from a comms standpoint than witnessing a founder make a big statement in a tweet or writing a blog to the silent roll of tumbleweed. Not only is it embarrassing, I've also seen it lead to anxiety in some people who, quite frankly, have more than enough on their plate already.

Think about the topics you can really *own* as a company

Back in 2007, internet guru Jeff Jarvis famously advised publishers on his blog BuzzMachine: 'Cover what you do best. Link to the rest.' The same applies to communications strategy. Instead of voicing opinions on subjects which are unrelated to your business, ask yourself what the topics are that are most relevant for you. And double down on them.

Say you're a workplace tech company, and you want to talk about a 'big picture' area such as the future of work. Spend time figuring out what the major trends are that you want to be associated with in the space – and the more genuinely fresh and interesting you can make your viewpoint, the more traction you will have.

As you start to own some of those talking points, you can deploy them, not just on social media but in any earned media coverage, in speeches and at events. Consistency is key here.

These are the ideas that show your company in the best light and chime with your core ethos. The ultimate accolade in this scenario is that – if you're successful at it – you'll hear others associate you with those ideas. This is why the time you invest in the strategic plotting of the central messages you want to communicate is so important. You need to be confident in them so that you can stick with them over months and even years, and not be seen as a leader who vacillates on big issues every time the wind changes.

The wheel of success for a startup's communications strategy has those same key ideas and messages at the centre of all its activities, including social, PR, content, events, data and insights, even if they place more emphasis on some of these than others.

Early-stage companies can't afford
to waste precious resources

Recently I came across a startup team who were so adept at social media and PR generally that their efforts were repaid with great media coverage across the board. But then another company, which launched pretty much at the same time with a similar product but with far less fanfare, steadily built market share under the radar.

The second company successfully closed its Series B round, while I have doubts that the first company will. What does that tell you? In isolation, nothing. Except to say this: while there are no hard and fast rules, early-stage companies need to devote their scarce resources, and time and sweat, to getting their product right. Yes, communications (especially when they're built around news announcements) can have a powerful impact when scaling a business, but if the product/service isn't quite right, you probably won't be around long enough for it to matter.

In the end, it doesn't matter how many Twitter followers you have. What matters is your business performance, not your social media reach. The latter may help the former. But without the first, you're nowhere.

PR is often more about slow-burn impact than instant gratification

Communications folks have always been asked to demonstrate their value and ROI for often-sceptical clients in all industries. Back in the digital dark ages, we used tools like Advertising Value Equivalency (AVE) to guesstimate value. In today's terms, that's perhaps a notch above reading tea leaves.

Obviously, digital native startup founders are unlikely to buy into anything that isn't data-driven. Yet at the same time, many of the companies we work with at Burlington are very good at being able to track traffic or sales spikes against, say, a piece in the *Daily Mail* or on *Business Insider*. Founders also tell us that a great piece of coverage or thought leadership, especially in tech titles, can help hugely with attracting new customers or star hires.

Sometimes a campaign can have impacts that are hard to measure. A piece of thought leadership, for example, might not directly boost the bottom line, but it might plant a seed which comes to fruition a few months later, with an invitation to participate on a panel where the founder in question meets his/her next investor or a major customer. If it's high quality, it may become the most-read item about you on the internet – and something you can direct people to when they ask about your company.

Ultimately, when you're doing comms, you shouldn't be looking for instant gratification. Yes, a news event might generate one-time explosive coverage, but the real value is slow-burn and incremental. The ideal is to build your credibility, brand and presence bit by bit, over time.

However, if you figure out a differentiating angle for your startup, first-mover advantage is critical

The narrative in the tech space moves fast in communications terms. If you're an early-stage startup in a genuinely new or emerging category, don't hang about. Get your story out there. Not too long ago, we were pitching a trailblazer in the insurtech/insurance disruption startup space – a category which few journalists we spoke to had heard of at the time. As a result, we got mountains of coverage, because it was fresh.

Within six months, however, a number of other companies had launched in the space, and we were lucky enough to work with one or two of them. Pitching media that time around was far trickier. All the journalists who were excited the first time fed back to us that while it was an interesting company, the space had become overly familiar in the meantime and they were disinclined to return to it too soon, for reasons of reader fatigue.

Moral of the story? New categories and technologies are highly time-sensitive – if a rival or similar company moves first, you'll get caught in their wake.

Never, ever overhype your company, compare yourself to a tech giant or exaggerate the size of the problem you're solving

If you can talk about how you're breaking ground and developing a new category, that's a good story. But at the same time, it's vital to guard against overdoing it with what you say. We come across companies who make claims like 'We're building the next Google Maps' or 'We're democratising healthcare', and as a startup you won't be taken seriously if you make grandiose statements like that.

Similarly, avoid clichés, and any pitch that begins with the phrase 'We're the [insert your own tech giant here] of X…' is destined for the trash basket. It's OK for a journalist to make that comparison, but spoon-feeding them generally doesn't go down well.

Similarly, never run to the front of the parade

No one likes a limelight-hogger or credit-taker, so always err on the side of humility when you have a major achievement, accolade or award to share. Leave it to others to big you up.

Ignoring the media won't work in the medium term

Sometimes founders will say things like: 'X doesn't do any interviews/ has a low profile, and their company is doing really well.' My response to that is they aren't doing well because they're not doing interviews. They're far more than likely doing well because they've got their product or service spot on.

What a founder tends to mean when they say that is that they don't *like* doing interviews or speaking to journalists. In those cases, mostly, entrepreneurs will in time find someone else in their organisation who can take on the role of being the spokesperson – there's usually someone senior who relishes the challenge.

However, while a founder/CEO can get away with this in the early days, as the company starts to grow, so do their responsibilities. Dodging the spotlight is difficult, particularly if you are successful or you are in a controversial field (such as AI or the on-demand economy), as journalists will want to write about you. Rather than shrouding you in mystery, staying silent can make you look aloof, or worse, as if you have something to hide. And if, say, you are disrupting a mainstream sector and impacting on jobs, then it's incumbent upon you to be part of the conversation.

The ideal is to have a relationship with one or two reporters that is beyond the merely transactional, where you talk to them only when you need them. Far better for it to be an ongoing relationship where you can offer them the inside track on a complex topic. That will help establish trust which will bear fruit further down the line. Journalists like to repay people who are helpful to them, yet the number of people who do this are few.

If you don't get your message out there as a company, media will speculate and the wrong narrative can prove sticky

I can think of a very well-known tech company that suffered due to adopting a low profile, and they faced persistent rumours and speculation. Similarly, if you avoid the media it can be very difficult to cultivate those core journalist relationships which you will almost certainly need and even depend upon as your company grows – i.e. if you have a major announcement you want coverage for or if you find yourself embroiled in a crisis. A lot of journalists want to feel like they are with you from the start, if you are an exciting company, and it's harder to win hearts and minds the later it gets.

That said, it's fine to be sparing with your contacts with media, particularly if you are adept with your own channels. London-based startup Citymapper is a case in point: their CEO and founder Azmat Yusuf is very skilful at getting his point of view across in blogs, for example, which are often picked up and quoted from by the media.

Keep your powder dry for major announcements

It may sound blindingly obvious, but a problem many early-stage founders will recognise is that if they don't have any news, getting coverage can be a struggle and a distraction. Yes, they can churn out blogs and op-eds, but as a lesser-known entrepreneur, we're back to the shouting into the void and it fails the 'What impact am I actually having?' test.

One founder I spoke to came to the conclusion that, actually, once you've had that big news moment of your launch and your funding announcement, it doesn't make sense to keep banging the drum just for the sake of it. In fact, it can even be quite damaging to your brand. Journalists fielding constant calls from a startup or their PR agency with fluff stories are eventually going to get pissed off – even to the point where they won't take a call from your company ever again because they've just been harassed so much.

(Sidenote: And, by the way, if you hire a PR agency, make sure you know exactly how they're describing your company when pitching to media. Devise the pitch with them so that it's absolutely how you want to be described – while taking on board their advice on wording or what would appeal to publication X or journalist Y. An incorrect or misjudged pitch – where, for instance, the agency miscategorises your startup – could seriously harm your prospects.)

Far better to keep your powder dry for when you have those news moments. In the meantime, use your own media channels. Take part in events, if appropriate, and when there's a relevant conversation happening in your sector.

When you do have something to say, make it work across multiple channels

When you have found the big idea or topic you want to own, it makes sense to adapt a multi-channel approach. For something significant, it's a waste of effort simply telling the story through a press release. You need to take the action or thought and turn it into an event – perhaps a keynote speech that can be adapted to provide an opinion piece. If your idea is good enough, you could place it in a newspaper or on a tech site. If you don't yet have the sort of profile to secure prominent coverage, you could still write a blog that is shared on sites like Medium or LinkedIn.

Use social media to make sure that people know it's out there and link to it. A word of warning: startups can sometimes get so excited about their piece of news that they tweet it too soon, thereby killing the opportunity to craft a news story and place it for maximum impact.

Also don't tweet or share your blog before the press release is out. Press releases are usually embargoed so that different media outlets get them at the right time for their needs. This is a process that needs to be carefully managed, and one overly enthusiastic tweet can ruin weeks of work preparing for a news announcement and sour relations with individual reporters or editors. Over the years, I have seen even experienced investors and founders fall into just this trap. Sometimes their excitement gets the better of them.

Never, ever fake it

Index Ventures co-founder Neil Rimer (see Chapter 2) has said that he could, of course, blog monthly or even weekly, but he believes less is more and that it's best to wait until he has something meaningful to say. Blog posts and opinion pieces spun from the flimsiest of premises serve little purpose other than to add to the noise. And people will always smell a rat, i.e. when the writer is jumping on a bandwagon or saying something he/she doesn't believe in. We know this because TechCrunch stopped accepting contributed articles, as they said it had become obvious that far too many were churned out by ghostwriters – or PR agencies.

Now you may counter by saying that there are notable VCs such as Benchmark's Bill Gurley, Union Square Ventures' Fred Wilson, Accel's Fred Destin and Benedict Evans of Andreessen Horowitz who blog regularly and successfully. Very true. But all of the above blog *with conviction*, have slowly built audiences, and their presence has become part of their personal brand. In the case of Evans, he has also established a hugely successful distribution channel – a newsletter which has become a media outlet in its own right. (Indeed, we recently had a client mentioned in one of his newsletters, which the CEO in question considered a PR bull's eye.)

By contrast, we sometimes get asked by VCs and entrepreneurs: 'Should I do a podcast?' or 'Should I start a blog?' The answer is usually 'No', if it's not something you would do naturally or are prepared to invest time in to build an audience.

As a scaling early-stage startup, if you're going to hire an in-house comms person, then go for a young, scrappy hustler

One question I get a lot is: 'When is the right moment in a startup's life to bring in a comms person or put an agency on retainer?' In part, the answer to this is 'It depends on the company'. However, if I think back to my time as communications director at Index Ventures, there were two great companies in the Index portfolio which still stand out for me in terms of their approach to comms: one was TransferWise, the other Deliveroo. In both of those cases, they recognised that PR was integral to their growth, and they went out and found a young, hungry person who hadn't done a lot of comms, but could go out there and hustle and was good at writing. Both hires went on to be really effective.

But there's a sting in the tail to this story. Both these companies were growing so quickly that 12 months later those particular guys weren't the right people to run comms in – what were by then – sizeable businesses with multiple stakeholders. So they had to go out and start the search for a more traditional chief comms officer. In both cases, the person who had been doing the role so successfully in the early days ended up leaving the company.

There's an important lesson here: what both those hugely successful companies grasped is that comms plays a very different role as a business becomes more established. Gone are the days when you were scrapping for coverage in industry titles. You're now in the spotlight and often under global scrutiny, and a polished, professional approach becomes critical as PR blunders become increasingly costly.

One problem we often see when companies set up an in-house comms team is that they give the first senior PR hire the title of 'VP of Communications' (or similar). The trouble is, with the rarest of exceptions, they are not; they're a junior comms person and it then becomes difficult to bring in a genuine and experienced comms VP if someone already has that title. Plainly, the way to avoid that problem is to not give that first individual a title that suggests at least 10 years' experience, and to be very clear with them from the outset that this is their opportunity to get in early and prove themselves.

The other way to approach comms as you scale is to hire a PR agency. We've been in that position, as an agency on the outside of a small startup business, and one problem which can arise is that there's often no single individual within the company who 'owns' the relationship with the agency. What happens then is unaligned expectations: the agency is not properly briefed or kept up to speed with what's going on and what's potentially interesting in the business. In turn, that means you're unable to be proactive in the sense of seeing opportunities in the news or anticipating problems before they arise.

On balance, at the seed-to-Series A stage, it would be better to have a scrappy in-house PR person, but make that role more multifaceted than just comms, so that it spans social, community management, events and content too. Beyond Series A, a more experienced internal hire with an agency on retainer (or if there is insufficient news to justify a retainer, hired on an ad hoc/project basis instead) would usually be the way to go.

If you're looking for pan-European coverage, hiring agencies across a number of countries may not always be the best way to go

I worked with one venture-backed B2B company who told me they wanted to hire agencies in France, Germany, Switzerland, Italy and Portugal. But when we sat down with them to discuss it and went through how many reporters covering their particular niche there were in each of those locations, the answer was three or four at the most.

So it made far more sense to build up a database and work back from there with their UK agency, to craft an angle which would work with each individual reporter in each country. Not only did they save a ton of money, but they weren't in the time-consuming position of having to manage multilingual agency teams across Europe.

Never leave a vacuum in a crisis situation

The crisis scenario I come across the most with startups is when there are changes in key personnel, or if the business isn't going well and a company's reducing headcount or shuttering offices. Invariably, at that point you'll have journalists sniffing around. Some founders' first instinct is to take the 'ignore them and they'll go away' approach. That's exactly the wrong thing to do – speculation will fill a vacuum, and it's likely to be very unhelpful to your company's interests. Things can quickly escalate from there, pushing investors, employees and other stakeholders into panic mode. And once a narrative takes root, it's very hard to unpick it.

If a crisis happens (e.g. a CEO quits, a high-profile customer pulls out, a harassment complaint surfaces, user numbers plummet, a rogue tweet sends the company's reputation spinning, etc.), the same rules of communications engagement apply. Move fast. Develop a crafted message. Speak publicly to *acknowledge* the situation (denial will come back to bite you) and apologise if appropriate. And it should be the CEO or one of the founders who takes the lead. Lay out the facts. Be empathetic to those affected. And be very clear about what action you are urgently taking to fix things. Be visible and prepare for every negative question you might get asked. That's the only way to regain the initiative – and your stakeholders' trust.

Mark Zuckerberg's so-called apology tour, in the wake of Facebook's 2018 data-harvesting scandal, followed this playbook to the letter. A whirlwind round of measured, mea culpa media interviews, combined with full-page newspaper advertisements apologising for a 'breach of trust', contained a storm, which had been fast-developing into a very serious threat.

∨

Nadia Kelly is the founder of Burlington, London's leading specialist PR consultancy for venture capital and technology firms. Previously, she was Director of Marketing and Communications at Index Ventures. Her 20-year career in comms also includes senior positions at Sparkpr, Orange and IAC Search and Media.

CHAPTER 17

'Customer care calls would come through to my personal mobile in the early years.'

David Buttress, co-founder and ex-CEO of Just Eat, on bootstrapping and scaling operations.

In 2005, David Buttress, then still – just – in his 20s, met up with Jesper Buch, Just Eat's co-founder, for lunch. Over a utilitarian Nando's in West London, the pair had a conversation that would change both of their lives. Buttress was working for Coca-Cola UK at the time, which was how he had come to know Buch, but was itching for a new, ideally entrepreneurial, challenge. So when he heard Buch talk about the takeaway business he had co-founded in Copenhagen in 2001, Buttress was intrigued. Fast-forward a year, and he had quit his job to launch Just Eat with Buch in London.

The earliest days of a startup are rarely glamorous, and Just Eat's were no exception. Wedged in a one-bedroom flat in the Docklands, with a couple of computers bought at Currys, the pair spent their first day assembling desks. 'I'd left a "proper job", and then all of a sudden you realise that the realities of starting a business are somewhat more humbling than you imagine them to be when you tell people you're going to be an entrepreneur,' Buttress recalls.

'There's just so much to do. When you start a company, you're everything, aren't you? From sales to customer care, to marketing and finance to putting desks together. And I'd come from Coke, a global organisation where if your phone broke you'd make a call and someone would appear with a new one, plug it in and show you how to use it.'

At the same time, he says, it was hugely exciting, because while he'd always wanted to start his own business, he hadn't come from a background where either access to finance or the entrepreneurial world were realistic options. 'As a result of that, we bootstrapped Just Eat. I think, looking back on it now, we bootstrapped it for too long. Probably partly because of our backgrounds. We're both very conservative financially, and worried about losing money because we never had it to lose in the first place, so we probably bootstrapped Just Eat for 12 months or maybe even 18 months longer than we should have. We raised money from Index Ventures in early 2009, and I always look back and think we should have done that earlier.'

Backgrounds aside, why does he reckon they delayed raising VC funding?

Buttress doesn't hesitate: 'Because the traction was so good. If I look back at the first month of Just Eat, March 2006, we turned over £36 between two of us, 18 quid each – which we spent in All Bar One. It felt like the logical thing to do when you'd spent a month of your life and made 18 quid. You just want to go and drink.' He smiles.

'As humbling as that £18 was, the reality was that the business grew quickly. It went from £18 to £236 the second month, which doesn't sound a lot, but then £236 then went to £700-odd, and then by the fourth month we were making nearly £2,000. Then by month six we earned about £6,000–7,000 a month net revenues from Just Eat, and as a result we added a salesperson. I could quickly see that that salesperson, within three months, paid for themselves, and we were also making a small margin on B2B sales [by supplying restaurants with hardware]. Forget the consumer revenues for delivering orders. So I thought: "This feels really scalable as a business model."'

At that time, Just Eat was still only operating in a single London postcode – E14 in the Docklands. 'So all of a sudden, all I did was a simple back-of-the-envelope calculation on the way home from work one day in the August of 2006 and went: "If I take the number of postcodes in the UK and extrapolate this out – and of course you can't do that because all the postcodes are different in size, but if I discount E14 by 30–40% and say that's the average – then wow! This business could turn over tens of millions of pounds.'"

That was six months in, and Buttress felt a growing conviction that they had a scalable business on their hands. 'I remember going home really excited and saying to my wife: "I really think we can build something exciting here." And she looked at me as if I was mad and reminded me that only a few months earlier we'd turned over £36. But the funny thing was that then, by month 13 or 14, so just over a year in, we were turning over £30,000–40,000 a month – and at this time we were still only in East London.'

Postcode by postcode

In the early days, the fledgling team were acquiring customers in three main ways. First, they were signing up restaurants postcode by postcode, ensuring they had three or four of all the major takeaway cuisine categories online within each postcode. Second, they would 'activate' restaurants by supplying Just Eat branding to them, while doing the same on the delivery side by branding drivers, bags and menus. Third, they used digital channels – primarily SEO and SEM – to generate users of the platform.

'On the local marketing side, I pretty much lifted everything from my Coca-Cola days, where the team did a phenomenal job branding up local newsagents. I basically copied everything Coke did in newsagents and brought it into Just Eat. And that's how we grew and why I said we should have done our [investment] round earlier, because certainly by the end of 2007 we were at a point where, if we were raising money today, we would probably have done an initial £10m round on a £100m valuation. And as a result, we would have done our IPO [initial public offering] twelve months earlier than we did and all the rest of it. But things were different 10 years ago. It turned out OK, but I now think we should have been less conservative and we should have raised earlier.'

Does Buttress think that – because food-delivery tech is considered a winner-takes-all category, where the UK competition includes heavy-hitters Deliveroo and Uber Eats – scaling as rapidly as possible was the only surefire route to success?

'Just Eat is a very different model to some of the last-mile delivery players like Uber Eats and Deliveroo,' he replies. 'The reason they have to scale fast is that without the efficiencies of delivery, your business model is terrible and you lose lots of money. So you need to find scale because that's how you find efficiency. That's the important differentiator, because the quality of the marketplace business model [like Just Eat's] within pretty much all verticals, but definitely with food, is actually – even when you are sub-scale, while you've got low revenues – the underlying economics of the model are very, very good. Then, as you build scale, you see you have a very scalable business.'

He expands: 'We were very ambitious, and healthy competitiveness was in our DNA from the start. If I look at Just Eat, we were market leader in every market we operated in by the time we IPO'd. When you build a market leader everywhere from Brazil to the UK to Australia, Canada, France, Spain, Italy and Denmark, that tells you something about the DNA of the organisation. And in some cases – in Spain and Italy, for example – we managed to build startups organically, and replicate the DNA of the organisation and our processes, deploy into that market and then build a market leader. That's not an easy thing to do. So I was quite proud of that.'

When it comes to adapting Just Eat to new markets, Buttress describes himself as 'militant' in sharing Amazon founder Jeff Bezos's belief that 'culture eats strategy for breakfast' (a phrase attributed to Peter Drucker, the management guru).

'I say to every entrepreneur I meet that when you've defined a clear set of guiding cultural principles and behaviours – and you've also coupled that to what Coca-Cola used to call "execution excellence", or what most others call good operations and processes – then it feels to me completely illogical to try and do some liberal management-style thing where you change the business to be culturally sensitive because you are now, for example, in Canada.

'I just don't believe that works. It's better for a leader to say: "This is our organisation, our culture matters, being good operators matters. We really think we've gone and cracked it and we've got a clear set of principles." Then you recruit to that, hiring people who are culturally aligned, (albeit there are differences in every market, which is great and you embrace that). But while you enjoy working with different cultures, at the same time you say: "This is the set of behaviours that matter at Just Eat."

'At the time, those defining values for us were "Frank", "Innovative", "Team" and "Fun". They were the four cultural things. We said people have to have at least a minimum level of those characteristics, and then they can bring their own flavour to them. Then with operations/processes, we took a highly disciplined cookie-cutter approach to new markets, where we said "These are our processes and we need to apply them in Spain to win Spain." And so on.'

Mongolian barbeque grill

Buttress offers two supporting examples. First, in Madrid, where Just Eat's sales team drew up a list of postcodes and then measured precisely the restaurant coverage in each one by cuisine. 'That way we [map out] the major cuisine categories that consumers want in Madrid, Barcelona, Milan, Toronto, and so on. Then the sales team very accurately measures on a day-to-day basis which restaurants they are adding in each of those categories in each postcode.

'Of course, one of your sales team might say: "Oh, I've spoken to the Mongolian barbeque grill or whatever and they want to join Just Eat." Well, that's fine, but actually we don't need another grill in that particular postcode, what we urgently need is a sushi place. So, yes, that salesperson can bring on that restaurant, but it won't count towards their numbers and they won't be paid a bonus. They'll get their bonus when they add the sushi place and develop the right mix of cuisine into each postcode, because on the consumer side there's a network effect, where once you add in the right mix of cuisine categories the customer will come back more frequently and become more loyal.

'So it was really important that we were very, very granular around that detail. It was no good looking at our cuisine coverage globally and massaging our own ego about how many different cuisine categories we had across the world. What really mattered was what was in each individual postcode – and making sure you added restaurants to grow your coverage accordingly.'

His second example of sticking to a process that worked was around partner restaurant 'activation' and branding. 'When I'd visit the local market, I'd walk the streets and if the branding wasn't done properly, like how Coke would brand a newsagent, I would personally brand it there and then and I would really drive the salespeople and say: "You have to brand up local investments." There's a reason why Mars and Coke do branding at a local level, and that's because it drives consumer transaction, it builds the brand and creates a network effect on the B2B side, because local restaurant owners look at other restaurants and when they see our brand they get to know Just Eat and they want to join us.

'So there were a few areas like those where I was really passionate about making sure the quality of our operational execution was of a high standard because it drove both growth and loyalty. It also meant we grew efficiently and didn't have to spend lots of money on expensive marketing because we did it the hard way.'

'They forgot my popadoms...'

From the outset, operational rigour was a watchword for Buttress, now a partner at VC firm 83North, and his co-founder. 'When we were raising our Series A and we were asked to describe Just Eat, I used to call us "a gritty business". Today food-tech, as it's now called, has become a sexy thing. But when we started Just Eat, I can tell you barely a venture capitalist would have heard of [the category] and probably wouldn't want to have even met us because what we really were was an online platform for local takeaway restaurants. And a local kebab shop is not your typical VC's idea of a sexy industry to be involved with.' He laughs.

Operations for Just Eat, from its earliest days in that Docklands flat, meant sweating the small stuff. 'With the restaurant owners, it was a case of: "Do they have a driver? Does their oven work? Do they have all the ingredients they need? Do they have paper in their printing machine to make sure they can receive orders?" And so on. On the consumer side it was literally phone calls to our "customer care" line that used to come through to my personal mobile in the early years because we didn't have any customer care, and it was things like "My food's late" or "They forgot my popadoms" or "I thought it came with fries". So we'd then have to call the restaurants ourselves to sort it out.

'It was painful and difficult in those early years as a bootstrapped business, and as soon as we had the capital we started employing a call centre, thank the Lord. But operations for us, particularly in the early days, was gritty at a very local level, dealing with real issues from real customers in real time, and the same for restaurant owners. We used to have restaurants' money, because obviously often it'd be paid by credit card over the web. We used to reconcile their accounts with us every two weeks, but of course some restaurants, which are small businesses, would be calling us up to ask when the money was coming because they needed to pay their staff.

'It was even down to the level of detail where I became an expert in explaining VAT to restaurant owners, because we were charging restaurants VAT on our service and it wasn't something they were familiar with. They'd never used a service provider before. They were used to paying their wholesale bills, their printing bills and their electricity bills, and so on, but they weren't used to paying for a third-party service, especially an online digital one that charged VAT. Many of them would be on the phone asking, "What's this VAT all about?"' Buttress recalls. 'So there were some fun learning experiences along the way.'

The right technology

Looking back over his time as CEO, Buttress admits that, like most entrepreneurs, there were 'a million things that we did wrong'. But, he continues, the one thing they got right, 'other than being crazily ambitious', was the technology.

He explains: 'Everyone else – including, at the time, lastminute. com, Hungry House, and all our competitors across Europe – was using fax machines to send orders to restaurants, which were unreliable; restaurants wouldn't turn them on, or the paper would run out. Some of our competitors were even phoning orders through to the restaurant. What's the point of being a digital platform if you're having to get on the phone? That's what the consumer does anyway. So one thing we did right was to build this technology platform from scratch.'

Buttress credits his co-founder, Buch, for designing a box or terminal known as a Just Connect box that was years ahead of its time. 'I'll always maintain that he built the chip and PIN machine that you see everywhere today a decade earlier than everyone else. All you had to do as a local restaurant owner was take the Just Connect box, which was literally a data-SIM card, a circuit and thermal printer all built in, and plug it into the wall, and all of a sudden you had two things: access to a digital platform, and the ability to accept orders using a two-way communication tool (because the box had four buttons on it, of which one was a green tick which basically said "Confirm order").

'That meant that a small local restaurant had better technology than they would if they were a Domino's Pizza franchise, because the order would come in 1.6 seconds from a customer's laptop, it would print out in real time in the restaurant's kitchen, the kitchen could push "Yes", which would close the loop and send a message back to the consumer at home saying their order has been accepted and confirmed.

'That for us was a total game-changer because it gave a unique experience to our consumers at home because they could communicate in real time with a restaurant, while for the restaurant owner it took away all the pain of phone calls at busy times, when it's difficult for them to take orders. It also meant that, with a push of a button, they could send a message to a consumer at home and they could also change the delivery time if they wanted to.'

Just Connect's technology became a huge competitive advantage for the startup. 'We put those boxes into every restaurant and we were very disciplined around it. The boxes used to cost £250 plus VAT, and lots of restaurants would tell us, "I don't need the box. Just phone me the orders like Hungry House or send me it by the fax machine." And we would very strongly reply: "No, you need this technology." And of course what that technology meant was, as we scaled, we scaled very efficiently because everything was fully automated, front and back end.

'After that it was only when the customer order went wrong that we ever had to call a restaurant. Which meant that probably 98% of our orders required no manual intervention at all, which is why Just Eat became the global leader from a scalability and efficiency perspective, and why you then saw us become very profitable in 2013 and onwards because as we built scale it was hugely efficient. Adding another restaurant and order to the platform didn't really cost us a lot, as we'd already built the infrastructure out.'

Get your hands dirty

Asked for his tips for scaling operations for high-growth businesses, Buttress offers two pieces of advice. 'First of all, hire people who're better than you, and don't be precious about letting go of the operational know-how of your business. Trust me, no matter how good an entrepreneur you are, how good you are at building a business and at the vision and strategy, there are better operational people out there than you, who have worked in other organisations that come with excellent operational practices and scale efficiencies – so bring them in and give them the keys to your operations.

'What that will help you to do is: a) professionalise and grow your organisation, and b) I guarantee it'll result in a better experience for your customers, whoever they might be and whatever industry you are in. So hire great people as early as you can on the operational side.'

Second, says Buttress, whereas good businesses throw money at a problem and hire lots of people to help scale their business, great ones think long-term and strategically about how technology can be used to scale more effectively.

'If you take the Just Eat example of the Just Connect terminal, the easiest thing in the world for us to have done would have been to have piggybacked off the likes of fax machines and phone lines,' he says. 'But as a technology business, we really wanted to try to change how the industry operated.

'So really challenge yourself to think, whatever the operational task, how technology can be deployed in order to do it better, quicker, smarter, give a greater product experience. And if you really challenge yourself to think hard about that and then are equally disciplined around operationally deploying it, it can 10x your business. It might be painful in the short term, but it can differentiate your business in the long term and it certainly did with ours in terms of competitive advantage and scale.'

Underpinning both of these, Buttress goes on to argue, is the fact that the best operational leaders get their hands dirty (in his case by pounding the streets). 'You've got to do it first,' he says. 'If you've done all the operational processes yourself, it gives you credibility internally, and even if they can do it better than you, your team will respect the fact that you've had a good go at it.

'It'll also give you insight that stays with you throughout the growth of your business. Throughout all my time as a CEO and four years as a public CEO, there were many occasions when, even though I was no longer doing those tasks, if someone told me something about any aspect of operations, I instinctively knew whether what they were saying was rubbish or not. I just knew if something didn't sound right or didn't make sense.'

Buttress thinks that Series A is usually too early for a startup to hire a COO – although he concedes there will be some companies which are exceptions to the rule. Instead, he advocates waiting until the business is looking to deploy into multiple markets or geographies – at which point the CEO is likely to have six or seven people reporting to them directly.

'That's because if you're going to end up with nine, ten or eleven direct reports, as CEO, what that really says is that you are not going to manage people properly. And when you are simultaneously covering more than one or two geographies, it's impossible to do that well [without a COO]. Obviously every business is different, but in my experience that would the right moment to start your search.'

⌄

David Buttress is the former CEO of Just Eat, an entrepreneur, angel investor and partner at 83North Venture Capital. After a successful eight-year stint in the FMCG environment with Coca-Cola Enterprises, David spent the next 11 years co-founding, building, living and breathing Just Eat in the UK, and leading the Just Eat global business. In 2014, 2015 and 2016, he was named in *Debrett's 500* most influential people in Britain, and in 2016 was one of Glassdoor's top five 'Highest Rated CEOs'.

CHAPTER 18

'Pay your technical debt continuously' and 'Start with *why*'.

Carlos Gonzalez-Cadenas, Chief Product and Technology Officer at GoCardless, has these 11 rules for scaling product.

Here, Spanish-born Gonzalez-Cadenas, who hails from Zamora in the country's northwest and is also an investor and advisor to early- and growth-stage businesses, offers his 11 golden rules on scaling product for scale-up companies (which he defines as post-product/ market fit organisations).

'The businesses I'm talking about have built something that works for a growing number of customers, which the founders know how to monetise, and now they're stepping on the accelerator towards building a company and scaling revenue, product delivery and international footprint,' he says. 'That's my particular focus and has been for close to a decade.'

1.
The three essential elements to get right in a high-functioning product development organisation are VELOCITY, IMPACT and QUALITY OF THE CUSTOMER EXPERIENCE

It's very important that founders have people in their product teams focusing on the three key dimensions of product development,' says Gonzalez-Cadenas. 'The first is **velocity**, which is about being able to ship products very quickly into market and generally move fast.

'Second is **impact** – ensuring that the product development organisation is not only shipping things quickly, but also that the things they are shipping have a genuine and meaningful impact for customers, whether individuals or businesses.

'One of the main issues I see in organisations, especially when you move from startup to scale-up phase, is that founders tend to get the velocity part right, but then say "We're shipping a ton of stuff, but it doesn't move the needle" or "It doesn't shift the KPIs" or "It doesn't do much for customers, despite the fact we're investing a lot of money", and so on. In other words, they're not getting anything like the ROI they need from the product development organisation.'

'The third one is **quality of the customer experience (CX)**. There are multiple definitions in the market about concepts like CX and UX (user experience), but what I particularly care about is making the product frictionless – that is, ensuring that customers can achieve their goal with as little pain as possible.'

Gonzalez-Cadenas goes on to say that although everyone in the organisation is responsible for making progress along these dimensions, it's important in practice to ensure that a different function is accountable for each of them.

'The "velocity" side of things I tend to give to the engineering function. The engineering team's focus should be on shipping high-quality software quickly and confidently.

'The "impact" bit I give to product management. So the main point of having a product management team in the business, which many founders struggle to build quickly enough, is that it's all about figuring out the things that are going to have the maximum impact for customers and for the company, and ensuring that the product development organisation focuses on those.

'The third dimension, "quality of the customer experience", I leave to the product design function. They must ensure that the product development organisation understands the entirety of the customer journey and how to reduce friction at every point of the journey.

'Product development teams must be equipped with people that successfully deliver on these three dimensions to have a realistic shot of scaling successfully,' he says.

2.
Always have clarity on who you serve – and then focus all your firepower on them

It may sound obvious to say 'Be clear about who your customer is', but when you're a startup you are very often shooting at everything that moves because you're still trying to figure out what works, and you end up trying to serve everyone by default, says Gonzalez-Cadenas.

'That scattergun-discovery approach is fine for the startup phase, but once you've figured out what works and you're scaling up, if you want to grow very fast you need to narrow your focus and figure out what's working in terms of individual customer segments, then double down on those. Ensure that you really understand what those target customer segments need and how to provide it for them more efficiently and successfully than ever before.'

3.
Long-term vision isn't everything – you also need to clearly articulate how to get there

'Many businesses end up in a situation where the long-term product vision is reasonably well defined, but they don't know the sequence of steps required to get there,' he says. 'So being able to clearly articulate the product strategy is crucial.'

'This is something that's often missing in a lot of product organisations, where there's a vague sense of direction but there's not a clear articulation of: "Here are the three key things that are aligned to our long-term vision that we really need to nail over the next 12 months."

'Being clear about the product strategy enables everyone in the business to make the right short-term decisions, and ensures that the product vision is not a pipe dream but instead an achievable objective that draws closer every day.'

4.
Make sure that your product development organisation is decentralised

On organisational design, Gonzalez-Cadenas says: 'When you're starting up you will typically have a small product team. But what often happens as you raise your product ambitions and consequently you start to grow the team, counterintuitively you end up doing less and not more.

'This is because at the beginning, you have 5 or 10 people in a room, and communication, coordination and decision-making are quite simple; everyone is on the same page without much effort. By the time you move to 50, 70 or 100 people, the opposite is true, and from a product development perspective, you need to pay much more attention to how you organise your team.

'By that I mean it's critical, when you scale, that your organisation is decentralised. You need to ensure that you have teams that specifically own one part of your product, so they have a mission and can operate, ship product and make decisions as independently as possible. Although no organisational design is perfect, Spotify's "squads & tribes" model for engineering teams provides a great blueprint for product organisations at scale.

'There is nothing worse for a product development organisation than adding scores of people without much thought about how to organise them. There's a lack of clarity about who does what, about how decisions get made, and the organisation becomes full of bottlenecks. As a result, you end up doing less and not more,' he says.

5.
Decisions should be made using the
right balance between intuition and data

There's a much-repeated mantra about how product organisations should be data-driven, but frequently teams go too far, and being overly data-driven carries its own dangers, he continues.

'Instead you should ensure that product decisions are made using the right balance between data and intuition, which is just as important as data and why you have to use both.

'What I've seen in many organisations that overdo the "data-driven" mantra is that they end up being too incremental. They end up focusing on the short-term, incremental improvements that are easy to back up with data, and they miss big things simply because they are less certain and cannot be fully evidenced with data.

'At the same time, you don't want to have a data-less conversation, where essentially everything is decided on gut feeling, because you also need the basic diligence data provides on, for example, how customers use your product. That's why that combination of data and intuition is key.'

6.
Standardisation and dissemination
of tools and best practices is something
all the best product teams excel at

It's absolutely vital – when you are scaling and gaining velocity – to ensure that every team and team member is fundamentally using, more or less, the same tools, says Gonzalez-Cadenas.

'Otherwise the risk is you end up reinventing the wheel 20 times, where one team is using a particular tool for testing, while another team is using a different one. That sort of duplication is just a waste of time and effort.

'The second thing is that best practice – where some teams are executing very effectively – needs to be disseminated and implemented by other product teams, so that all the boats in the harbour are being raised simultaneously.'

7.
Ship product frequently, quickly and confidently

'Frequently' means product teams should ship product improvements at least once a week, says Gonzalez-Cadenas. 'The shipping process itself must be quick and highly efficient – it should never take three hours to ship something to production. And by "confidently", I mean you need to have the measures in place to ensure that you cannot inadvertently break the product for your customers as you ship new changes.'

He adds that those qualities tend to be present in the early days of a startup, but they often fade away when a company begins to scale, because by then its product and infrastructure are more complex and multilayered, and as a result shipping becomes incrementally harder. 'That's a killer of productivity and a killer of morale from the point of view of the product development team,' he says.

He recalls that when he first started working at Skyscanner, it took six weeks to ship a new version of the product. 'Shipping stuff was painful and super slow back in those days, and the product development team was very demoralised. But since then there's been a total transformation where today the company has tens of different teams shipping on their own, doing it multiple times per week and running a big number of experiments in production every month.'

The way this was achieved was by investing heavily in infrastructure, automation and developer tooling, he explains. 'By the end, we'd made a habit of shipping stuff to production so frequently that it had become a non-event. That's where you want to be because the success of the business in many ways depends on it.'

8.
Ensure you pay your technical debt continuously

'I've lost count of the number of times I've heard companies say "We've got to rewrite our platform" because of reasons such as: "It doesn't scale" or "The quality of the code isn't good enough" or "We have too much technical debt",' says Gonzalez-Cadenas.

'People then spend two or three years rewriting their entire codebase, only to end up with a new codebase but more or less where they started from a product and customer point of view. In some cases they end up in an even worse position because some of the features that they had previously – and that customers depended on – are no longer in the new version.'

The upshot is that many businesses in this position lose their competitive edge and become paralysed after three years without shipping anything. 'So the big lesson here is make sure you pay your technical debt continuously. Spend 10–20% of each quarter on technical investments (paying back technical debt or preparing for the future), instead of waiting until you're in a very bad situation, because it's going to seriously damage your business if you don't.'

9.
Build (internally) only when you have to

'This is crucial: when it comes to non-core stuff, always try to partner with others instead of building it internally,' Gonzalez-Cadenas cautions.

'Typically, the best product development organisations often have brilliant engineers who think they can build everything better than almost everyone else out there. However, the reality is there are not enough years in a lifetime to build everything yourself in-house, when there are any number of perfectly good off-the-shelf solutions out there.'

He goes on to give an example from his time at Skyscanner, where the product development team was discussing the introduction of a new internal tool.

'Not unusually, the team's first instinct was "Let's see what we need to build to enable this", and my challenge back to the team was there are probably tens of companies out there that offer that same exact functionality and we can integrate with their API tomorrow, and avoid the multiple months of development that it's going to take us to build something ourselves.

'For me, the crucial thing is to "build only when you have to" and therefore focus your product development team resources on your core stuff, where you can add value to customers and differentiate from competitors. Doing that will substantially accelerate impact for customers and for the business.'

10.
Make people management a top priority

'When you're a startup, you often don't know if you're going to die tomorrow or next week, because it's too early to know whether you have a business or not,' he continues. 'So at that stage, founders are – understandably – not really focused on people management. But the moment you get into scale-up mode, and it dawns on your team that they're in a business that might actually be successful, they start to think about their future and how they might progress professionally; how they can take on more responsibility and develop their role.

'That's why, when you're scaling, it's so important to ensure that you invest enough in people management, because the bigger you get, the more this matters. Many companies that are scaling up fast put a lot of focus on attracting talent, but they don't put enough focus on developing and retaining their talent, which are two key aspects of people management.

'On the development side of things, as you're scaling you need to hire strong leaders from outside the company, while simultaneously also developing leaders internally. In my career, I've come across many people who have great potential, but too many companies don't spend the necessary time and resources helping them develop.'

As the product leader, it's your responsibility to ensure there's a brilliant future in the business for your key team members, says Gonzalez-Cadenas. 'Retention is a really big problem in the technology sector, and particularly so in tier-one technology hubs like London and San Francisco where there's a huge amount of competition for talent.

'So do whatever you can to create a great work environment and keep your best people in the business. Losing key talent is very disruptive because those individuals are not only highly skilled, but in addition they typically have a lot of context and are highly effective in the business.

'If you end up losing your key people you are losing economic value for the business and undermining your productivity. Companies that underinvest in developing and retaining their people typically struggle to scale up their business at a fast pace.'

11. Start with *why*

Gonzalez-Cadenas argues that a key cultural element found in the best product teams is customer orientation – that is, a strong sense of doing the right thing for the customers.

'This may sound obvious, but product development teams often have a tendency towards being inward-looking compared with the rest of the business, which is why it's so important to instil a culture which is built around the customer.'

At GoCardless, for example, one of the company's key values is 'Start with *why*', he says. 'When our engineers are writing down the specifications for a problem they want to solve, they always use the first paragraph to address the question of why they're doing this and what difference it will make to our customers.

'One of the best signs of a product organisation that has a strong customer-centric culture is when there is a grass-roots "allergic response" when someone suggests implementing a functionality that might not be in the best interest of the customers.'

During his three-year tenure at Skyscanner, where he rose to be Chief Product Officer, **Carlos Gonzalez-Cadenas** scaled the leading travel search site's product development team (which covers engineering, design and product management) from 150 to 400 people across 10 offices around the world. As Chief Product Officer, he saw Skyscanner's product delivery soar by 15x, while delivering dozens of large programmes, product improvements and new launches, as well as revamping the company's mobile product offering. In 2017 he joined GoCardless as the online payments company's Chief Product and Technology Officer.

CHAPTER 19

'Don't sell umbrellas to camels.'

**Partnerize CEO Malcolm Cowley on
scaling an enterprise startup and why 'B2B
companies are judged on revenues early'.**

Of the three major scaling challenges his business initially faced, Malcolm Cowley says the first was its birthplace of Newcastle, in the northeast of England, where the company – which provides SaaS solutions for digital partner marketing – is still headquartered today.

'To get a business such as Partnerize off the ground when your ambition is to build a large global company, you need to take into account the limited funding available in a city like Newcastle compared with the major metropolitan centres. So, whilst Newcastle is a great place to start a business for many reasons, it's still a struggle for companies to find the right investment partner to help them scale,' he says, before adding: 'although I do think that situation's getting better.'

Speaking from San Francisco where he's now based, Cowley argues that if a startup is able to present a business plan which shows a) a serious chance of scaling, b) a talented team and c) a verifiable track record, then because early-stage investment tends to be more about confidence in the team than anything else, where it's based isn't a make-or-break factor.

'In that scenario, like ourselves, you are able to secure capital outside of your location. The first venture capital firm that seed-funded us was [London and Berlin-based] DN Capital.

'But I don't think it's the same for everyone. The profile of companies outside of London can be a little hidden, just like in

Silicon Valley, where if you're outside of that 35-mile radius of the Valley then that can be a problem. While it's less of an issue in England, if you're a company based out of the northeast, that still means you're not around the corner from the big investors, and you can't just take a walk from your office to theirs. And that proximity, that personal contact, does matter in the early stages.'

Another related early challenge, which almost all technology businesses face, is sourcing talent, Cowley continues. 'I've been involved in two businesses that were founded in Newcastle and there is incredible talent in the region on the technical side. Unfortunately, it's still a limited pool compared with one of the major hubs. And while there's less competition for that talent, which is a positive, certainly there just simply aren't as many people locally with those kinds of skills.'

While he acknowledges that the UK government and the Tech Nation network have been making a dent in the problem, the only way cities like Newcastle can really build an ecosystem is through having a number of successful founders scale up large businesses, exit and then bring that exit money back in to reinvest at the grassroots level, he says. 'That's when people will really take notice and start to pick those careers that would lead them towards that goal of working for an entrepreneurial high-growth business.'

The next big challenge Cowley and his co-founders encountered was that the business was international in outlook and operation almost from the outset. 'We were founded to enable companies to more easily create measurable partnerships to drive business growth – and those partnerships could very well be located in Japan, China, or anywhere in Europe, America or Australia.

'If you're a business that can sell to consumers or other businesses in those locations, then you don't want to limit yourself to partnerships in your local area. Therefore, if we were going to build the platform that really connects those two together to create a new business opportunity for clients, then we needed to be truly global pretty early on.'

Expansion can't be faked

Today Partnerize – which was formerly known as Performance Horizon – has eight offices in the UK, the US, Germany, Japan and Australia, while its platform drives $6bn+ in advertiser top-line revenues across 275,000 marketing partners in over 214 countries and territories. 'International expansion can't be faked. Our technology platform handles the tracking, reporting and payments for partners in all those countries, and so we had to create a local corporate entity for many of these markets. You need to have a corporate entity in countries like Japan, and in China, and you need to have local bank accounts in places like Brazil, in order to make local payments to partners for the sales/referrals they've driven.'

The way Cowley cracked that was by bringing the right sort of heavy-hitting support onto the board, as well as the right investors who were aligned with a rapid-expansion strategy. 'You need to know that your investors can access the right sort of resources, so that if you need local advice in Japan, for example, then that connection can be made and you can have the right experience on the ground to be able to help you. Or it might be access to the right people from a tax or governance perspective.

'A lot of it is about surrounding yourself with the right people as early as possible to enable you to achieve your plan. Also, for a company that is VC-backed, growth is essential and some of the things that enable that growth take time. If you want to set up a business in China, for example, what we've found is that there is a very prescribed set-up process which can take up to 12 months.

'As a business that has to move quickly, establish itself and generate revenues, it can be quite a challenge to manage expectations with your board, because you're not going to generate near-term revenue in that region over that period. It's a long-range bet for a company that's two years old.' He adds: 'But what's great is it really pays off on the back end.'

Building a high-growth startup is all about understanding your business goals and having the necessary firepower at the table when you need it to help you achieve them, he continues. 'It's always been a mantra of ours to "think big". We stepped forward without fear of things like scaling internationally, but a lot of that was down to the fact that we'd planned in advance. I'm not saying we got everything right all the time, far from it, but the majority of the time we had the right preparation.'

Be predictable

For all enterprise businesses, predictability is something you should obsess about, Cowley says. 'If you think about that path to becoming a much larger business that could potentially withstand being in the public markets, for instance, to be able to make that leap from private to public, then predictability is key.

'Being able to accurately forecast how the revenues will build and where you're going to be in four, five or six quarters' time is a challenge when you're on-boarding your first 30 customers and you're still trying to learn about your business.

'With an early-stage enterprise business, it's easy to run into forecasting difficulties, so you should be thinking about raising more capital than you need; you've got to be hot on managing your burn [rate], and you've really got to stay in your lane as much as you possibly can in the early days while you [achieve] product/ market fit.

'Again, you should bring that sort of support and experience to the table as early as possible – and you shouldn't have any fear of that, as a founder. People say "Hire people who are smarter than you" – specifically in areas where you're weak – and I think doing exactly that can keep you out ahead.'

Hiring for a B2B business

Cowley advocates one hire in particular for B2B businesses: 'I don't think it's ever too early to hire an experienced CFO. Certainly, from my perspective that has been the number-one transformational hire. It's somebody that can help you think through some of the scaling challenges, with the board management piece and with strategic thinking.' He adds: 'I'm not talking about a Head of Finance here, but more of a fully fledged CFO. I think investing in that hire early will save you a lot of grey hairs.'

He also has a tweak to the notion of hiring slow and firing fast – for the enterprise sector, he says that while it's true that founders should fire fast, where necessary, they shouldn't hire too slowly. 'It's a very competitive market out there for talent, especially in the major metros. You certainly don't want to have a great candidate languishing in that process because you will miss [out on] them. Get your hiring profiles right in the first place, and then run a tight process – effectively double-timing it, where you still spend a lot of time with the candidate but, in aggregate, it's not a huge amount of time.'

Cowley emphasises the importance to high-growth businesses of hiring 'people who scale'. He says: 'The whole idea of these businesses is that they're pumping in money to grow at a massively accelerated rate, and so they need to get to scale quickly sometimes, to dominate the market. So, the person who is experienced this year for what you need today, *that* person is likely to struggle tomorrow when you're growing fast. You're really trying to look for people who have a history and profile of growth themselves throughout their career, rather than somebody who is very experienced but is sort of at their ceiling.'

Don't try to solve too many problems

Focus is key for a B2B company in the early stages, he continues. 'Don't try and run off and solve the next problem. Really zero in on being good at what you're good at, and understand if you can own that area and really achieve for a customer at enterprise level. Then they'll help to champion your expansion within their business – and beyond. But if you're sort of half-hearted with that initial engagement, then you'll come a cropper.'

Don't obsess about valuation

People really focus too much on optimising their valuation in those early funding rounds, argues Cowley, when to a certain degree the valuation that really matters is the one when you exit the business. 'People should focus less on optimising valuation in between rounds. Leave some room for new investors. You don't know what's around the corner, and having that little bit of a cushion rather than a high hurdle can certainly help you keep the business moving and remove friction at later stages if things haven't quite gone to plan.'

Focus instead on optimising to build a great business with solid fundamentals, because that will increase your options along the way as a CEO. 'Don't worry about the market. You can't control it, but you can control the type of business that you build.'

Remember: 'Nothing is ever as bad or as good as it seems'

'That's somebody else's quote, but it's an idea I really subscribe to. There are wild swings in these businesses, and that takes a lot of mental fortitude. But you realise, after a while, that these things kind of even out, and so help yourself emotionally, remembering that it's never as bad or as good as it seems at first glance.'

Enterprise customers are expensive to acquire – so you need to ensure the investment will pay off

Partnerize has about 170 clients, 90% of whom are direct customers as opposed to via a third party such as a digital agency. 'Many of those clients are paying us a six- or even seven-figure sum, and if you are paying that kind of money, there's going to be a process behind being chosen, and that may involve procurement and so on. So as a B2B founder, you've got to understand that sales cycles will run long and plan accordingly, because at this level you could spend over £100,000 to acquire a single customer.

'That's a heavy investment for one customer so you'd better be sure that that's going to pay off at the back end. You need to be on top of the cost of acquisition versus payback. In the early stages, you want this to be under 12 months. There are a lot of processes to optimise from pre-sales to contracting, and on-boarding to post-sales and making them successful and, importantly from your point of view, referenceable needs to be your priority.

'There are a lot of things going on there, and if you're outside the parameters that you're looking for, then you'd better be over-indexing on qualified pipeline generation, because something's got to be there to see you through to the next milestone.'

Bring on the smart money, because nothing helps more than people or access

The two best things a great investor brings to the table for a B2B startup, beyond capital, are people and access, says Cowley. 'Those are the two main things that we look for in an investor, because if you can fast-track your sales process by getting a warm introduction at the executive level, then that really helps you to grow quickly and efficiently.

'Obviously you want to hire great people – quickly, too. We're well known for having great technology, but business success is all about people at the end of the day – and in the early stages even one great (as opposed to good) hire can make all the difference.'

Focus on referenceable customers

'Our CRO Pete Mycock says: "Don't sell umbrellas to camels." Really what he's talking about is to make sure you understand who your ideal customer is and to stay in that lane, where they will really get the most benefit from your product and/or service, and focus almost exclusively on them. They are far more likely to become referenceable customers, who can then provide air cover for your sales leads [by giving your company] a great reference.

'If you're an enterprise business like us, then referenceable customers are huge. Without them, it becomes a difficult chicken-and-egg situation. So, my advice is to try extremely hard to get those first referenceable customers, and over-index on keeping them happy. The theory is that it should get markedly easier the more of them that you have. So always ask yourself: "Are these clients really referenceable? Will they help me to reduce the sales cycle?"'

Cowley on... scaling tech

On scaling the technology side of the business, Cowley says he and his leadership team prioritised hiring people who had a proven track record of scaling tech. 'There's $6bn-worth of e-commerce being driven and tracked across the platform today by partners of our customers. So that's a huge amount of data. Again, a little bit like the internationalisation process, you can't fake it. You're selling to some of the biggest companies in the world, and they are quite reasonably expecting everything to work all the time – and for it to scale.'

That entails really thinking about scaling early on and understanding what that architecture needs to look like in a few years' time, he says. 'Because that means knowing what to invest in *today*; you've got to have people who've done this before. So again, a lot of this is about bringing in that experience level to help you get ahead of the learning curve, anticipate the scaling technology problems you'll have 12–18 months out and then build for that now.'

Partnerize currently runs at 99.99% uptime, giving customers a service-level agreement (SLA) that is 'not a long way from that', says Cowley. 'In the early stage of the business, what did being able to build out capacity mean for us? Sometimes it meant doubling our infrastructure. Back then we used a managed service provider because in the early days that was the most efficient way to be able to quickly add new infrastructure to our platform. This allowed planning to be a little more fluid. But as the business has grown, we've adopted a much more forward-looking capacity management process, and the tech team look at current capacity and utilisation as it is now, and then project where we're going to need additional capacity.'

Scaling and uptime, he says, are by definition among the company's biggest concerns. 'We really wanted to be certain that we could scale the platform without any major issues when we on-boarded these large clients. And in the early years of the business, that could mean a significant percentage uplift in traffic overnight, so you always want to make sure the tech's robust and the client's first impression was really good.'

Cowley also says he always makes a point of effusively thanking his tech leadership for hitting their year-end KPIs, because their performance is absolutely critical to the business. 'They're often the unsung heroes – when things are going well, they don't get a lot of praise, but the alarm bells would be going off if there was a problem, because downtime could be an existential threat.

'Fortunately, we were able to stay ahead of the curve long enough until we had the kind of scale we have now, so it's a little less of a concern although still extremely important, as customers rely on us to track critical information that helps them run their business. We have a lot of experience in the team now, and although it may seem a little table stakes to us today, we never forget it's taken a lot of work for us to get in that position and to get those key people in place who can help me to sleep at night.'

Once again, it's a matter of investing in the right leadership, he says. 'In a B2B company, this stuff *has* to happen. It *has to work* – otherwise the whole thing falls apart.'

Cowley on... raising money

When it comes to how a B2B business raises money, Cowley has some hard-won advice. 'If you're growing a B2B business, you'll be judged on revenues early. So, if you're a Series A company coming from the UK looking to raise your B round in America, you have to remember that – to put it bluntly – no one cares about you. You'd have to be very hot, with the best metrics, a real superstar, to get around and over some of the biases that still exist,' he explains.

'If you're determined to do it [i.e. raise a B round in the US], you can increase your chances by setting up locally, because if you're going to raise money in Silicon Valley and you're only over here for a couple of weeks, which is what we did for our Series B, it will be challenging.

'As soon as people hear that you're only here for two weeks and then you're heading back to the UK, it's a red flag. Investors say "No" a lot more than they say "Yes", so you're just giving them an easy out. I think that dynamic is something that people underestimate.'

There are, he says, plenty of great funding options in the UK and Europe these days, and if you're not yet ready to set up in the Valley, you may want to leave raising money in the US to further down the line – or alternatively start thinking about it and building the necessary relationships on the ground in the Valley (or on the East Coast) much earlier. 'The best way to do that is to get the right early backers, who can [open doors].

'But still always remember that you're going to be judged on revenues early. Just make sure you really think about how much you're going to need to raise to achieve your plan and reach that next milestone with the right profile, if you will be raising again.

'Really understand your runway and have a Plan B with investors in case Plan A doesn't work out. Leave a lot of room in your plan, because plans tend not to work out as well as you think they will, and make sure you know that your investors have got your back if that happens. That's something you really need to take the time to discuss with them, to understand where they'll sit in that eventuality. It's not something you want to be getting to grips with in the midst of a firefight,' he adds.

'Ensure you know the metrics you're going to need to get to that next stage of fundraising. Those are really important things for B2B entrepreneurs to think about anyway, because whether it's now or sometime in the very near future, you will be judged on those revenues. If they don't match [your investors'] profile for that stage of funding, then that could be a serious challenge for you.'

Cowley also advocates playing it safe by always raising a little bit more money than you think you need. 'That was a good tip from my chairman in the early days, and I'm certainly glad we did that. Without a doubt, it enabled us to get to where we are today.'

Malcolm Cowley is the co-founder and CEO of Partnerize and the driving force behind the dramatic growth of the partner marketing platform (PMP) company. Prior to Partnerize, Malcolm was a co-founder and president of Buy.at, a UK-based global affiliate network that he and the team built into a market leader and later sold to AOL. Partnerize helps fulfil Malcolm's vision to broaden the partnership channel for leading brands, bringing data-driven marketing, real-time optimisation and AI-powered predictive analytics to the industry. Now based in San Francisco, he is from Newcastle-upon-Tyne, UK.

CHAPTER 20

Sheffield Steel.

Aldo Monteforte, CEO and co-founder of
The Floow, on design choices, compensation
and attracting talent outside a major hub.

Back in 2011, Aldo Monteforte, CEO of The Floow, was introduced
to his co-founders by fellow Italian Fabio Ciravegna, a professor in
the computer science department at the University of Sheffield. 'At
the time I was talking to Imperial College and to Stanford University
– my own alma mater – because the diverse skills I was searching for
are typically found in universities and I thought those two would be
my best bet,' says Monteforte.

'But then my friend said: "Look no further than the University of
Sheffield for this project. I have a team of two who might be able to help
you." It turned out he was right. I founded the company with those two
individuals – Paul Ridgway, my CTO, and my CIO [Chief Information
Officer] Sam Chapman – and we've been together ever since.'

Today The Floow – which supports the motor insurance and
automotive industries in the Americas, Europe and Asia with telematics
comprising predictive analytics and digital end-user services – has
soared to over 110 people, the vast majority of whom are based in
Sheffield, where the company is headquartered. So what – if any – role
has The Floow's South Yorkshire location played in its ability to scale?

Given that over 70% of the company's team are scientists – a
mix of computer, data and social scientists – Monteforte identifies
the principal scaling challenge that The Floow encountered as a
human one.

'As producers of software, without a doubt our biggest issue has been attracting talent in the quantity and of the quality necessary to match the opportunity that the company is trying to go after,' he says, before going on to detail three 'design choices' made in The Floow's earliest days which have been critical in shaping its evolution.

Under one roof

'We made a bet in the beginning that as a company our product would be comparatively better if we kept all our technical resources under one roof. As a boot-strapped startup, of course there are arguments for outsourcing when it comes to technology, whether that's India or Eastern Europe or another region. But we made a design choice from day one that we didn't want to do that. We felt there would be a distinct advantage to having everybody together, particularly bearing in mind the diverse range of technology people in the company.'

The second design choice Monteforte and his co-founders made was to build The Floow in Sheffield, due in part to the fact that the city provided the backdrop to their initial meetings.

'Of course, being based in Sheffield carried pros and cons,' he concedes. 'On the plus side, being very closely associated with the university would give us access to other talent. There is always a magnetic effect at work in the vicinity of large, particularly technical engineering universities – I was very familiar with that phenomenon at Stanford, for example. But the cons are that the supply of talent is limited. It's not the kind of supply you could have in London, given its sheer size.

'So for us, the biggest challenge has been attracting in Sheffield a steady supply of human talent qualified for the type of venture that we are building. I have to say, we've been quite fortunate in the sense that we've been able not only to tap into the local ecosystem, but more and more as the numbers have started to grow and scale, we're beginning to attract people from other parts of the UK and recently other parts of Europe too.'

An organisation with soul

Asked how that has been achieved, Monteforte replies that many people will gravitate towards an organisation that they feel has 'a soul' and an objective that they can really get behind – one that goes beyond simply profit-making.

'And at The Floow we offer that in spades. At its core, our technology makes individual mobility safer, smarter, and saves people's lives and limbs. We channel it to insurance companies who then deploy our technology with hundreds of thousands – and we hope, in the future, millions – of policy-holders, with a view to conditioning their behaviour (hence the social science element to the company). So there's a clear attraction associated with what we're building, and that's one important element that draws people to what is, we recognise, not an obvious location.'

Technology outliers

There is a second pull-factor too. Technical people, continues Monteforte, love working for other brilliant technical people, and he describes both his co-founders as 'outliers' in terms of their technical competences.

'I have been able to build, with their help, a team that has – for the vast part – stuck together and stuck with us in the knowledge that the technical leadership was top class, of Rolls Royce standard. That has been truly remarkable, and, clearly as their team has expanded, it has developed its own magnetic capabilities of attracting even more talent to the organisation.

'Of course, you need salespeople, marketing, account managers and other specialists too. So what worked really well for us was the calibre of the early clients we've attracted to the company – including Direct Line, RSA Group and AIG. They are world leaders in their space, whose reputation speaks very loudly.

'The fact that we could then go out and say, "We are serving these industry leaders, these very demanding organisations," meant that we could attract more talent – people like David James, our COO, who joined us after 22 years at GE Capital, and many others who complemented the organisation on the operations, sales and marketing side of things.

'So overall, we attracted talent to Sheffield with a combination of an inspiring vision for the company, combined with an outstanding team of technologists that tackled and built the early prototypes and platforms, and clients in whose light we could shine and win credibility from their references. All of those elements worked very well for us,' he says. 'But I'd argue there's another one too – and it's one which pervades the entire organisation.'

The lack of turnover in the senior team from the very beginning of the company, Monteforte claims, has not only had a stabilising effect, but it has allowed a very consistent company culture to develop.

'We recently carried out an exercise to codify the culture of The Floow. When you are 20 or 30 people, as founders you have the opportunity to meet everybody pretty much on a daily basis. But once you scale to a certain threshold, that gradually becomes impossible. Particularly when you have clients across the world and you're travelling a lot, which takes so much time away from the office.

'So to keep the cultural elements in place, we codified our culture, and it turned out that the company was built on four pillars – innovation, ambition, collaboration and commitment – and at every opportunity we emphasise these four pillars for the benefit of everyone joining the business. I believe the stability of our senior team has allowed us to build and maintain those core values.'

Compensation & stock options

Sheffield's relatively inexpensive cost of living – compared with London and the other major hubs – has also played a vital role in attracting and keeping key talent at The Floow, as has a generous employee equity scheme, he emphasises.

'All the other factors would have been unsustainable without a consistent policy around compensation. We are a company that has grown organically – we wanted to be self-sufficient and able to attract investors off the back of being a cash-flow self-sufficient company. That has meant that we have always been extremely careful about salary levels, and we have been aided in this in part by the fact that the cost of living in Sheffield is clearly more contained than other locations, like London.'

The knock-on effect of this means that while The Floow operates at a compensation level that is 'good for Sheffield', an experienced engineer could expect to earn significantly more in the capital. However, Monteforte has tackled this potentially inflammatory issue with a 'very aggressive' policy around employee equity.

'Our policy is very simple: anybody who is with the company for at least six months is entitled to equity in the form of stock options. The company, in fact, is majority-owned by management and staff, which is also a key part of our narrative.

'I can look into the eyes of my colleagues and my clients and tell them: "The company is ours." Yes, we have a board of directors, but the majority of the members of that board are appointed by and represent the management team. That gives us a huge advantage in terms of the ability to focus on the mission of the company and avoid some of the conflicts of interest that sometimes unfortunately emerge in the life of a company, where, for example, investors may want to exit when management doesn't.

'What we wanted to achieve with this particular ownership structure was to focus everybody's minds as much as possible. So we've tried to be very careful and prudent on the cash components, but much more generous on the equity piece.'

However, Monteforte does admit to harbouring doubts – initially, at least – about whether offering compensation packages which prioritise employee equity would serve as an inducement to prospective hires.

'You can pay your mortgage with your salary and your bonus, of course, but you cannot use stock options for that purpose. But it works for us. If all the other elements are present – if you have the clarity of purpose, you have a good strong example from the leadership of the business, and you give your team ownership – they will act more like owners and deploy more of themselves into the business, which is all you want.'

Capital can be incredibly costly if taken too early

A third 'day one' design choice Monteforte took was to hold fire when it came to taking on investment – something becoming cash-flow self-sufficient enabled him to do. 'We wanted to build the product, ship it and start generating revenues before taking capital from investors,' he says.

'The key motivation for us was always to retain control of this business for as long as possible. There was acute awareness that having investors early on is a great thing in many ways, but it can sometimes also be a curse. It's very much a lottery, in a way.

'We bootstrapped, which meant a lot of sacrifice from our standpoint in different ways, but it paid off. It meant the ability not only to attract investors, as we did at a later stage, but to influence the terms of the investment that we received as well. The key term that we have influenced is the fact that management is in control of the company, which means we could afford to be more generous with equity with our colleagues.'

The last five or so years have been incredibly favourable to entrepreneurs, he adds, with an abundance of capital available, and

The Floow has been approached on at least a weekly basis by venture capitalists or private equity investors wanting to find out more about the company.

'So it would have been quite possible to take capital earlier and from a wide range of different investors – and the level of appetite [from prospective investors] has been increasing over time, in part because the company has become larger and more recognisable, and in part because the fintech space in general now has a whole narrative about it that didn't exist before.'

Nevertheless, Monteforte held his nerve and didn't waver: 'Capital is great, but it can be incredibly costly to an entrepreneur if taken too early, particularly if you have a strong vision, if you really want to shape the organisation and have certain principles like the importance and the centrality of customers and staff. Though investors may share those principles, at some point they may actually remind you that they are more important than both of those.

'That influenced our approach a lot vis-à-vis investors, and we have been very, very selective in taking money. The deal that we closed in March 2017 saw Fosun, the largest private equity investor in China, coming in, because we see China as a great market for us and we need help there. So compared to other stories that I am aware of, I think the capital-raising front hasn't been much of a preoccupation for us. Instead, we've been preoccupied with winning client organisations, generating revenues in the knowledge that if the business does that well and creates a market, then investors will manifest themselves. And that's what happened.'

Lessons were learned

While talent acquisition remains the predominant challenge for Monteforte and his team, growing his client base – especially in the early days – ran a close second. 'There was a lot of learning there,' he says. 'Our technical team in particular had to perform a few miracles in the early years, and we were able to pull a good number of them off because of the outstanding quality of the technical team and our operational resources.

'Ultimately, it came down to the level of commitment. We were working pretty much day and night across many months to deliver to specifications, to budget. Inevitably, on some occasions, we got things wrong, clients were upset, but lessons were learned.

'We were very fortunate in that we were able to persuade major insurance companies to start experimenting with our early products that admittedly in those days were not fully baked – and the vast majority of those organisations, though not all, decided to stick with us and understood that we were building something very much at the leading edge of the technical frontier, that nobody had done before. They were supportive of us even when we failed.'

Looking back, what does he put those 'failures' down to?

'They were pretty much due to lack of resources. We realised we needed to continue to invest and expand the technical team and that challenge is ongoing. We are now well over 100, but we are still, in numerical terms, insufficient; I could do with two or three times the size of the organisation to meet the challenges that we face.

'I wouldn't want to impress upon you that our story has a successful outcome necessarily, because we are still on a journey and the journey is far from over.'

He concludes: 'The Floow is living through the most unprecedented proliferation of sensor-generated data that humanity has ever experienced. We exist and we are developing because of this underlying phenomenon that requires organisations like ours that can make sense of all of it. That's why, for us, success is an organisation of 1,000 people, not 100, because that is the size of the opportunity out there.'

∨

In 2000, after several years in investment banking with Nomura, **Aldo Monteforte** became an entrepreneur and investor in high-growth telematics companies. From 2000–2011 he was co-CEO and investor in Cobra Automotive Technologies, an early player in telematics and usage-based insurance (UBI). He founded The Floow in 2012, with the vision of making mobility safer and smarter for everyone. Aldo is a graduate of the Stanford Graduate School of Business, where he earned an MSc in Management (Sloan Fellows).

CHAPTER 21

'Five years ago, we were talking to people who had never heard of machine learning.'

Martina King, CEO of Featurespace,
on pivoting a business and making the most
of her company's Cambridge roots.

Born in 2005 in the University of Cambridge's engineering department, Featurespace was the brainchild of Dave Excell and the late Professor Bill Fitzgerald, then head of Applied Statistics and Signal Processing, applying the techniques researched in the lab to commercial problems.

The 'predictive analytics' technology they and other leading Cambridge engineering and mathematics academics were pioneering could identify individual changes of behaviour in a data set in real time – a technique that was not only years ahead of its time, but something with almost unlimited potential, albeit yet to be applied in a business context.

Indeed, it wasn't until 2008, when online betting giant Betfair asked Featurespace to find a way to apply its machine learning technology to outmanoeuvring fraudsters, that the enterprise startup set off on its long and somewhat tortuous journey from classroom to commerce.

Fast-forward four years, to when Martina King joined the company as CEO and Featurespace had still not settled on a particular sector, let alone go-to-market strategy, which was something the former Yahoo! Europe and Capital Radio MD was brought in to address. 'The company hadn't quite found its way,' she recalls. 'It had been trying to work with the marketing services industry, predicting the churn of customers and which customers would be most likely to purchase.

'And then there was also another – very different – piece of work that we undertook around trying to predict cancerous cells in skin melanomas: from images of skin lesions, could you predict the change that occurs just by looking at the images over time? What we learned from this data analysis was that the maths was there to identify the moment of change and you could certainly create a system to do it, but the problem was the quality of the images themselves. At that stage, the images being input into the system weren't reliable enough to be able to produce predictive analytics.

'So there are a whole host of different challenges that Featurespace had attempted to tackle, but we began to focus more and more on the fraud challenge, and protecting customers and consumers from real-time fraud attacks.'

The more the company spoke to both people in the gaming sector and in financial services, particularly in banks and payment processing, the more a common theme began to emerge, she says. 'We kept hearing that existing risk prevention systems weren't good enough and they weren't keeping up with the changing modus operandi of fraud attackers. So we set about building those industries a fraud prevention system to their brief, and that's how we then came to develop a product.'

The 'reverse-engineered' pivot

Reflecting on how Featurespace gradually zeroed in on its commercial sweet spot of 'Adaptive Behavioural Analytics' for fraud and risk management, King says initially it was a case of setting wide parameters for use cases and testing them out individually. 'It was going broad, speaking to lots of different organisations in different sectors, from oil and gas to marketing, and the gaming sector to financial services and insurance.

'What we were trying to do was understand a company's problem to see if we could build a better solution than the ones that currently existed in the market. We soon discovered – and we're going back now over five years ago – that the technology was so new that we were talking to people who had never heard of machine learning, who didn't really understand what the uplift of the technology can achieve.'

She qualifies this: 'To be fair, neither did we, and it wasn't until we applied our academic and business minds to our gaming and financial services customer data that we began to see the significant business uplift we could provide for companies.'

In contrast to some of the tech sector's most celebrated pivots – such as those of Instagram, Flickr and Groupon – Featurespace almost reverse-engineered their strategy, by first identifying business areas with endemic and longstanding problems which could be more effectively solved by machine learning technology.

'We worked with different sectors and then started to find people who understood the language of predictive analytics – and it turned out that an awful lot of those individuals were fraud experts,' says King. 'They were already used to building data models, they were already trying to use systems to solve their business problems.'

She explains: 'When you're using machine learning, every time you get an answer right, that's good. However, every time you get an answer wrong, it's called a "false positive". There were very few people in the world at that stage that we met that even understood the terminology. So finding the guys that were fighting the fraud battles initially was brilliant, because we spoke the same data-science language, that was the first thing.

'Then they were able to tell us about the problems they were having with their existing suppliers. We replied: "If we were able to build you something that actually worked better, would that be of interest to you?" And the answer to that was: "Yes, please."'

King and her team were thus in the enviable position of designing and building a product with continuous input from the customer. 'By working collaboratively with the industry, we were able to give them the product they wanted.'

Start with the problem

Asked for her tips on pivoting a company, King says that, based on her own experience, leadership teams need to be rigorous about first digging into the market they want to disrupt. 'By that I mean that you need to know for certain, not least on behalf of your investors, that it doesn't matter if you've built the world's best solution to a problem, if there isn't actually a commercial market for it.

'It sounds obvious, but with Featurespace, we had a lot of very noble ideas about what we could do with our technology, but the kind of backing that we'd have had to receive from investors to get that long-term proof point – very few of them are prepared to hang around that long. As a young company, we needed to prove our commercial way in the world very quickly in order to be able to secure our financing and then our future.'

That approach also enabled Featurespace to solve product/ market fit, something that King describes as the only way of ensuring a B2B company's survival. While she concedes there are consumer products which can be tested on groups of customers to glean early feedback – and then iterated accordingly – that requires significant investment, not least in the area of marketing spend, and can be quite a precarious route to go down as a result.

'For a business-to-business company – if you've identified the market that you are going to work with – I don't think there is any other way than making sure that your product fits the customer requirements. That's the only way you can do it.

'Prototyping, testing and creating a measurable, market-leading return on investment for your customers, leads to a product developed to meet their needs. The market will tell you what they will buy – if you ask,' she says.

Knocking on doors

The company's technology-first evolution meant that its quest to identify a core problem to solve took time and diligence. King advises entrepreneurs and startup leaders in a similar position to hold their nerve. 'Initially it takes an awful lot of trial and error and knocking on doors until you find open-minded business people to work with, to be able to experiment with – and only then can you find the place where you hit your Eureka moment.

'But in reality, you can only do that by working collaboratively with companies and working with their data and immersing yourself in what their problems are. The great thing for us was that because the fraud prevention market is a relatively small one in the UK, the guys all know each other because they're all aligned in trying to solve the same problems.'

First, you – as the startup – need to earn their respect, she continues. 'But then being able to ensure you're building a product to their requirements means that when you finally deliver it to them they're deliriously happy. So it's that relationship-building – and trust that then starts to exist between vendor and customer – that enables you to make sure that you can grow as a business.

'Ultimately, this is all about working with your customers to give them a product that's going to solve their specific problem. If they see that you can do that and your technology is tried and tested better than the incumbents in the market – and you deliver it on time and on budget, exceeding their expectations, then that's the best way for you to build a lasting reputation.'

Scaling a machine learning-focused company

So what, then, are the key challenges to scaling a machine learning-focused company like Featurespace?

King replies that as a tech pioneer, the company is only ever as good as the quality of people it attracts, and their propensity towards being open and receptive to experimentation. That takes a particular mindset, she argues, and finding talent that fitted the bill required the company to be some way down the road to being proven and commercially viable.

'When you're doing something that is as important as protecting consumers from fraud attacks, it's very motivating for people working in these new technologies. But, in my experience, they want to be part of something that is [already] commercially successful.

'That the company is not too early in its journey, that its product is developed and it has customers who are advocates of what you're doing means that a lot of the risks are behind it – and that's very attractive to potential star recruits,' she says. 'But then, it's also about offering a mission for bright minds to crack.'

Cambridge heritage

Somewhat unusually for the CEO of a fast-growth VC-backed tech company, King has a largely non-tech background which encompasses media organisations including the Guardian Media Group, Capital Radio and the Radio Advertising Bureau (which she chaired after her stint at Yahoo!). So how has that diverse backstory helped prepare her for her current role of scaling Featurespace?

'I've worked as an executive and as a non-executive of small and large organisations: public, private, commercial and charitable,' she says. 'Wherever you look, the challenges are universal: direction, management/leadership, product/customer management, revenue generation/cash management, ambition, execution and funding.

Case study: Featurespace founder Dave Excell on the company's stateside push

Another critical strand of the scaling process has been taking the company to America, from where founder Dave Excell leads Featurespace's global push. Based in Atlanta, Georgia, he says an early priority was 'learning to speak like a local'.

'We've had to ensure our US customers have confidence that we understand their specific needs and that we're here to support them,' he explains. 'Providing this confidence has touched all areas of the business, including the very nuanced ways in which we describe how our product works – for example, referencing an "ACH" or "wire transfer" rather than the "faster payment" that is common in the UK.'

Paying close attention to detail is crucial too, he says. 'It sounds obvious, but we need to ensure all figures are presented in dollars, that we always use American spellings, and remember to start with +1 when we share conference line numbers. Unfortunately, missing these small details sends the wrong signal and can distract potential customers from listening to your key messages.'

Featurespace's turning point in the US, Excell recalls, was obtaining 'referenceable customers' in the country. 'This is a bit like the old chicken-and-egg scenario. We invested a lot of blood, sweat and tears in winning our first US customers, and the non-monetary payback has been enormous. Demonstrating our ability to deliver the same successful outcomes in multiple markets has made it an easier decision for our customers to choose Featurespace as their fraud prevention partner.

'The US is a huge market, and it's easy to get lost in the noise,' he says. 'So my advice is identify a set of realistic early-adopting customers, and make a concerted effort to win them over instead of adopting a "spray and pray" approach and potentially running out of money.'

'Today I'm running a machine learning company. Our technology is world class, however our success is built by the people who work at Featurespace. It was built by our customers joining our mission and by our investors who provide us with the funds to innovate. "It's all about the people" may be a cliché, but I've never witnessed an organisation create a long-term legacy or value without an exceptional leadership team. Those qualities are universal,' she says.

'And with an exceptional team comes the need to delegate and trust. No general manager, MD or CEO can be an expert in all departments, and neither should they be. Running a radio station taught me that I couldn't be a DJ, or keep the studios broadcasting, or pick the best playlist, or make good commercials, or be an accountant, but we *could* attract the best people who could do all of those things.'

While she concedes that coming in as an outsider and 'getting [her] head around what machine learning can do and how it can change the world', wasn't the easiest of tasks, it was always intellectually stimulating. 'How exciting to be trusted with a technology that was very nascent, and to be able to see if we could find our commercial place in the world.

'My job within that is about creating a safe environment for our people to know that we're trying different things, and if something fails then we try something else. And now that we've found our way [in terms of product], we're facing a different kind of challenge: we've got to hire more people and we're scaling.'

One thing that has helped both phases of growth has been the company's strong association with the city of its birth. Being based in Cambridge, particularly when you're launching and scaling a company that has 'a great technological leap forward' at its heart, confers great credibility and kudos on you, says King. 'We've been selected by customers across the world, and that heritage – coming out of one of the very best academic institutions – is both reassuring and attractive to them.'

The company, which frequently hires from the university's exceptional talent pool, is also based on campus – handy for keeping an eye on the brightest and the best, and for ensuring links between the business and the university's engineering department endure.

'We are very much committed to Cambridge, and have, for example, a student cinema club that we organise, so that we maintain close ties not only with today's students, but past ones too. That's something that's proving very important to us a company, as we grow.'

∨

Martina King is CEO of Featurespace and joined the company in 2012. Former MD of augmented reality company Aurasma, Martina has had an extensive career in media technology, including leadership roles at Yahoo! Europe and Capital Radio. Martina is non-executive director of Debenhams, and was named one of the Top 40 powerful women leaders in tech by Silicon Republic.

part three
FINANCE & FUNDING

CHAPTER 22

'Shareholders are looking for reassurance from the CFO, who must be "the voice of reason" in the business.'

Alex Gayer, ex-CFO at SwiftKey and CFO at Receipt Bank, on scaling finance.

Kicking off his Upscale session on chief financial officers in scaling businesses, Alex Gayer – who was CFO at SwiftKey as it grew from revenues of half a million pounds in 2012 to £10m a year just three years later, ahead of its acquisition by Microsoft – recounted an experience from early in his career. At the time, he was working for Helveta, a startup which, among other things, was tracking and tracing trees through the timber supply chain into Europe.

'We were bar-coding trees in the forests of the Amazon and the Congo, and tracing them, literally from standing trees to high street retailers, to prove they came from legal sustainable sources,' he recalled. 'I was the first finance employee – the CEO and founder didn't want a finance guy, but the investors who'd recently invested in the company essentially said: "You're not having Series A without a finance person."

'In the end, they came up with a compromise of hiring someone who was both finance and commercial, which meant that the investors wanted me focused on finance, while the CEO wanted me to focus on growing the business – so I had to do both.'

The company was later invited to participate in two tenders, the first in Peru, the second in Ghana. 'As I didn't speak Spanish, I went to Ghana. Soon, we were negotiating with the government of Ghana for a multimillion-dollar contract which would have been brilliant for a startup – except no one told me it takes about six months to negotiate a contract with the Ghanaian government.

'So, there I was in Ghana for six months, while the CEO was in Peru, and there was no one running finance. We were suddenly burning through cash much quicker than anyone realised. And the board were calling me up asking for my financial reporting, while I was in the middle of a negotiation that [felt like it would never end].'

That experience taught Gayer one great lesson: 'How you manage the competing demands from different stakeholders with very different desires and aspirations is one of the key issues startups face.'

Later, in an interview after the session, Gayer warms to his theme, arguing that because early-stage companies are often still grappling with product/market fit, they are forced to balance, often precariously, experimentation and 'trying things out' against not running through their cash too quickly. 'Then the next question becomes: when do you bring in financial resources to help you manage all that, which is in itself a cost?' he says.

And that dilemma, in turn, spawns others. 'Normally you need a CFO to help you with those types of decisions. But CFOs, in themselves, are very expensive, and quite often that's not a resource that you've contemplated at the early stage of the business. So should you just go for a slightly less experienced finance person instead, who can manage the function but couldn't quite give you that value-add that you need as you go through those decisions...?'

Adding to the complexity is that raising money is usually an ever-present challenge for first-time founders. 'Some founders are more connected in terms of who they know than others. Some are very competent in finance, whereas others are far more technical in nature, which is why the timing of when you bring in the more experienced financial resource to help you will invariably depend on the skill set of the founders themselves.

'If your founders are very technical, it's going to be earlier. If your founders are very commercial and seasoned, serial founders and entrepreneurs, they could probably do a lot more themselves and you can bring in a more strategic finance person a bit later.'

But once a finance lead is on board, how does their role evolve as the company scales, from seed through Series A, to B and beyond?

Gayer replies: 'The way I see it is that as a seed-stage company, you're literally just proving the concept. So the finance resource needed at that stage is very much operational: it's just about financial transactions and processing. As you move to Series A, you start to get into commercial contracts and pricing. You're just starting to get some customers and you tend to need a little bit more advice.

'And then obviously as you get to Series B, that's typically when you've got a bit more of a product/market fit and you're talking really around starting to invest and scale out your distribution channels. You start to raise more serious amounts of investment and you're starting to have more complex board structures.'

While there's no definitive playbook answer on when a startup needs a CFO, clearly as it moves from Series A to Series B, the scope of work that falls onto the senior management team starts to get more complex, particularly around financial issues: there's more analysis, more forward thinking and more board management, he says. 'So I definitely think as you gear up for your Series B, there's a need for that more strategic financial input.

'Particularly, of course, as the challenge once you've raised your Series B is application of resources and trying to work out what's going to have the biggest impact, the biggest return on investment, and that's absolutely a strategic finance role at that stage. So it's definitely between A and B in my mind where that strategic level of finance is really needed.'

Have the hard conversations

Once in the role, a financial lead's top priority – whether they're a CFO or not – will be to ensure that in the early stages a company has a long-enough financial runway for the team to work out what their business model is and exactly what their strategy is going to be, Gayer says. But once that's established, that individual has to 'keep everyone honest and aligned more or less to that strategy'.

And that involves more than a few tricky conversations, which any CFO or finance lead worth his or her salt shouldn't balk at having. The reason for this is that a mindset shift occurs with some founders at this point in the company journey, argues Gayer.

'In the early stages, they seize all of the opportunities that present themselves and then work out almost afterwards which is the better one to do. There's a bit of post-rationalisation here, I think, where they say, "We took that particular course of action because we thought it was the best at the time," which isn't always the truth.

'But once you've settled upon a business model, you need to somewhat rein in all of the experimentation. You need to focus and you need to refine your strategy, because otherwise you're going to end up wasting energy and resources and have a lack of focus. And I think those are some of the hard conversations that the CFO has to have.'

Be 'transaction ready'

Alongside focusing on strategy, Gayer argues forcefully that, given the nature of high-growth tech businesses, for companies who have taken on institutional investment not only will further rounds of funding in all likelihood follow, but also, ultimately, an exit or liquidity event – i.e. an IPO or M&A.

In any of the above scenarios, a raft of due diligence will be necessary. 'And that due diligence is obviously designed to expose any of the material risks in the business and any flaws in its governance structure,' he continues. 'So it's a really good discipline to keep your business prepared for those certain events.

'By that I mean making sure your filing is up to date, that you know about your tax liabilities and risks, ensuring the company has minuted its meetings, that you have good structures in place for controls and approvals, because the last thing you want, as a CFO in particular, is to go through those transactions and for it all to fall over just because you've come across a skeleton in the closet that you weren't aware of.

'It's a good discipline to be prepared for those events, and going through the rigour of an annual audit is a bit of a stepping stone towards doing that, even when there's no statutory requirement for it.'

Delegate authority

During his stint at SwiftKey, Gayer ran what he describes as a 'very small and efficient finance function' – just four or five individuals in a company that was operating, through the app stores, in over 140 countries with a physical presence in five or six. 'So [that's] probably not a typical experience of how a company's finance function grows. The reason we managed to be very lean and efficient is that a) we had a relatively small handful of customers that were very high-value, and then b) distributing through the app stores is an incredibly efficient and light (in an administrative sense) way of generating lots of revenue.'

The company initially covered the standard operational bases, including accounts payable, accounts receivable, payroll and basic reporting. Yet as it grew and became increasingly successful, operating in more territories, Gayer needed to delegate authority to more people within the organisation.

'As you do that, I found one of the best tools for empowering people and giving them authority is to give them [control over] a budget. Along with that budget they have to develop an operating plan, and then they have to be held accountable for delivering against both that plan and the financial performance.

'Once you get to that stage of organisational development, you need financial resource to do the planning, to do the monthly reporting, the variance analysis, to sit with the managers throughout the business and help them become financially accountable. So you need to then start building out from the finance resources, the planning and reporting capability within the team, in addition to the financial operations that you had earlier.'

Bring in a dedicated tax manager

But it's when a company starts to go global that another layer of complexity is added – namely, the tax risk element to the business ramps up significantly.

In line with his belief of 'always trying to be one step ahead and be transaction ready', Gayer advises scale-up founders to invest in bringing in a dedicated tax manager to oversee the firm's international expansion and address all of its tax risks both domestically and internationally. 'The risk particularly ratchets up as you start to sell overseas and as you start putting more people on the ground internationally.

'So the way I build my teams is transactional first. Then you start thinking about budgeting, forecasting and planning. Next, you bring in some sort of business-decision support resources to help manage the business as you're scaling and become more financially accountable. Then, as you expand overseas, you get into things like tax resources.'

If you go global, don't skimp on advice

There is often a belief in early-stage companies that they should spend as little as possible on strategic financial advice on expanding overseas. Gayer says this is a false economy – and invariably leaves startups paying over the odds, both in terms of financial outlay and wasted time, in the long run.

With that in mind, he cautions startups against cutting costs by favouring small (and far less costly) advisory firms over the 'Big Four' professional services giants. 'It might sound like I'm on commission for the Big Four, but they simply have the right networks globally, and you can speak to someone from their firm in the UK who can talk to their counterparts in the territories you're moving into.

'This type of advice is their bread and butter, they've been through it many times before, whereas with some of the small firms you're asking them for advice when they don't have the specialist knowledge and they're learning themselves.

'In my experience, international expansion is absolutely one of the areas where you should pay for proper advice. It would just be more efficient in terms of time, and they probably give you the right answer with much less risk.'

Gayer speaks from painful personal experience. He recalls paying a smaller firm for advice on scaling to the US while at SwiftKey, which turned out to be plain wrong. 'It took months and months, and then we had such little confidence in the advice we were given that we just discarded it and went with one of the Big Four instead, who gave us completely different advice.'

Similarly, at Helveta, he was urged to use a smaller (and far cheaper) accountancy firm in the UK for advice on tax legislation in Africa, which is often opaque and difficult to navigate. 'That firm supposedly had an international network, but it turned out that it wasn't overly developed and I was having to try to speak to people on the ground in places like the Congo. Everything was difficult – communications and logistics in particular – and getting the advice written in a way that I actually understood was just challenging. It also took a fantastic amount of time.'

Go with the global firms instead, he advises. 'The Big Four just have better processes and methodologies, and I would guess they've got more standardised ways of describing situations that just make it much easier to understand and a lot less effort on my part, as the engaging company, to get an answer.'

Invest early in systems and processes

Another area where Gayer advocates startups investing is in software tools – to support finance and accounting systems and processes. 'The reason for this is that finance has two roles in a high-growth company. First, the information that people make decisions on is critically important, and the accuracy of that information is obviously essential. Financing is often the source of much of that information. So it's obviously quite right that the finance team invest lots of time and resources in providing and doing the reporting, and surfacing that information for the business to use.

'If generating that information and generating it accurately takes you a full month to do, then by the time you've generated it, it's a month out of date and the business has moved on. If it takes you a full month, then all you've done is your accounting or reporting, but you haven't been proactive and added any value to the business. So your focus has to be on making that really efficient.

'The reason I say that is if you can get your month-end closed and all your information down and out in the first five or six days of the month, then that gives you another 15 working days in the month to actually get into the business and help add value.'

Small companies need to deploy all the resources they can get their hands on, continues Gayer, and the finance team tend to be analytical and have a unique holistic overview of the whole business, because of where they sit as well as the nature of the finance function.

'My view is always try to make the team as efficient as possible in the routine monthly close, so that you can free up as much time as possible to really just be a business advisor to the rest of the business. Constructively challenge them on their decisions and help them try to make more executive decisions based on logic and analysis, which to my mind is often where the finance team's core skills lie.'

Finance should be the 'voice of reason' in a business

It's that same sense of the finance team having a reasoned and analytical approach to problem-solving, and being able to act independently of any other agendas in the business, which leads Gayer to say that finance can and should be 'the voice of reason in a business'.

He argues: 'I think one of my strengths that I bring to the business is an understanding of the value-creation agenda: how you can create value both in terms of what drives revenues, but also a company's strategic value. As an experienced CFO, I also understand the risks in the business and how to make those trade-offs in a logical and reasoned way. That's what I mean by the "voice of reason".'

The CEO and CFO should be business sparring partners

As the two individuals with a 360-degree view of the business, ideally the CEO and CFO should be good-natured sparring partners, able to bounce ideas off each other (without falling out).

'You spend a lot of time talking about the issues in the business, and if particularly the CEO has got some ideas, they'll want to talk them through with someone who has that holistic view of the business – and the CFO is the natural candidate.'

He concedes that there can be tensions between the pair too. 'The level of tension comes down to personalities as much as anything else. But the CEO typically will be slightly more bullish, while obviously one of the CFO's prime objectives is making sure the business has a sound finance strategy and the resources [to support it].

'If, as the CFO, you're being the custodian of the commercial strategy, then holding people true to that, particularly when their

CEO has a great new idea, can often be challenging. So of course at times you have to have a fairly robust conversation about "Well if we do this, that means we can't do that and the impact would be this…"

'At times you'll agree and at times you won't. But if you don't agree, ultimately you have to come to a unified position that you present externally. And that comes down to working at the relationship between yourself and the CEO. At certain times you might not be able to present that unified message and my advice when people ask me "How do you deal with that situation?" is always try to make sure there are no surprises: so if you can't agree, then at least before publicly disagreeing, both of you should be aware of each other's positions, and when quizzed the other one should know what you are likely to say. That's just the way you manage that conflict.'

The CFO has to represent the shareholders, says Gayer. 'Obviously the board will look to the CFO for independent verification. They'll want to trust the CFO. They'll ask the CEO and they sort of expect the marketing spin, the vision.' He laughs.

'Then they'll want the CFO to be able to say: "This is the range of possible outcomes… if it goes well it could be this, and if it goes a little less well it could be that." And then they'll want them to lay out the implications of both scenarios. Ultimately, what they're looking for from the CFO is reassurance.'

∨

Alex Gayer is CFO of Receipt Bank and an advisor to a number of technology startups. Alex has over 20 years' experience in scaling and transforming businesses, with a career that has included both blue chip organisations and high-growth technology ventures. Prior to Receipt Bank, Alex was CFO of SwiftKey, a highly successful mobile software company that was acquired by Microsoft in early 2016. Alex is a graduate of UMIST, he qualified as a chartered accountant with PwC and holds an MBA from London Business School.

CHAPTER 23

'Negotiation isn't about bluster and bluffing.'

Cherry Freeman, co-founder of LoveCrafts,
on how to raise venture money, when to fight
your corner – and what to look for in investors.

When LoveCrafts raised a Series C round of £26m ($33m) in the spring of 2017, it brought the total amount raised by the social network and e-commerce site for home crafters to over $60m in less than five years. Co-founder Cherry Freeman, who ran the fundraising process in each of the company's four rounds, says entrepreneurs should approach taking on investment in one-to-three-year cycles, depending on how fast their particular market is moving or what their product is.

'As a founder you need to know what the key milestones are going to be to build confidence that you are making progress towards your vision,' she says. 'Obviously, no financial plan stays the same and you change course continuously, but you do need to start out with a plan and then work out how much cash is required to get you from, say, Series A to B, what you're going to be spending it on and what the business is going to look like in two years' time as a consequence. You also need to consider what the return is going to be, because that equation needs to make sense for investors.'

But, she emphasises, raising money should never be a goal in itself. After all, profitable businesses don't need to raise money unless the profits that they generate are insufficient to achieve the level of growth or development that the founders are looking for. 'So you've got to be very careful with how you think about this: raising money is not a marker of success,' she says. 'It's not the goal.'

However, she does concede that it is a benchmark used by fellow entrepreneurs, investors and the media to assess a startup's progress. 'It's the only objective piece of information that you have from the outside looking in. It's also the only objective bit of data that the management team have that the external market values what they've done. So in that respect, it's probably why it's portrayed as [a marker of success].'

She urges founders to think of fundraising as a campaign that ends up in a deal or a sale. 'You're selling a vision, and what you get is investment in return,' she continues. 'Because it's an all-encompassing task that takes many months to complete and it results in a push to get it over the finish line, it can feel like raising money is the result.' She smiles wryly. 'But, of course, every time we raised money, that's just been the beginning of an enormous amount of work. The moment you say "Thank goodness I got that done" is when the real work starts.'

Here are the things Cherry Freeman says founders need to think about when fundraising for their startup:

1.
Finding the right investors
(Seed stage)

'With a seed round, it's definitely all about network,' says Freeman, 'and I think it must be very challenging for founders who don't have one – although being able to build a network is part of the talent that an entrepreneur needs to have.'

'Network' covers a broad spectrum, she says. 'It may be someone you know, but more likely it's an introduction to someone who has an interest in what you're doing or your company's sector or niche.

'Very often it's an investor who has had a good experience with something that they see as being analogous in some respects to your startup. And that's true through every single stage: if they can see something about a company that they've had success with in the past, then that founder is going to be pushing on an open door.

'But, ultimately, it is very much network, and for seed stage it's a mixture of [high net-worth] individuals and small funds.'

Having the right backers at seed stage is critically important, she emphasises. 'These are the people who are going to be the most heavily invested – literally – in helping you build your next stage relationships.'

Doing this without 'warm' introductions is hard, because many investors prefer to back someone they've got to know. 'Of course, if you're a serial entrepreneur and you've done it before, it's easy, but if you're doing it for the first time, you can't just walk in the door and/ or send in your pitch deck. You need an introduction – so make it your job to find someone to introduce you to an investor you want.'

(Series A stage)

'One of the criteria for deciding who you're going to work with at Series A should be the nature of their relationships with other funds for investment further down the road,' says Freeman.

'There's a hierarchy of brands in the VC world, and you can look at their existing and historic investments and see which of those investments has gone on to raise subsequent rounds of funding.

'Then you can look at who else has invested alongside them. Typically the lead investor at Series A will follow on – i.e. take a small part of the next round – and there'll be another investor who comes in and takes the majority of it. Say you've taken money from a certain VC, you can easily check which other VCs they sit around the table with on other boards. If you look on Crunchbase, for example, all this data is readily available.

'Then you can see whether they've got the relationships for subsequent investment rounds. Whereas if they've only made a handful of investments and it doesn't look like any of those have gone on to raise B and C rounds, it means one of two things: either those investments haven't been successful, or it means it was a different sort of investment that doesn't require a huge amount of funding, and is about helping the business become self-sustaining.'

One thing entrepreneurs need to consider is their appetite for risk, because taking on investment from early-stage investors is far from a guarantee of success, cautions Freeman. 'Early-stage VCs aren't looking for nine out of ten companies they invest in to go on to be successful, profitable businesses. What they need is a couple of breakout successes, and that's what returns the fund.

'So you have to be quite clear, as a founder, that just because you've raised your Series A, it doesn't mean you've got a high likelihood of success. Actually, the odds are a lot better than they were [without VC funding], but they're still quite heavily stacked against you. I say this because there are many businesses that raise Series A that could have carved a path to profitability without it. They'd just be smaller, less valuable businesses. But for some entrepreneurs, that's OK.'

(Series B stage and beyond)

When it comes to Series B onwards, Freeman says entrepreneurs should seek out founder-orientated investors. 'At that point, investors should see their role as supporting and enabling the founders and broader management team (as opposed to seeking to manage them and/or the business).

'The chemistry between organisations (i.e. VC firm and portfolio company) is also critical. It can be a fantastic relationship that adds disproportionate value, or it can be an incredible drain and one more thing founders have to manage.

'Founders should also look for relevant knowledge and experience, as well as top-tier smarts, so investors can add value as a non-executive board member and through their network. Ideally there should be something self-selecting here.'

2.

Balancing the time demands of the fundraising process against the day-to-day running of the business

The fundraising process unavoidably drains your time and is only exacerbated by the fact that as an early-stage founder, you really have to run the whole thing yourself. 'Being able to raise money and to present yourself in an articulate and a cogent way – backed up with data – is part of what the investor is looking for when they're deciding where to put their money,' Freeman says. 'So if you can't front that up, then that raises questions.

'You can possibly delegate the fundraising process to a third party or advisor with a D or an E round, but up to this point at LoveCrafts we've done it all ourselves. I'm quite lucky because I'm one of three founders here, and historically part of my responsibility has been to do with fundraising. But when I've been fundraising, I haven't been doing much else, because it is all-consuming.'

The amount of work involved with fundraising increases with each successive stage, she continues. 'Our Series A round took maybe three weeks until we got a term sheet, from start to finish: three weeks of pitch meetings, then providing the first set of data, then responding to enquiries and then getting to the terms. Then from a term sheet to signature was about another week. Then it was about six weeks to get all the legals and the diligence done.

'That process at Series A is not particularly onerous and didn't consume a lot of my time: six weeks, maybe, and then part of my time for another six weeks.'

However, by the time you get to Series C, the entire process ramps up significantly. 'It's probably three months, full-time, from starting the process to term sheet,' she says. 'Then from there to signature, it's another two and a half months, still full-time.'

3.
Managing the process (part 1): Weed out the wrong investors

Freeman's first tip on the fundraising process itself is to try to weed the 'wrong' investors out of the process as quickly as possible.

'I don't know for sure, but I suspect that not doing that is a mistake that a lot of founders make. The reason for this is, as a founder, you pitch continuously to everyone, from your first employee to the person who's going to rent you an office, to the first individual who's going to supply you with goods or services, who's never heard of you and you probably can't pay. So you're always pitching, you're always in sales mode, and you want to convert everybody to your cause.

'Actually, fundraising is like running a sales process, in which you need to work out quite quickly who your runners and riders are, and not waste time on people who aren't going to get to completion. When you hear an objection, don't try to overcome it, but try to work out whether they've just misunderstood – in which case you need to do a better job of setting your stall out – or if actually their objection is a valid one. It doesn't matter if you don't think their objection is important, the fact is *they* think it is, so move on to somebody else.'

It's crucial to understand the currency of your proposition when you start pitching to investors. In essence, if your startup is in a 'red hot' sector, you might only need a handful of prospective investors at the top of the sales funnel. But if your company is complex or it's in an area that's unfashionable, you'll require a much broader selection. 'Doing the work up front to try to figure out what's going to make a more likely completer, before you put them at the top of the funnel, is definitely worth it,' says Freeman.

'Do they have similar investments in an equivalent sector? Or can you draw some parallel between your company and one of their own where they've had success before? It might be the same business model, or it could be a market with similar dynamics or a similar approach to how you address a problem in consumer demand.

'Whatever it is, find those parallels, and that's effectively what your message is going to be to that investor.

'You'll be a bit subtle about it, of course, but make sure you play those things out because "pattern recognition" is what these guys are all about. They've seen a certain thing work before, and although they might not have seen it in your space, they can see why it works.'

She expands: 'That's the way a lot of venture capital funders approach [investing]. They're looking for patterns they've seen before, in their own portfolio ideally, or that they might have seen in the wider market. Take a look at what they're writing or blogging about. Have they got a thesis-led strategy for their investments? Does it match with what you're doing? There's a lot of research you can do at the top of the funnel.

'But you do need to understand how broad you need to go – whether you think [your startup] is something that is going to be of interest to a minority of funds, in which case you probably want to go quite wide, or you think actually it's so hot it's just about getting enough [VCs] in the top of funnel to create some competition at the end.'

While that shapes the beginning of the process, argues Freeman, the trick is whittling contenders down as quickly as possible, so that you don't have a large number of VCs in the data room [the virtual space where you put all of the documentation that a potential investor is going to want to look at before they're able to make an offer, or post-offer, as they do their due diligence] towards the end of the process. 'That's because as soon as they're in the data room, they start coming at you with enquiries. And each of those enquiries typically requires you to go off and do a bespoke piece of work.'

The amount of information that needs to go in the data room will increase with each stage of investment and each size of cheque, because the later-stage funds will do a lot more diligence, she continues. 'Once they start asking questions, that's when, actually no matter how much prep work you've done, you've got to go and do a lot more bespoke work. It's very difficult to do a great job of bringing investors over the line when you're stretched very thinly. So you really want to get your funnel quickly down to a handful that you think are very likely to get over the line.'

In an ideal world, founders want to end up with no more than three or four term sheets, she says. 'That's three or four VCs you'd be happy to work with, all with good offers. Then you've got something you can use to try to generate the best deal for yourself.'

4.
Managing the process (part 2):
Valuation isn't everything

When it comes to negotiating, Freeman says it's a mistake just to consider your company's valuation – rather, you should think about 'the whole package'.

'You'll read about companies raising $500m rounds in TechCrunch. But if you knew the full details, you'd probably find that those investors get their $500m back before anybody else does. It might also carry coupons: in other words, it pays them interest as well, so by the time the company pays it back it's $800m – and they get that before anybody else gets their money. Even if the valuation is, say, $2bn, there's $800m coming out to the first investor – and they've probably still got their 25% stake on top of that as well.

'So it's not just about the valuation. You definitely want to look at the "preference stacks" – who takes their money out first. There's also "anti-dilution protection", where if you hit a speed bump and you need to raise some more money at a lower valuation, then existing investors may seek to maintain their shareholding. If that happens, then of course the management and founders are getting absolutely crucified. There's various shades of grey between that extreme and everybody diluting.'

Another element to keep top of mind is the host of terms around the nature of negative controls that an investor will have in the business, she continues. 'So, typically an investor will come in and they'll require a veto over certain types of decision that the company might want to make, like using all the money to buy another company or raising lots of debt or appointing a chairman. Or they might want to have a veto of the annual budget if they don't agree with it, or they may want a veto over the employee option scheme, and so on.

'The list goes on. What they effectively mean to a founder is the nature of their role and their independence is changing. Each founder will have a different perspective on this, but they just need to understand that, and they need to be very clear if there are things they're not happy giving away control over, or giving a negative control over, then they need to make sure they're clear about that in the term sheet, not when they're two weeks away from running out of cash.

'You need to know as a founder what's important to you. If you're working with a fund you really trust, and you think they've got great expertise, you may be very happy for them to have vetoes on a whole range of things. But then again, you might not.'

5.
Managing the process (part 3): The term sheet

Once you've got through the funnel, and two or three funds have decided they'd like to make an offer to invest in your business, they offer you a term sheet, continues Freeman. The term sheet will have on it a number of terms which, if you agree to them, will then be the instruction that is given to both sets of lawyers: the company's lawyers and the venture fund's lawyers.

'They basically say that the contract between the two parties should reflect "the following terms…" So the key question for the company then becomes: "Are these terms acceptable for me? Are there other terms that are very important to me that aren't documented here – and that I need to check we're in agreement on and that's stated up front, before we go into the next phase?" (The next phase is typically a period of exclusivity in which to negotiate the final contract.)'

Depending on the fund and the process that the startup has run, in principle all commercial due diligence should be done prior to issuing a term sheet and all, if you like, confirmatory diligence – legal, technical and financial – could be done subsequent to the term sheet.

'So effectively, at the point at which you've got a term sheet, the venture fund should be saying: "Any questions about the market, the product/market fit, your strategy, what it is that you're seeking to do – all those questions have all been answered. We understand your financial projections, we like your financial projections, we're in agreement with your plan more or less." There should be no digging into that kind of stuff later.

'But then, in the post-signature phase, it moves on to: "Is the financial information you gave us a true and accurate reflection of your actual accounts? Do you have any kind of enormous legal exposures that we need to know about and may even make us want to walk away? Is your technical platform robust and fit for purpose, or are there gaping great holes in it which mean that actually the business is not nearly as strong as we thought it was?"

'In those particular situations, you – as the company – have to concede that if they change their mind, they change their terms, then fair enough. But if they sign the term sheet and *then* say "Actually, we don't think the market is that big" or "We're worried about this competitor", and at *that point* they want to change their terms, then I'd say: "Go jump!"'

She points out that a lot of funds would rather not do the obligatory deep dive into a company until after they've entered the period of exclusivity with them, simply because they do not want to invest internal resources until they know the deal is all but in the bag. For that reason, Freeman advocates asking potential investors to confirm in the term sheet itself that they have completed all of the exploratory and commercial due diligence before it's signed, as well as specifying exactly what their diligence between signing the term sheet and signing the contract will consist of.

'It's worth getting them to be very specific about that, because that's the point in which you can flush out that actually they've been in the data room but didn't bother to put any serious time into really getting under the skin of your company, and they'd rather you were off the market when they did that,' she counsels. 'If that means they potentially change their mind or change their offer, well you're probably stuck with them by now, because you've probably told everyone: "No thanks, I've already agreed a different offer."'

She adds: 'A credible fund with a good reputation would not do that, but you do hear of it happening from time to time.'

6.
Managing the process (part 4): 'Get a law firm who know their way around a term sheet

'If this is the first fundraise you've led, you need to sit down with someone who can make sure you understand what each clause means, and can tell you what the other things are that possibly could go into a term sheet that you may not be aware of,' she explains.

'Then you can have a discussion with your lawyer about what's important and what's not. Really you should get your lawyer to help you do a mark-up of the term sheet. Even if you like the terms enough to say "Yes, I think we can work with this", there's usually still, in our experience, a negotiation around the term sheet before you sign it.'

7.
Managing the process (part 5):
Negotiation isn't about bluster and bluffing

Freeman argues that 'being true to yourself and who you are' should always underscore your negotiating stance. 'Negotiation is not about confrontation and bluster and bluffing. Decide what your values are. If you want to be honest, straightforward and transparent, that's absolutely fine in terms of raising funding, but at the same time you don't have to give all your information away.'

Investors don't need to know, for example, who else you're talking to, their valuations, whether it's three or five term sheets, and so on, she says. 'I would keep that very much to myself. But certainly I would be clear with investors, saying: "We will, of course, go through a process and we are talking to a number of parties. We'll do our best to respond to you as quickly as we can."

'I don't think you need to say "I've got three other bidders" or whatever it may be. You can be more classy than that, and actually the strength in negotiation comes from your confidence that you're going to get a number of good offers. Each venture fund will imagine that if they like your proposition, others are going to like it as well.'

While founders wouldn't ordinarily ask VCs to sign a non-disclosure agreement (NDA) up front, they should be clear that they expect everything to be kept confidential. 'Certainly when they go into the data room, you would give them an NDA or ask them for whatever their standard NDA is,' she adds. 'The reputable VC won't be talking about your fundraising round, because they'll know that their reputation does somewhat depend on not colluding with other people in the market.'

8.
Managing the process (part 6): 'Say 'Thank you!'.

When you get to a term sheet, be very clear about what it is that you want, says Freeman, who urges founders to be positive and complimentary about VCs, who are usually putting a great deal of time and effort into understanding a prospective investment – something they're not obliged to do. 'They've got other choices of where they put their money and I'd be appreciative of that; I'd be grateful for it and I'd certainly be grateful for a term sheet. Somebody making an offer to put millions of pounds into your business? I think the first thing you do is you say "Thank you!'

'Then you say, "I would like to work with you, but I wonder if you can see your way to moving on a number of things that are very important to me and are really an important part of our evaluation." (That's kind of subtext for: "And how I will compare you to others" – but you don't need to say that; it's implicit. No one likes to feel as if they're being held against a wall and told they have to get somewhere otherwise they're not going to get the deal; someone else is. So treat people the way you would wanted to be treated yourself.)

As someone who has led no fewer than four fundraising rounds for LoveCrafts, and with a background in general management and M&A, Freeman has clocked up considerable negotiating mileage.

'But while I had quite a lot of experience of looking at contracts, I'd never done fundraising before LoveCrafts, which is obviously quite different and has its own set of terms that are attached to it.' However, she says early-stage founders can quickly pick up the technical elements – i.e. what goes into a shareholders' agreement and so on.

'What's harder to learn is the art of negotiation,' she says, 'particularly when what you're raising money for is so important to you – you put your whole life into it. It's hard to be dispassionate.'

Where does she stand on the idea that founders should raise as much financing as possible with each round?

She replies that it is very dependent on the company and sector. However, she says there is an argument that because the investment market is sentiment- and confidence-driven, founders should seize their opportunity when it arises.

'You don't know when those changes in sentiment are going to take place, and, of course, you don't want to be at the end of your cash cycle when everyone's worrying about the future of the world economy and isn't investing any money. So you definitely need to have some contingency in your financial plans,' she says, 'which means you need to raise a bit more than you need.'

You should also know what your BATNA (best alternative to a negotiated agreement) is. In other words, founders should always have a Plan B, she says.

'You need to know what you're going to do if you can't raise money. You need an alternative plan, where you cut your overheads and ideally carve out a path to profitability. Sometimes that will be an awful option, like cutting 50% of your staff, but you know that you can do that if you absolutely have to. That gives you some backbone, so you know that in your next round you're not going to end up giving away 80% of the company just to keep it going.'

On the all-important question of a founder's relationship with his or her investors, and the qualities they should look for in a VC, Freeman says the most important thing is trust – because there are ups and downs in venture-backed businesses. Will they have your back and support you? Or will they simply add to your workload and stress? Fundamentally, will their contribution help you to build a more valuable business?

'You should also consider their ability to help you with your next stage of funding through introductions to other investors or through their own fund,' she advises. 'That's absolutely critical. Plus, there's a whole market that provides venture debt, which a lot of VCs will turn their nose up at, but effectively it's a way of raising additional funding if you want to stretch your runway out a little bit further or maybe fund a small acquisition, if an opportunity presented itself, that you don't want to pay for out of the money you've got earmarked to get you to your two-year plan.

'The venture debt providers will only come in on the back of a top-tier venture investor. They'll look at that brand and that'll give them the confidence that they're backing something that's got legs.'

Another thing to look for in a VC is their portfolio of businesses. 'Your investor will typically try to make them available to you as a network – by which I mean, say, all the marketing directors/CMOs [in their portfolio] will get together and you can pick other people's brains who may be grappling with similar problems. Particularly if it's a fund with a number of investments in analogous businesses, then there's quite a lot of value to you as a founder in that.'

What a VC won't generally do (and you wouldn't want them to, anyway) is parachute in with their colleagues to advise you on the day-to-day running of your business. 'That's not how they would describe their value,' she says. 'It's much more from their network. If you're facing a particular business challenge, they might say it will be interesting for you to talk to this company who successfully addressed a quite similar set of issues.'

On whether VCs can help source talent for a company they invest in, Freeman is rather more sceptical. 'I think that comes down to luck and circumstances. We've had a few introductions to some incredible people who now work at LoveCrafts, but it's not something founders should be banking on,' she says. 'As a rule, that's something you'll need to do yourself.'

Cherry Freeman co-founded LoveCrafts, the online home for crafting communities, in 2012. Based in London's Soho, with a development centre in Kiev, LoveCrafts has distribution hubs in the UK and US which supply knitters and crocheters globally. Cherry manages the trading business at LoveCrafts and has led four rounds of fundraising, securing over $60m in capital raised. She has deep tech sector experience, as an advisor to venture-backed companies such as Mimecast and New Voice Media, and as director of the software business at Computacenter plc. Cherry's career began as a consultant at the Boston Consulting Group.

CHAPTER 24

'Be upfront about past mistakes' and 'Why every signal matters at meetings'

Megumi Ikeda, GM and MD at Hearst Ventures Europe, gives 12 tips on navigating due diligence with investors.

The due diligence process undertaken by investors in the run-up to fundraising is not for the fainthearted. From copies of office leases to customer contracts, and shareholder minutes to employee equity schemes, entrepreneurs are required to produce a blizzard of paperwork, as well as set up a data room. Your legal advisors – and always opt for venture capital specialists, by the way – will guide you through this documentary and evidentiary maze.

However, from an investor's perspective, some of the most important parts of the due diligence process aren't to be found buried deep in the data or contractual sub-clauses. Yes, of course startups seeking investors should be 'transaction ready', but when it comes to personal relationships investors will also 'go with their gut' and on the chemistry in the room. After all, investing in a company means working closely with its leadership team for a period of years, and no one wants to be stuck in a dysfunctional marriage. So here are some of the things to bear in mind, according to Hearst Ventures Europe's Megumi Ikeda:

1.
Due diligence is your last chance to pull out of the wedding

From an investor's point of view, once a term sheet has been issued, the last thing we want to do is pull out of a process. Once an investor says they're going to invest, they should be all in. So for both sides of the table, the due diligence period is your last opportunity to make sure the numbers, market opportunity, chemistry and professional relationships all align. If they don't, and you foresee trouble ahead, pull out. As a founder, you're going to be spending a lot of time with your backers, and while a few pre-wedding jitters are normal, be sure – and I mean really sure – before you take your vows.

2.
We've had to walk away from some deals at the 11th hour

Sometimes, due diligence personal checks on founders have thrown up undisclosed fraud and/or legal issues, which of course derail the whole process. We've also had an instance where everything was lined up and we were good to go, and then the personal checks on the founder came back as 'deeply problematic'. We've had to walk away from those deals, however good things looked on paper.

As investors, we trust you – the entrepreneur – to approach a prospective investment in the spirit of openness, and even if it's something relatively minor, you would always hope and expect the founder or CEO to disclose it in advance rather than for your due diligence to unearth it very late in the day. No one wants to waste time, on either side, and trust is a critical component of any founder/investor relationship.

3.
ALWAYS be upfront

Because if you're upfront about where you went wrong, it won't come across as you attempting to conceal something or sweep it under the carpet. If, say, an entrepreneur never mentions a falling out with the head of sales, resulting in delayed monetisation, or says they graduated from a particular university when they did not, it leaves investors wondering what else they might have 'forgotten' to mention and whether there's more to this person than meets the eye. Absolute clarity is always the way to go, because everything's going to be – in theory, at least – exposed to daylight after the investment's been made.

4.
When it comes to chemistry, every signal matters

Often the 'softer' side of the due diligence process – the part that's about chemistry and relationships and that has nothing to do with financials, business plans or market opportunity – can scupper a potential deal. One time I remember the palpable tension between two members of a startup's management team at a pitch just made us feel something was awry: if they can't get along in public, just imagine what goes on behind the scenes? (And in fact, our instincts proved correct; we later learned that one of the founders was removed soon afterwards, and a new CEO was installed.)

While we, as investors, should probably spend much more time than we do with potential portfolio companies, and in an ideal world just camp out at their office to get a real feel for the team, in reality that isn't a luxury that we can afford. Therefore, when we do meet the founding team, particularly at those early meetings, every signal matters to us. You'll often pick things up without looking for them. One investor colleague told me he once attended a pitch where the CEO didn't allow the technical founder to speak at all. Now that's a problem, especially at Seed stage, where the technical founder and what he or she can do, and how involved they are, is very important when selling the dream.

5.
Trust your gut

Gut feeling matters a lot in any business where you're measuring talent. At some point you'll have to feel comfortable with that individual or founding team, particularly given the length of the relationship you have once you're an investor in the company. So founders meeting investors should apply a similar rule of thumb: if your gut tells you something's wrong or that you might not get along with a particular investor or firm, then by definition he or she isn't the right investor for you.

6.
Your investor doesn't need to be a friend you'll see at the weekend – just someone you want to spend time with over the next four or five years (or more)

Founder/investor relations work best when there's a good fit in terms of personality and culture. They don't have to be a person you see on Sunday afternoon with your family (if you have one), but they do need to be someone you respect, want to seek out for advice and/or a friendly ear, and ideally someone you enjoy spending time with. Awkwardness and discomfort are likely to be magnified over time.

Founders should look for someone with integrity, who treats them with respect and professionalism. They're going to be sitting around a board table and giving up part of the cap table to their investors, so they need to feel comfortable that these are trustworthy partners for the journey, at least to the next investment milestone, and hopefully beyond.

7.
Avoid investors who reply to emails during meetings

Investors should be fully engaged in the due diligence process. They should be enthusiastic. Listen for the questions they ask – they should be searching rather than simply the obligatory ones you'd expect. But they should be asked respectfully. Avoid investors who don't make you feel like a priority – particularly the ones who check their phones or reply to emails during meetings, or who are forever in a hurry and poised to rush out the door to their next appointment. VCs are invariably harried, but they should be focused on your company alone when they're with you.

8.
Always ask investors for references from founders of other companies they've invested in

As part of your due diligence, ask to speak to other CEOs from their portfolio. Making your own independent approaches, by tracking down another portfolio founder through your own network or via LinkedIn, pays dividends too. The kinds of things you should be digging into are issues such as conduct on the board, availability at other times, and responsiveness to emails and requests. Practically every VC today says they offer various ancillary services – but is that actually true? And if it is, does it genuinely add value or is it just window-dressing for their website?

Also find out how your prospective investor behaves when the shit hits the fan. Do they cool off a founder they've invested in if quarterly metrics are missed? Do they take longer to respond to emails? Is there a trend you should be aware of?

You wouldn't get a roommate without finding out if you can live with that person, so approach a relationship with your investor in the same way.

9.
The CEO should always lead the fundraise and due diligence process, particularly with an early-stage company

CEOs have to endure something akin to a marathon each time they go through the fundraising process. They are expected to be at the top of their game in terms of how they present themselves and the company, and how they interact with people, as well as providing all of the requisite data – and all that while running the business day-to-day. Each one of those is difficult, but they're being asked to do all of them simultaneously. However, especially at the earlier stages, if someone other than the CEO is leading the fundraising process, it doesn't really work, because as VCs we invest in the founders and have to feel conviction about their story.

10.
Always hire specialist legal advisors who know startups and the VC industry

Find a legal firm with a good track record in dealing with venture investing. You're going to have to pick your fights during the negotiation, and having someone on hand who can advise you and help you separate the important fights from the ones that you can let slide is going to be very useful, particularly if you're a first-time founder. They can show you what's considered common practice, and even better, if they're able to say, 'Look, I've negotiated with this VC a dozen times, so I know where they'll push back and where they'll give up,' then that's not only immensely helpful, but it'll also save you a lot of money.

Good advisors will help with finishing the process on time – if you're an early-stage business, an investor's cheque often cannot arrive too soon.

The best way to track down the right legal firm is, as ever, through personal recommendations from other founders who've used them. They also do market themselves, of course – but always do your own due diligence. Ask for references and don't hold back with your questions. You may have a bit of an issue around the stage you're at and how much money you can pay them, but they pretty much all do early-stage legal advisory work, because they all want to land the next Google when it's just 10 people.

11.
Be ready

Even if it seems a long way off on the horizon, if you know you're going to be looking to raise money, the best thing you can do is prepare early. And the best way to do that is to make sure all necessary company documentation, data and metrics are continually updated and good to go. The last thing you want to do is to be scrambling to get everything together at the last minute, which will not only cause delays to the entire fundraising process, but won't impress investors.

Invest early in capacity to do this, which may mean adding an early hire to your finance team, otherwise you're going to be pulling people away from their day-to-day job to gather data. You're going to be doing that anyway, of course, but if you get the logistical work done early, you'll impact far less on their output. That's prudent, because investors will still be evaluating your company's performance during the fundraising period itself, and they won't cut you any slack because you were distracted by getting your numbers together.

Similarly, founders must be on top of the company's core metrics before they talk to investors – few things put off a potential backer more than an entrepreneur being unable to rattle off those numbers on demand.

12.
If an investor passes on backing your startup, they owe you the courtesy of explaining why

If they've taken your time, it's only reasonable that they talk you (albeit briefly) through why they've decided to pass. You might not agree with their reasons – and that's a separate issue – but that data point is worthwhile getting. It may help you address issues that require your urgent attention, as well as prepare for the next time you come face to face with an investor.

∨

Megumi Ikeda is a MD of Hearst Ventures and the GM of Hearst Ventures Europe, where she oversees investments and non-organic acquisitions across Europe. Hearst Ventures' investments include Broadcast.com (Yahoo), Buzzfeed, HootSuite, Netscape, Otonomo, Pandora (NASDAQ: P), and Roku (NASDAQ: ROKU). Based in London, Megumi previously ran the European arm of the Peacock Equity Fund, GE Capital and NBCUniversal's $250m venture fund.

CHAPTER 25

'Companies born in up-cycles often don't develop resilience.'

Entrepreneur-turned-investor, BGF advisor and co-founder of Moonfruit, **Wendy Tan White**, on scaling strategy and growing a business at a time of adversity.

I
When there are headwinds…

'If you want to found and grow a business over a long period of time, then there will always be some sort of existential threat somewhere on the horizon,' says Wendy Tan White, who co-founded the SaaS web-building service Moonfruit in 2000, which was acquired by Yell for $37m 12 years later.

'And by "existential threat", I mean things that maybe feel more out of your control. When I was an entrepreneur at Moonfruit, I went through two major existential threats. One was the dot-com crash, when funding dried up everywhere overnight. If you went to Silicon Valley from 2001–2006, there was just tumbleweed. It was even worse over here, because there wasn't any particular tech VC ecosystem to speak of in the first place.' The second 'existential threat' was the financial crisis of 2007–2009. Back to that later.

'So, as a founder, you just need to be prepared,' she says. 'The truth is, being an entrepreneur, the biggest trait you probably have is being adaptive and resilient anyway. To really grow and run a business, you're going to need both those attributes.'

Always try to see the bigger picture

'Sometimes people can have a bit of a panic about a looming crisis, when nothing is yet based in reality – they're just generalised concerns,' says Tan White. 'As an entrepreneur, you need to be able to manage both long-term strategic goals and your short-term immediate issues. You've got to sit in both spaces at once.

'I sit on the UK Digital Economy Council, and with Brexit, for example, the common issues that get raised are around talent. Yes, there may be issues around capital. And there is an issue around universities not having enough teaching staff… These and other things may affect you as an entrepreneur trying to build your business, but there is almost always a way around them, and often there are advantages too.

'Often, periods of uncertainty force you not to be lazy and take the easy options. Often they produce more interesting opportunities. With Brexit, there are opportunities to make relationships outside of Europe, for example. Could your startup bring in talent from Asia or the United States?

'One of the great advantages of being in the UK is we've got some of the best educational institutions in the world, and there is brilliant talent coming from the world globally who still want to work here for a period at least. So can you harness that early graduate talent, for example?'

She points out that government initiatives are trying to ease concerns over talent post-Brexit, particularly in the tech-nology industry. 'There are now 500 visas a year set up for exceptional talent, so for things like machine learning, artificial intelligence and other specialist skill sets. Those visas exist, so you should go get them, and they can be fast-trackable too. The appalling thing is that not enough of them are taken up, because people don't even realise that they exist. And, by the way, you can always fight for good talent to be here anyway.'

She adds that there is also plenty of home-grown talent in the UK. 'When you go looking across UK universities, there is lots of good talent, and startups don't just need the pure AI-type talent anyway, they also need web designers, developers, product people, marketers and so on – you need all of those to run a business. So founders should get out there and look.'

Moonfruit grew during the financial crisis

Even as the credit crunch bit back in 2007–8, sucking oxygen from the economy, Tan White found, to her initial surprise, that Moonfruit grew. 'We were a DIY website builder for small businesses, and we actually found when people left jobs in the finance industry or were otherwise impacted by the financial crisis, they used the opportunity to set up their own business. So actually, we grew through that era.

'The thing to bear in mind, depending on what your products or services are, is that there are also opportunities that happen during periods of uncertainty, including recessions. The question for founders to ask themselves is can they adapt?

'With Brexit, there will probably be even more demand to skill up the UK population or to automate. Is your business in education? Is there something you can do to help meet that demand? Could you help skilled people get visas to work over here? Would there be a business in that? There will always be opportunities for entrepreneurs.'

Capital flows to opportunity

'In the end, the thing that saves you as an entrepreneur is whether your company actually works or not,' says Tan White. 'If you're proving there's a market for your product or service, if you're out-innovating the competition, capital will find you no matter what the climate.

'Capital tends to flow where there is opportunity, and the best way to save your company during a financial crisis, or post-Brexit when there may be less capital about, is run a strong business and do your damnedest to make sure your unit economics work.'

It's not just about being capital efficient, it's also about doing your homework, she says. 'Let's say capital flow does die down a bit after Brexit; you can still go out there and find it. When I started Moonfruit, I went to France and to the US for capital because UK investors at the time still hadn't got their heads around pure digital tech outlier companies. If you're prepared to get on a plane, you will find that capital; it's a global world.'

Be prepared to strip your company back in a crisis

Before the dot-com crash, Moonfruit had raised $8m from VCs in what Tan White terms 'a classic venture-backed outlier business model'.

'The way that model works is that you invest for growth, and once you've got a scaling customer base, you work out how to truly monetise that base. But that relies on [subsequent] stages of VC funding, and because of the dot-com crash the funding dried up and we were suddenly in a situation where we hadn't hit that revenue engine yet, but we had a lot of staff – a team of around 60.'

So Tan White and her co-founders Joe White (now her husband) and Eirik Pettersen faced a stark choice. 'Were we going to really strip the company right back so that we could make ends meet and then grow the business the old-fashioned way – i.e. by making a profit – or were we just going to pack up and decide the whole thing wasn't viable?'

Opting for the former, they began the painful process of shedding staff. 'Letting people go is always stressful, and as a young entrepreneur you've never done it before either,' she says.

'These are people who had, in some cases, families to feed, and it affects them emotionally as well as literally; learning how to look after people through that cycle is not easy. In my case, some of them were my friends too.'

What impact did it have on her? 'Looking back on it, I was pretty depressed during that era. To have gone from the front pages of the newspapers and raising a lot of capital back to an attic, and trying to work through that, was seriously challenging. You end up questioning yourself: "'Did I fuck up? Am I cut out for this? Can I really do this?" You do a lot of questioning, a lot of soul searching.'

Moonfruit grew the old-fashioned way; nowadays people call it 'bootstrapping'

With hindsight, Tan White thinks the thing that 'saved' Moonfruit in the end was that enough people were already using the service to demonstrate that, even though they weren't yet paying, there was pent-up demand. 'People wanted to build their own websites, because in those days most people couldn't do any sort of development themselves,' she explains.

'We asked our customers whether they'd pay, and enough of them did for us to grow the business the old-fashioned way, by reinvesting the money we earned back in the company. Nowadays people want to call it "bootstrapping". Most traditional businesses have always worked that way. It was tougher, but we became much better business people and entrepreneurs during that era than during the high-publicity, high-octane, raising-capital-type game.

'In a funny way, it gave us a second wind. It meant that once we knew how our revenue metrics, margins and cost base worked, and how much it cost us to grow, when we hit the mobile/social wave we really had to start to build our products to take advantage of that distribution and we really grew. We started to make a lot of money. At that point, of course, we attracted more capital too.'

While it was a bumpy ride at times, the whole experience of going through different cycles of a journey taught Tan White and her co-founders a great deal about business and made her a far better mentor and investor. 'Sometimes companies that are born during up-cycles haven't got the resilience,' she says. 'Some companies are lucky, for instance with timing, and some just have money. But they won't have discovered the hard way how things really work. You learn a lot in hard times, I would say.'

If your company genuinely uses emerging technology, then make the most of that with investors

Tan White acknowledges that – at the time of writing – it's possible that, post-Brexit, there may be less capital available to startups in the UK. However, the UK's growing global reputation in key areas such as artificial intelligence/machine learning – in the wake of acquisitions by US tech giants of UK companies like Evi (Amazon), DeepMind (Google), SwiftKey (Microsoft), Magic Pony (Twitter) and Vocal IQ (Apple) – means capital will continue to flow here, and startups can capitalise on that.

'It may be that as a founder you need to be strategic about how you're going to stay current,' she says. 'I don't mean every startup should describe themselves as "a machine learning company" when it's not fundamental to their business, because all investors will just see through that. But if you genuinely know that your company is using AI to disrupt a particular business model, say, and that will help you scale, then make the most of that emerging technology because it is absolutely relevant.'

An investor's world view is essentially Darwinian

Founders should think laterally about the likely impact of major upheaval, as well as keep an eye on how competitors respond, says

Tan White. 'The way investors look at it is that there will always be someone else who will spring up in your place and adapt to changing environments or sudden shocks if you don't.'

The truth is, she says, most startups fail. 'Between 2007 and today, globally around 11–12% got acquired, that's all. Significantly fewer than that ever reach IPO. So there's a huge amount of failure, and the odds are overwhelmingly against you.'

But, she adds, unlike investors, who tend to view the startup world as essentially Darwinian, as an entrepreneur you are making a one-on-one bet. 'You shouldn't care about any other company, and you shouldn't be thinking about what the percentage chance of you succeeding is. You should decide that you're going for it, and it's 100% within your power to make it happen.'

Build some contingency into your fundraising

When asked whether she advocates raising as much as possible during times of uncertainty, Tan White replies: 'You should raise what you need to run the most ambitious business you are going to build. There's a fine balance when you're fundraising – you want to get enough capital in, especially if you're an early-stage startup, to experiment and then really build out product/market fit (when you don't yet have key metrics).

'Key metrics really come down to: do you know the growth dynamics and the cost base of your company yet? And is there a market to sell your stuff to or not? If you don't know those things yet, you've got to experiment. So depending on what stage you are, you'll need contingency to get to that point.'

Similarly, for later-stage companies, where you've got that growth engine and you're trying to scale, you may want contingency to floor the gas if things go really well, or cushion you if something unexpected goes wrong. 'So yes, you should build some contingency into your fundraising, but you also need to weigh that up against the fact that you dilute [your shareholding] every time you do that.'

Ultimately it comes down to your specific situation as a founder. If a startup is in a position where it's fighting off investors at a time of heightened uncertainty, then it may well make sense to take the extra money rather than gamble. 'However, if you're in a very fertile environment and you're doing extraordinarily well, you may decide to take more investment later in the journey, because you know you'll increase the value of the company before you take capital, so it's less dilutive.'

II
Scaling strategy

At seed stage, founders are selling a vision to investors – they invariably don't yet have true unit economics, says Tan White. It's too early for them to know how much it costs to a) acquire a customer, b) convert them into a paying customer, c) how much they will sustainably pay and d) the value of that customer in the long term and the cost of maintaining them and so on.

'That solid economics doesn't normally happen until you have product/market fit,' she says. 'It's usually only then that people want to invest in you to scale, if you are venture-backed, ideally globally. Before that, your job as a founder is to have the biggest vision that you can, and explore it, gathering as many proof points as possible to show that you are the right team to actually bring it to life. You'll have proxy unit economics like a) user growth, b) user engagement, c) referral rate, d) NPS and e) customer pipeline.

Pitching strategy is like an hourglass

Tan White says that the best slide decks she sees are succinct but the culmination of an awful lot of work behind the scenes – they are often living documents that evolve as a team gets feedback from investors and customers, and as traction accelerates. Ideally they are the roadmap the business is actually following. 'I always say to founders that pitching strategy is a bit like an hourglass. At the wide point of the hourglass you have your big vision – if you're Airbnb, for instance, being the biggest property provider in the world that owns no property. The narrow part of the hourglass represents the product and customer traction you need to make today, to place you on the trajectory towards that big vision and make you credible: with Airbnb that would be increasing numbers of hosts advertising their spare room in San Francisco, and people paying to rent them, through your platform.

'Then, when you go out to fundraise again for Series A, you are actually saying: "I need, say, £5m for the next 18 months to take me on these next five steps towards my big goal, and you should believe me because I have evidence I can build product and get customers engaged." So at each stage you're measuring your progress by showing how far along the trajectory towards your big vision you've travelled. Very few companies ever do this in a linear fashion. Everyone hits bumps in the road. Occasionally they'll hit on something else and then they'll have to retrofit their story. The overall trend of traction, though, is up and to the right.'

Why is the big vision so crucial? Because it has a direct bearing on the size of market you could ultimately own and on the product roadmap and the technology you build today, she says. Get it wrong and it will box you into a smaller business, leaving – often fatally – little room for manoeuvre. 'The problem with tech is it creates legacy quickly, and it's not easy to redevelop it if you've gone down the wrong tech stack – unless you raise even more capital to re-engineer it afterwards, which isn't easy to do.

'If you totally screwed up your UX, there's a cost to redeveloping that, and will you have already burnt your brand in the process? The older your company gets, the harder it is for it to genuinely pivot to a whole different strategy.'

What you also see, depending on how successful companies have been, is that their original, declared strategy gets masked, Tan White continues. 'If they didn't quite hit the trajectory they wanted to get to, you will often find their vision and their goals become more prosaic and practical.

'Staying with the Airbnb example, let's say they hadn't managed to build a community of hosts and couch-surfers on a global tech stack and then build up enough trust in the community to move the business into whole properties, they would have ended up revising themselves downwards to a smaller market, as a niche bed-and-breakfast business platform.

'You can usually tell a founder's appetite and how well they've actually executed from the way they start to tailor the information/vision they show you as an investor.'

Remember your vision

Another thing Tan White says to founders is that if they've got a big vision for their company, try to step away from the daily grind of building their business to remember what it is.

'Sometimes the day-to-day execution drags you down into such a level of pragmatism that you forget (or at least lose sight of) your bigger vision,' she says. 'When that vision may be the very reason you started your company in the first place.'

There's nothing wrong with starting out to build a sustainable, long-term, profitable business – perhaps because you never wanted to work for someone else – if that's what you set out to do, she says. Not every founder wants to, or is cut out to, build a venture-backed outlier business with global potential. And that's OK – just be honest with yourself that that's what you're trying to build.

'What I sometimes see is companies who aren't quite sure what they are, and they sometimes end up with investors that are misaligned with them. If you want to build an outlier business then make sure you have the right investors to do that,' she says.

Growth versus early monetisation

A note of caution: some investors want to de-risk and will push founders towards revenue, sometimes at the cost of doing the bigger vision. The Valley companies are known for scaling for growth, just pushing that growth and not necessarily worrying about monetisation until much, much later, explains Tan White. 'Whereas, on the whole, in Europe you'll find they still want to see monetisation a bit earlier,' she says, adding that companies will have to tailor their strategy accordingly.

When selling a pivot, zero-base your pitch

Tan White advocates approaching each round of funding as if it's fresh and standalone. Founders cannot take any investment for granted, even if the company's firing on all cylinders, and they in effect have to re-pitch each time. 'You still have to come up with a compelling vision from where you are.'

All the more so if you're planning to pivot your business, she says. 'When you're trying to pivot, you have to be very compelling with investors around why you have the experience, knowledge and insight to succeed by pivoting [where you failed before]. So I'd zero-base it. Almost pretend you're [starting again] from scratch.

'Even if you're going to your existing investors, behave as if you're starting again afresh. Only this time you actually have more experience and evidence, because you'll have done something – you'll have a team and you'll probably have customers by then, and you'll have learned something from them.'

Pitching to pivot a business boils down to the same approach – spelling out your big (albeit transformed) vision, Tan White continues. 'Why is it you believe this is the right way to go now? What's changed? What external market evidence and what internal primary insights do you have, because of what you've done so far?'

Twitter was famously carved out of Odeo, a podcasting company, and was reinvested in – so pivots can work, she says. 'But you have to have evidence and the belief again, and sell the narrative as to why this is now the way to go.'

Don't drink your own Kool-Aid

Founders have to pull off a near-impossible trick, where simultaneously they have to distort reality – because they are selling a vision of something that doesn't yet exist – and yet not bullshit themselves, cautions Tan White. 'As the Americans say: "Don't drink your own Kool-Aid."

'You need to have a massive amount of self-awareness to be able to say to yourself: "I know I could get there, I believe in myself, I believe in the team, I believe in the vision – but at the same time I know I'm actually way back over here right now."

'The best founders can actually be in both places. They can be self-aware and know what is real. Then they can paint the bigger picture and get people to believe they can get there. Personally, I was a belief-based founder; I had to believe that I had found a way to get there, that I could see a path through. I also appreciated that my co-founders and team used that to execute and build the robust trellis that makes a vision reality.'

As an investor, she looks for the entrepreneurs who can describe their strategy in level-headed terms and articulate the steps they need to take. 'What I'm often looking for is: "What is their insight/unfair advantage that makes me believe they are the ones that can achieve what they say they can?"

'In pitch meetings, I'm mostly digging into the strategy with questions. I want to find out what the real blockers have been, and be sure that they have genuine insight in how to get around them. But also what opportunities have they got coming up, that they can see but maybe someone else can't? How do you capitalise on this?'

Distil your strategy into a few words

Being able to summarise a vision and a strategy in a few words is vital too. 'I know it sounds simplistic, but the reason why that's so important is that if you can't articulate your vision in a way that's really straightforward – and your vision needs to have real clarity about the problem you're solving and why people should come to you – then it's a hard sell to customers and to investors and it's hard to hire people into your company,' she says.

'It's hard to create a culture as well. That distillation tends to drive the brand, so the proposition and the products need to fit into it too.

'I look for that a lot with my teams. For me, it's almost the first page of their deck. If founders can't articulate what they're trying to achieve, then they haven't got clarity – and the problem with lack of clarity is that, as your team grows it magnifies through an organisation. When you are three people you can keep re-iterating it. Once you are 50, if you can't summarise it then everybody else will have a slightly different spin on it, and eventually you'll find the big vision and how to get there becomes muddled and just erodes.

'Being able to articulate it is also a good way to bring yourself back when you are in the weeds. Are you actually building towards the right thing or not?'

Clarity also matters, even among co-founders. 'If you don't articulate and align on vision/strategy, you might find that you both (or all) end up with slightly different interpretations of your company's purpose. So being able to sum it up in a few words or a single phrase is very helpful for staying aligned not only with your co-founders but with your investors too.'

Your slide deck will stay pretty
much the same (unless you pivot)

A startup's vision tends not to evolve much over time, which means the slide deck you started with when you were just a couple of people will be refined along the way, but won't change much either, says Tan White.

What *does* tend to change is the execution. 'If you think about it, you're learning how to execute your business, because if it's a new business, especially if it's a disruptive, outlier business, then it hasn't been done before, therefore nobody has the playbook for it either.

'When I think back to Moonfruit, my first slide deck was actually entitled FireBlaze – it wasn't even called Moonfruit –but it was always about people sharing their passions by publishing online. Even though it became more of a business builder, it was still fundamentally about allowing people to share their passions online and democratising the web for the person on the street. That never really changed.'

∨

Wendy Tan White MBE is an advisor to BGF. She was a partner at BGF Ventures and a general partner at Entrepreneur First, building deep tech companies with a £40m Next Stage Fund and programme. Wendy was CEO and co-founder of the SaaS website builder Moonfruit, before selling to Yell Group. She is a board trustee of the Alan Turing Institute, a member of the UK Digital Economy Council, and on the boards of Tech Nation and the Department of Computing and Dyson School of Design Engineering at Imperial College London.

CHAPTER 26

'The average person doesn't get married after two or three dates; the same goes for finding the right investor.'

Balderton Capital partner **Suranga Chandratillake**
on the pathway to Series B.

While his firm doesn't invest at Series B, it does steer many of its Series A-stage companies through that milestone, which Balderton Capital partner Suranga Chandratillake describes as 'the hardest round of all to raise… because it's the in-betweener round'.

He explains: 'In the earlier rounds, a big part of what you're really trying to use to sell your story is a narrative, and it's a narrative which weaves in a combination of the founders, the quality, power and skills of the team, with the scale of the market opportunity, mixed with fascinating insight into the problem you propose to solve in that existing market – and of course some early data that shows that product/market fit might be there, although it's early. It's still on pretty shaky ground.

'So it's very much about the future. It's very much about the potential and it's therefore highly narrative-driven.'

Series C and beyond – which are effectively growth rounds – are highly quantitatively driven, he continues.

'Generally, those investment rounds, apart from a handful of exceptions, are all about metrics. At that point, whether it's revenue or whether it's users or whatever else it is, it's fairly well modelled, people are going to crunch the numbers. Of course they want to understand the broad vision and everything else, but there's going to be a lot of time spent on this numerical, measurable quantitative nature of where you are and where you can get to next.'

Series B is something of a mash-up of Series A and Series C, which is why, as founders hit the ramp towards it, they need to take its unique, in-betweener status into account when they prepare, says Chandratillake.

'Ultimately it's going to end up with me – as the founder or one of the founders – sitting in front of a range of investors, and I'm going to have to tell a story for about an hour or so to each of them. That story is going to have to really take them on a journey, because my business is bigger than it was in Series A, but it's still pretty small. We're still probably doing single-digit millions of dollars of revenue, if we're doing revenue, and therefore I can't pretend that I've got some kind of massive business. I probably have a similar turnover or revenue to the average branch of Burger King or McDonalds, so I can't pretend that I'm this huge organisation yet.

'On the other hand, I'm going to have real numbers, whether that's users, whether that's engagement, whether that's revenue or whatever. They're real, they should be growing, there should be a steady story, there should be a really pretty solid model or engine that shows that I've put x in here and then y comes out over there, that the input-to-output ratio is profitable and efficient and everything else.

'So it's a tough one. You have to look at it both ways and say, "This is that funny round where I have to do a bit of both of these things." You almost have to compartmentalise your thinking and ask: "What is the narrative aspect of what I'm going to talk about, and what is the quantitative aspect that I'm going to talk about?" Then you make sure you've almost got both bits of it going, and then sit down and start to weave the two together.'

Approaching investors

When it comes to investing, Chandratillake is a firm believer in backing founders with whom he has an ongoing relationship, even if only recently sparked.

'Certainly, I really struggle to invest in someone I've just met,' he says. 'It can be done; my firm has invested as quickly as four days after a meeting – and that was literally from first meeting to cash in the bank. But that's extremely rare; certainly in Series A, it's extremely rare. I'd much rather get to know the person first.

'As a founder you should want the same. People focus on the investment process itself, which is usually a couple of months long – it takes 10–15 meetings – but remember if you get this person [as an investor], they're probably going to have the right to a seat on your board for the next seven or eight years, which by the way is about the same length as an average marriage in the West.

'The average person doesn't get married on the basis of two or three dates and a month of courting. Most of us spend a bit longer than that before deciding to get married. So you want to do the same [with a prospective investor]. That doesn't mean that you have to be full-on dating for the whole period, but you do need to have met each other a few times, spent time together and developed a real sense of each other and what your values are.'

And the better you know your investor(s), the more clarity you'll have with regard to your own position further down the road, he continues. 'If you're worried about being kicked out as CEO one day, for example, the easiest way to know the answer to that kind of question is to have spent meaningful time with that person. You know how they react and how they respond to you giving them bad news when you miss [key targets], as well as good news when you beat them.

'That's way more powerful and a much stronger signal that you'll be able to read than just saying in one of five meetings: "Do you promise to avoid firing me in the future?" Naturally, everyone is going to say "Of course I won't" to your face, but whether or not you can believe that is another question altogether.'

How to pitch VCs at Series B

For founders who are pitching a venture firm – particularly when pitching the whole firm simultaneously – Chandratillake has three key tips.

1) *Work with the individual you are working with at the venture firm on the pitch itself.*
If you, as a founder, are doing what Chandratillake suggested earlier, i.e. meeting your contact at a particular VC firm multiple times, you should do dry-run versions of your pitch in front of them to get their feedback, he suggests.

'They know more than you will ever know about how their particular team will react to the pitch, what kind of questions will get proposed (and how to deal with those questions before they even come up), and what the black holes will be and so on.

'Every firm is different, and every partner at every VC firm is different, so while you can have a good generic pitch, it's massively valuable to have specific advice. So work with whoever you're pitching to, and the person you know best at that firm, to really make sure you're saying the right stuff, in the right way, and you're answering the right questions up front.'

2) *Take at least one other person with you to the pitch – but make sure they speak for a substantial amount of time too.*
Chandratillake argues that it's crucial to have more than one person at a pitch, because it's very hard for one person to do all the talking, and also listen enough and be able to answer questions as well as remember critical facts and numbers.

'There are some individuals who can pull all of that off, but they're few and far between. In my opinion, until you know you're one of those guys, you might as well take another person.

'However, if you do take another person, they have to do two or three slides, and they have to do them well and be as thoughtful and polished as you are on it. Otherwise, it's just weird; they sit there and it becomes very awkward. Also, it's a human thing that it's very difficult to ask questions of someone who hasn't spoken at all during the pitch. So you want to avoid that, and make sure that person is bought into the conversation as well.'

3) Keep it short.

At every venture partner meeting that Chandratillake has ever seen at his own firm, but also at other firms to whom he's pitched his company as CEO in the past, the partners always have a huge number of questions. 'So I'm always staggered by the founders who come in with an hour's worth of presentation material [up front].

'If you've got a one-hour pitch slot or an hour and a half, as we do at Balderton because we like to give people a bit more time, you don't want to spend even a majority of it on PowerPoint. You've got to realise that at least half of it is going to be Q&A. So keep your pitch short, and keep it sharp.

'You can even, if you want to, say: "Look, I've purposely kept this down to 20 minutes, so let me just whizz though it first and then we can do all the questions." But even if they stop you and start asking questions in the middle of it, you need to know you've got enough time to get back on track and make sure the full story gets out.

'If you don't do that, there's a massive danger that you won't get to the end of the story, and usually there are equally valuable things towards the end as there are at the front. That means huge chunks of your story can get missed and left behind, and that's a travesty given that you had this wonderful, valuable, magical period of time in which to tell them everything you can about yourselves and your company.'